White-Collar Workers

White-Collar Workers

ALBERT A. BLUM
Michigan State University

MARTEN ESTEY
University of Pennsylvania

JAMES W. KUHN
Columbia University

WESLEY A. WILDMAN
University of Chicago

LEO TROY
Rutgers—The State University

 RANDOM HOUSE New York

Copyright © 1971 by Random House, Inc.

All rights reserved under International and Pan-American Copyright
Conventions. Published in the United States by Random House, Inc.,
New York, and simultaneously in Canada by Random House of
Canada Limited, Toronto

ISBN 0-394-30111-0
Library of Congress Catalog Card Number: 76-120146

Manufactured in the United States of America by H. Wolff Book Mfg. Co., Inc.,
New York, N.Y.

Design by J. M. Wall

First Edition
9 8 7 6 5 4 3 2 1

Preface

A few years ago, I gave a lecture at a conference in Germany on the implications of the computer for clerical workers. Other sessions, which dealt with the computer's impact on technicians, engineers, and management, were scheduled at the same time. After my lecture, I talked with a few economists from a Marxist country who apologized for not attending my session but reported that they had gone instead to hear the talk about the computer's effect on management. I laughed and pointed out that Marxists were no longer concerned with the proletariat—in this case the salaried proletariat—but were now mainly interested in the problems of management.

But, of course, Marxists are not the only ones who have shifted their focus. In the past decade or so, scholarly concern with labor in the United States has mainly focused on the unemployed and disadvantaged. Interest in labor-management relations has centered principally on organizational behavior. Furthermore, those studying white-collar workers have emphasized professionals, such as teachers, rather than the lowly clerk in the office. Dagwood is not as dramatic a character as Mr. Chips or Rap Brown; a program to fulfill his needs is not as exciting as a course in sensitivity training. And yet, however important these other topics are, there is one inexorable fact: The proportion of white-collar employees in the labor force will continue to increase for some time to come, and how they think and behave will have an impact on American society.

In this book, my colleagues and I have focused on one aspect of white-collar life: the relationships between the white-collar workers and the unions. We have looked at clerical employees, engineers, retail clerks, white-collar employees in the federal government, and teachers. Each author has been responsible for his own

v

chapter although each contribution was sent to the other authors for comments.

It would be presumptuous for me to attempt to sift out the main themes present in all of the chapters. I simply suggest that the relationship that develops between unions and white-collar workers will help determine the future of the American labor movement and, as a result, will greatly influence the nature of American life. It is, therefore, important to understand this change since most textbooks on labor focus on the blue-collar worker.

A book with five authors has its own unique problems: authors go abroad, change jobs, work around other commitments. But finally, it is done. As the end man on the receiving line of the manuscripts, I would like to thank, for all of my associates, the large number of people who spent so much time with us in helping us learn enough to finish the volume.

Albert A. Blum
East Lansing, Michigan
June 1969

Contents

White-Collar Workers

THE OFFICE EMPLOYEE

by ALBERT A. BLUM*

To organize the unorganized has been the enduring goal of the American labor movement. Thus, George Meany, head of the AFL-CIO, at the federation's 1961 convention, announced that "The greatest unresolved trade-union problem remains . . . the essential task of organizing the unorganized. . . ." He then referred specifically to the white-collar workers "where the benefits of union organization are largely unknown." Although one union leader after another has reiterated Meany's wish, most white-collar employees still refuse to enter the house of labor.[1]

But why is the failure to organize this group of workers such a pressing problem for the unions today? First, the "real" level of trade union membership has generally remained unchanged in the decades since the end of World War II. In fact, since 1956, the number of trade union members as a percentage of the employees in nonagricultural establishments has been steadily declining. In 1956, 33.4 percent of employees in nonagricultural establishments belonged to unions; in 1968, the percentage had dropped to 27.9. Although these statistics have troubled union leaders, they have also disturbed commentators outside of organized labor who, partially as a result of this data, have begun to talk about a crisis facing the American labor movement.

Critics who are concerned with the unions' inability to grow blame labor leaders for failing to organize the unorganized workers, a challenge they had met in the 1930s, when, after the depression, massive numbers of unskilled and semiskilled industrial workers had joined the unions. Today, organized labor seems unable to attract the largest unorganized group, the white-collar employees, a group that has been making up an ever-increasing share of the labor force.

The statistics back up the critics. As Table 1 indicates, in 1967,

* Professor, School of Labor and Industrial Relations and James Madison College, Michigan State University. I would like to thank my graduate assistants, James Spellicy and J. Douglas Smyth, for their assistance.

Table 1. "Organizable"* Segment of Nonfarm Employment, Sixteen Years of Age and Over, by Occupational Group and Sex, Selected Years, 1947–1967, and Projections to 1975

Sex and Year	Total "Organizable" Employment*	Number of White-Collar Workers Employed (thousands)				Blue-Collar Workers (Total)	Service Workers (Other Than Household)
		Total	Professional and Technical	Clerical Workers	Sales Workers		
Both Sexes							
1947†	41,799	14,202	3,795	7,171	3,236	23,401	4,190
1957†	49,694	19,526	6,469	9,119	3,938	24,716	5,452
1967	61,560	26,737	9,879	12,333	4,525	27,262	7,556
Projected 1975	72,700	33,300	12,900	14,800	5,600	29,700	9,700
Male							
1947†	29,193	7,105	2,321	2,883	1,901	19,735	2,353
1957†	33,011	9,386	4,080	2,952	2,354	20,913	2,712
1967	38,195	12,211	6,183	3,406	2,622	22,683	3,301
Female							
1947†	12,606	7,103	1,474	4,289	1,340	3,666	1,837
1957†	16,683	10,140	2,389	6,167	1,584	3,803	2,740
1967	23,365	14,529	3,697	8,928	1,904	4,581	4,255

Percentage Distribution

Both Sexes						
1947†	100.0	34.0	9.1	17.2	7.7	56.0	10.0
1957†	100.0	39.3	13.0	18.4	7.9	49.7	11.0
1967	100.0	43.4	16.0	20.0	7.4	44.3	12.3
Projected 1975	100.0	45.8	17.7	20.4	7.7	40.9	13.3
Male						
1947†	100.0	24.3	7.9	9.9	6.5	67.6	8.1
1957†	100.0	28.4	12.4	8.9	7.1	63.4	8.2
1967	100.0	32.0	16.2	8.9	6.9	59.4	8.6
Female						
1947†	100.0	56.3	11.7	34.0	10.6	29.1	14.6
1957†	100.0	60.8	14.3	37.0	9.5	22.8	16.4
1967	100.0	62.2	15.8	38.2	8.2	19.6	18.2

* Total "organizable" nonfarm employment excludes managers, officials, and proprietors; and service workers employed in households.

† The available data for 1947 and 1957 relate to the employment of persons fourteen years of age and over. These estimates were adjusted to apply to sixteen years and over by applying employment ratios for 1958, the earliest year for which data for the two series are available. Except for sales and service workers, the required adjustments were less than 1 percent.

SOURCE: Adapted from H. M. Douty, "Employment Trends and White-Collar Employee Organizations in the United States," paper delivered at the 1968 Labor Symposium, Wake Forest College, September 18–19, 1968, p. 3.

34.2 million employed persons over 16 wore a white collar. Some 7.5 million of these, however, were managers and others who hold similar high-level positions—unlikely candidates for union membership. Discarding these leaves 26.7 million white-collar employees —about 43.4 percent of the "organizable" segment of the work force (that is, excluding managers, officials, proprietors, and service workers employed in households) at work in nonagricultural establishments—an increase of about 88 percent since 1947.[2]

Blue-collar workers numbered about 44.3 percent of the organizable group in 1967, thus representing about the same union potential as white-collar employees, but this was only an increase of 16.5 percent in the number of blue-collar workers. Service workers, excluding those in private households, made up 12.3 percent of the organizable group—an increase of 80 percent in the number of service workers since 1947.

Thus by 1967, white-collar employees had equaled blue-collar workers as a major source of union potential. By 1975, if projections prove accurate, nonmanual workers will have even moved ahead of blue-collar workers in this respect. While total nonfarm employment will grow by 25 percent, white-collar employment will grow by 40 percent, and 46 percent of those considered organizable will be white-collar workers. Blue-collar workers in 1975 will reach only 41 percent and service workers will grow to 13 percent of the organizable potential.

Clearly, the future for union growth rests with the white-collar employee. Will he continue to reject labor's inducements, as his fellow clerks have done in the past? Union membership figures, which are normally put together by the unions themselves, are noticeably vague. The Bureau of Labor Statistics, the main official body to collect such data, started to include white-collar employees in its studies in 1956. Table 2 shows the results. There were 2.4 million white-collar union members in 1956; 12 years later there were 3.1 million. In 1956, white-collar union members made up 13.4 percent of total union membership; they made up 16.1 percent by 1968. But more important, 12.8 percent of white-collar employees in 1956 belonged to unions; 12 years later the percentage had dropped to 11.2 percent. (In contrast, about 43 percent of blue-collar and service workers, other than household workers, belonged to unions in 1968.) Since 1956, then, white-collar unionization, as a percent-

Table 2. White-Collar Union Membership in the United States as Proportion of Total Union Membership and of White-Collar Employment, 1956–1968

	Adjusted Union Membership* (millions)		White-Collar Union Membership as Percentage of	
Year	Total	White-Collar	Total Membership	White-Collar Employment†
1956	17,980	2,417	13.4	12.8
1958	17,506	2,143	12.2	10.7
1960	17,526	2,150	12.3	10.3
1962	17,050	2,242	13.1	10.1
1964	17,312	2,536	14.6	10.8
1966	18,391	2,693	14.6	10.5
1968	19,297	3,106	16.1	11.2

* Membership of national and international unions with headquarters in the United States adjusted to *exclude* Canadian membership and to *include* membership in unaffiliated local and single-employer unions.
† Employment includes professional, technical, clerical, and sales workers.

SOURCE: U.S. Department of Labor, Bureau of Labor Statistics, cited in H. M. Douty, "Employment Trends and White-Collar Employee Organizations in the United States," paper delivered at the 1968 Labor Symposium, Wake Forest University, September 18–19, 1968, p. 6. See also U.S. Department of Labor, Bureau of Labor Statistics, *Directory of National and International Labor Unions in the United States 1967*, Bulletin No. 1596, 1968, pp. 60–61, and recently collected BLS data.

age of those potentially organizable, has gone down. Thus, the proportional decline in white-collar unionization parallels the decline in over-all "real" union membership.

The failure of unions to attract white-collar employees into their ranks is reflected in the results of National Labor Relations Board elections (Table 3). From 1957, when the Bureau of National Affairs first began to collect such figures, through 1961, the unions lost a greater percentage of total elections than they won. In 1962, the trend changed and they began to win more elections. However, the elections they won were mainly in units with few workers; the unions tended to lose those elections involving the most white-collar employees. The average number of employees in the units in which the union was victorious was never larger in any given year than the average number in the units lost. In fact, only in 1967, which was probably the most successful year organized labor has had recently with respect to white-collar employees, did unions win unit elec-

Table 3. NLRB Elections in White-Collar and Clerical Units for the Period January 1, 1957–December 31, 1969

Year	Total Elections	Total Units Won by Unions	Total No. Employees in Bargaining Units Won by Unions*	Average No. Employees in Bargaining Units Won by Unions	Total No. Employees in Bargaining Units Lost by Unions*	Average No. Employees in Bargaining Units Lost by Unions	Percentage of Total Elections Won by Unions	Percentage of Total No. of Employees Involved in Unit Elections Won by Unions
				All White-Collar Units				
1957	154	70	5,500	78.6	7,000	83.3	45.5	44.0
1958	165	99	3,900	39.4	4,300	65.2	60.0	47.6
1959	209	101	3,660	36.2	6,860	63.5	48.3	34.8
1960	161	78	3,005	38.5	5,095	61.4	48.5	37.1
1961	395	177	4,660	26.3	6,845	31.4	44.8	40.5
1962	462	273	5,880	21.5	8,460	44.8	59.1	41.0
1963	443	255	6,495	25.5	15,250	81.1	57.6	29.9
1964	472	269	6,780	25.2	9,255	45.6	57.0	42.3
1965	514	318	7,605	23.9	10,125	51.7	61.9	42.9
1966	580	352	9,085	25.8	10,100	44.3	60.7	47.3

1967	868	567	15,090	26.6	11,940	39.7	65.3	55.8
1968	808	422	11,175	26.5	15,900	41.2	52.2	41.3
1969	752	422	10,695	25.3	14,885	45.1	56.1	41.8
Total	5,983	3,403	93,530	27.4	126,015	48.8	56.8	42.6

Clerical Units†

1961	188	84	2,320	27.6	4,250	40.9	44.7	35.3
1962	225	131	3,200	24.4	3,995	42.5	58.2	44.5
1963	230	136	2,965	21.8	5,135	54.6	59.1	36.6
1964	237	132	3,475	26.3	5,870	55.9	55.7	37.2
1965	276	165	5,160	31.3	7,455	67.2	59.8	40.9
1966	270	159	4,525	28.5	4,905	44.2	58.9	48.0
1967	313	188	7,485	39.8	8,110	64.9	60.1	48.0
1968	315	160	3,935	24.6	7,410	47.8	50.8	34.7
1969	—	187	4,110	21.9	—	—	—	—
Total‡	2,054	1,342	37,175	27.7	47,130	52.2	56.2	41.2

* Rounded estimates.
† No separate data were published on clerical elections until 1962. (This category includes clerical-technical units.)
‡ Totals are through 1968 except for those columns which include 1969 data.

SOURCE: *White Collar Report*, Bureau of National Affairs, Washington, D.C., No. 47, January 27, 1958; No. 99, January 26, 1959; No. 150, January 18, 1960; No. 205, February 2, 1961; No. 259, February 22, 1962; No. 311, February 21, 1963; No. 364, February 27, 1964; No. 417, March 4, 1965; No. 472, March 24, 1966; No. 521, March 2, 1967; No. 577, March 28, 1968; No. 628, March 20, 1969; No. 687, May 8, 1970.

tions in which the percentage of white-collar employees involved totaled more than 50 percent of all workers (55.8 percent to be exact) and this figure dropped to below 50 percent again in 1968. This failure to organize large offices was reflected in a 1966 message from the president of the Office and Professional Employees International Union (OPEIU), who exhorted the union to "think in terms of tackling companies which employ thousands of white collar workers."[3]

But white-collar employees fall into many categories. In this book, we have attempted to differentiate among some of these categories, including the retail clerk, the engineer, the school teacher, and the white-collar employee in the federal government. In this chapter, we shall look at the clerk who types or files and focus on her (the office employee is more frequently a woman) relationship with unions.

First, although the data are not exactly comparable, clerks appear no more willing to join unions than other white-collar employees. National Office Management Association surveys indicate that 7 to 8 percent of the offices studied had been either partially or wholly unionized in all of its analyses since 1961. (Surveys in 1951 and 1955, using smaller samples, had shown 9 percent partially or wholly unionized.) A Bureau of Labor Statistics study shows that 15 percent of the office workers were unionized in the 1966–1967 period, compared with 69 percent of the plant workers. The BLS figures for clerical employees are probably too high since they were based on an analysis of medium and large establishments in private industry located in metropolitan areas, which would be more likely to be unionized than small firms in towns. The BLS survey, however, does indicate that clerks are not well unionized in any industrial group except public utilities.

There have been other indications of the failure of unions to secure members among clerks. The BLS offers some comparative figures for 17 metropolitan areas for the periods 1953–1954 and 1966–1967. In 1953–1954, 16.5 percent of all office workers belonged to a union; by 1966–1967, the figure had dropped to 15.8 percent. The NLRB elections shown in Table 3 provide additional evidence. Elections involving clerical employees follow the over-all white-collar trend. Since 1962, the unions have won more elections than they have lost, but they have lost elections in units involving more clerks than the units in which they won.

The above data clearly indicate that organized labor is not growing, that one of the reasons for its stagnation has been its failure to attract the clerks, and that the potential expansion of trade union membership in the United States depends upon whether or not organized labor can break this white-collar barrier. Moreover, some argue that if that barrier is broken, the reverberations that ensue will alter and revitalize the labor movement because the clerks will introduce new ideas (perhaps of a more conservative nature) just as the semiskilled and unskilled factory workers did in the 1930s. Because of the importance of this group to the future of the American industrial relations system, managers, union officials, public servants and scholars have agreed on the necessity for seeking an understanding of the factors that influence white-collar unionization. In an attempt to further this understanding, I shall deal with four broad categories, economic factors, political factors, sociopsychological factors, and industrial relations, and explore the way in which selected factors subsumed under each category affect the decision of clerks to join unions. It should, however, be remembered that none of the factors or even the general categories are discrete entities. They all affect each other. Furthermore, some items could as easily be placed under more than one category, but they are separated here to give the discussion greater clarity. We will first turn to economic factors.

□ Economic Factors

One of the oldest theories concerning union growth attaches the level of trade union membership to the roller coaster of the business cycle. When times are good, the number of jobs will go up and so will union membership; when times are bad, membership will go down.[4] This explanation has been rejected by most scholars on the basis of very good evidence. Surely, in the last decade, union membership as a percentage of the organizable labor force has declined, whether or not there has been a recession. However, two economic factors are often legitimately suggested as determinants of the decision of clerks to join unions. One of these determinants, job security, will be discussed later when we deal with automation. We now turn to the other determinant, namely salaries.

Howard Coughlin, president of the Office and Professional Employees International Union, a major white-collar union, declared in 1966 that the "underlying reason for organization [of white-collar employees] and subsequent collective bargaining is money. . . . We must continue to emphasize money as the initial incentive for unionization and collective bargaining. It would be a mistake in instituting an organizing campaign to emphasize things other than 'bread and butter' issues as reasons for organization." Thus in the course of a campaign to organize a bank in Texas, his union tells its clerks, "The surest way to fight poverty [is to] join the Union."[5]

Union organizing literature frequently focuses on the clerks' resentments in the matter of salaries. "Do you know that a laborer who belongs to an AFL-CIO union gets paid more than a stenographer who is not in a union," asks a young lady in a piece of union organizing literature. She also sadly comments that "a union janitor gets more than a Class A typist." The lesson appears clear—at least to the union. Stenographers and typists ought to sign a union membership card if they want to be treated as well as laborers and janitors. Why is it then that so many office employees did not respond in the way anticipated to this kind of appeal? It is not that the facts in the pamphlet were wrong. Surely, from 1939 until 1955 (the year of the AFL-CIO merger), the gap between the salaries and fringes paid office employees and those paid blue-collar workers had narrowed steadily. Between 1939 and 1955 the median annual salary paid clerical and kindred workers increased by only 172.3 percent; operative and kindred workers (manual workers) had their wages raised 256.1 percent. Also, fringes that had often been given only to salaried people rapidly found their way into blue-collar workers' compensation plans during World War II and then in collective bargaining agreements in the 1950s and after. How close the blue-collar worker has come to the white-collar employee in fringes is indicated by some BLS surveys, which show that employers paid 27.6 percent of basic pay for supplementary benefits for production workers in 1962 and 25 percent of basic pay for these benefits for white-collar employees in 1963.[6] Clearly, manual workers now enjoy what once was the sole prerogative of nonmanual employees.

The white-collar employees were not unaware that the blue-collar worker had almost caught up with them in terms of salaries and fringes. A survey in late 1963 asked office employees to compare their reactions to the level of their compensation with the reactions of other workers. Fifty-four percent reported that they were *not* more satisfied than other workers; 38 percent declared that they were. Some earlier surveys indicated that two out of three white-collar people did not believe that they had done as well in terms of income as other groups since World War II and that only a slightly smaller percentage of unionized clerks gave "to get better pay" as the reason why a clerk would join a union. And yet most clerks did not.

One reason the clerks failed to join can be traced to the fact that management took steps to rectify the salary situation, partially, at least, as a result of fears concerning white-collar unionization. Using 1955 as a base, nonmanual salaries had increased by 28.9 percent by 1961 while wages for manual workers had increased by only 21.1 percent. In 1955 $284 had separated the clerical employees' median annual salary from that of manual workers. By 1961 clerks were making $646 more than manual workers. In 1961 clerical salaries were nearly 15 percent higher than the operatives' wages (in 1955 they had been 8 percent higher).

But conditions worsened for the clerk during the 1961–1966 period. By 1966 the gap had narrowed to $365. Clerical salaries had risen only 18 percent while operatives' wages had gone up 27 percent. The extent of the drop can be better seen by comparing the figures for 1964 with those for 1966. In 1964 clerks' salaries were 11.3 percent higher than operatives; in 1966 they were only 6.6 percent higher, one of the smallest percentage differences in recent years.[7]

Tentative figures for 1967 and 1968 indicate a marked rise from the 1966 low (but apparently not as significant an increase as that secured by technical and professional white-collar employees). However, the fact remains that for the past two decades, unions have had a chance to use the salary issue as a carrot to attract white-collar people and have not particularly succeeded. At times, the issue may cause resentments, particularly when one clerk compares her salary with that of another clerk in the same or another company (the Office Employees are using the comparison with Wall Street clerks); or with what a unionized clerk, at the same job with another company, is receiving (the Steelworkers have used the latter approach effectively) ; or with its actual worth as inflation eats away at it. But this resentment, since organized labor has permitted it to remain largely unfocused, has not particularly facilitated unionization. Economic factors, in fact, often have to filter through the other factors—such as the political ones that we will analyze next—in order to have a positive or negative effect on the decision to join a union.

□ Political Factors

Much has been written about the influence of politics on the growth of unionization. For example, it has been argued that the New Deal, and the Wagner Act, in particular, sparked the rapid growth in unionization during the 1930s. Similarly, the argument has been made that a favorable administration in Washington and a National Labor Relations Board sympathetic to unions will foster the expansion of white-collar unionization. Obviously, the way the NLRB determines bargaining units or unfair labor practices can easily facilitate or delay unionization. During the Eisenhower administration, for example, some white-collar employees, bitter over economic conditions and other complaints, tried to join or organize unions and were fired. The claim has been made that resolution of unfair labor cases by the NLRB took so long during this period that by the time the issue was decided the fired workers could no longer be helped. Therefore, the argument runs, clerks who lived in the uncertain atmosphere created by the NLRB and who were tied to weekly credit payments hesitated to join unions for fear they would lose their jobs. However, under Presidents Kennedy and Johnson, despite a more sympathetic administration and a more prolabor NLRB, white-collar union membership did not grow significantly except in federal and state governments, where executive orders and state and local legislation directly encouraged the formation and growth of unions.

The effect of governmental actions on the growth of unionization, though important, has been somewhat overemphasized. There has been a tendency to look at the impact of such formal political decisions as those expressed in laws and executive rulings rather than at the informal political decisions made by white-collar workers themselves. Nevertheless, the party affiliation of the clerks themselves may be more important in determining whether they will join unions or not than the fact that the government is controlled by Democrats or Republicans. Surely the evidence indicates that a white-collar union supporter is more sympathetic to a mixed economy and to the increased role of government in economic life than a white-collar union opponent.

Some management and union spokesmen recognize the importance of a clerk's political and economic philosophy in his decision whether or not to join a union. One West Coast firm has a communication program that is designed to keep its white-collar employees "profit-minded and oriented to a free economy" and the firm is not alone in carrying a "free enterprise" message as part of an antiunion program.[8]

On the other hand, some labor leaders argue that clerks can be attracted to union membership if they can be made to see the labor movement as "a social critic, an economic leveler, a stimulator to management, and a focal point of social idealism." Joseph A. Beirne, president of the Communications Workers of America (CWA) has suggested that one way to get clerks to join unions is "to change the hostile attitudes about unions that prevail among so many people today." He proposes to do this by involving the unions more and more in community action—the Boy Scouts, the blood bank and so forth—so that white-collar people and others will recognize that the CWA and other similarly inclined unions are "community minded," for "in organizing new members we must appeal to man's interest to give as well as his desires to get."[9]

And Walter Reuther had concluded:

> You cannot appeal to a [white-collar employee] strictly on the basis of improving his salary or economic condition. I think the labor movement has to take on the character of a social movement. It is dealing more and more with the problems of the whole community and will have to enlist these people, give them a sense of consciously participating in shaping the great issues that will determine the kind of society in which we are all going to be living.[10]

To trade unionists who hold this view, sympathetic administrations in federal and state capitals do not represent an adequate political prerequisite for marked union growth. They feel it is equally important that white-collar persons accept a social reform philosophy and develop the attitudes this commitment involves. Therefore, they contend that the struggle to unionize white-collar persons should be viewed in a broader context; that is, it may involve changing not only attitudes towards unionism but also attitudes towards society in general.

□ Sociopsychological Factors

Among the most frequently offered explanations of the failure of clerks to join unions is sociopsychological in nature. This view holds that clerks identify with management and will not reject this identification by entering into a labor organization. However, those who are convinced that unionization will become more attractive to clerks also have a sociopsychological explanation. Proponents of this idea believe that white-collar employees will develop a sense of group or class consciousness, a feeling that clerks they are and clerks they will be, and that this new awareness will help destroy the old identification with management.

That clerks have identified with management is practically a truism in labor and industrial relations, a belief held in common by both management and union leaders. And the evidence indicates that white-collar employees do indeed feel that they have more in common with management than with production workers and that they identify more with the middle class than with the working class. In fact, many clerks view the very act of joining a union as a lowering of status. One labor organizer reports that "most office workers say 'unions are for the Zerellis and the Ormmanskys, not for me.'" Moreover, management has spent a good deal of money and effort to ensure that the clerks will continue to hold this view.[11]

Despite the fact that many clerks do hold strong pro-management feelings, a large number of union officials believe that clerks will change these sentiments. These labor leaders are convinced that there is an important new force at the workplace that will make clerks begin to identify with the working class rather than with management.

They feel that clerks will thus come to recognize that clerical members of the working class they are and will be. Joseph Shister has argued that this sense of social immobility is an important reason for the growth of unionism. However, he adds that a "dramatic source of dissatisfaction" is also necessary if workers are to join unions. Those who are convinced that white-collar employees will join unions suggest that the new force in the workplace is just such a "dramatic source of dissatisfaction," and it will, among other things, make white-collar people more like the working class and will arrest their upward mobility. In the words of the president of the Office Employees Union, it will make white-collar workers "develop the same psychological outlook as manual workers in mass production" and, therefore, they will become "more receptive to unionism." The force we have been referring to is automation.[12]

Automation, the argument goes, is so altering the nature of white-collar work that the white collar will soon be blue (supposedly automation has the reverse effect on blue-collar workers, whose work is becoming more white-collar in nature). Automation has the following effects, among others, on the white-collar worker:

1. His skills are reduced or disappear and his work is becoming more like blue-collar work.
2. He is becoming convinced that his dreams of upward mobility are no longer true.
3. He has less job security.

Unionists believe that if they focus their efforts on these and related effects of automation, white-collar employees will join unions in large numbers.

Automation and Skills

In 1960, the Industrial Union Department of the AFL-CIO predicted that the "increasing mechanization of office processes routinizes the typical office worker to a point where he more and more resembles his brother in the factory." His need for skills would be diminished, claimed the AFL-CIO, and he would be reduced to operating a machine like any blue-collar worker. Instead of proving this prediction correct many researchers have on the contrary concluded that after the computer has entered the office, the number of lower level, routine jobs have decreased while the number of higher level, more skilled clerical jobs have increased. As a result, automation is actually raising the over-all skill level in the office. Eventually, they contend, one may see an inverted pyramid of skills in the office, with a greater number of jobs in the more skilled section of the hierarchy.[13]

There are those who argue against the idea of an inverted pyramid of skills and these are the writers most frequently quoted by union spokesmen. However, an analysis of their writings reveals that they tend to talk about the earlier stages of automation. In this period, it was true that a bookkeeper whose skill was no longer needed because of automation might be transferred to a routine position as a punch-card operator, a change that represented a decline in skill level. Such writers fail to note, however, that eventually punch-card operators disappear also.

In the long run then, the job and skill mix in an automated office seems to be changing in two ways. One trend is toward a greater proportion of highly skilled clerical employees. However, a cautionary note must be made—the over-all elevation in skill levels may hide a drop in total clerical employment. Let us assume that before the installation of a computer, an office unit had 200 employees, 150 of whom did routine clerical work and 50 of whom did highly skilled work. There was thus a 3:1 ratio of unskilled to skilled. After the computer was installed, only 100 workers, 60 unskilled and 40 skilled, remained. The mix had dropped to 3:2, representing a clear upgrading of the skill mix in the office but at the cost of 90 unskilled clerical jobs and 10 skilled ones. This possible drop in employment may have long-term implications for unionism, a problem we shall discuss shortly.

A second apparent trend is that as the office becomes more highly skilled, some office employees may be forced out of the nonsupervisory category, perhaps into management or into the ranks of the professional or near professionals. Those clerks who remain will thus be left in nonsupervisory jobs involved in machine-oriented, routinized work, opening a sharp gap between their level of work and that of their superiors. Thus, although the increase in routinized work does not appear to have resulted in a decline in the level of skills of clerks in general as the unions had hoped, there is some indication that automation may, in the long run, produce a decline in clerical employment as well as a growing gap between the clerk and the next step up in the job hierarchy, which will diminish his chances of upward mobility toward management levels.

Upward Mobility

"[T]he feeling that as an individual he cannot get ahead in his work," said sociologist C. Wright Mills, "is the job fact that predisposes the white-collar employee to go pro-union." Unionists often agree with Mills' claim. The head of the United Automobile Workers' (UAW) Technical, Office and Professional Department argued in 1969 that the clerks' "expectations" that they would advance to management positions were a major obstacle to organizing them. But the problem may disappear, according to this unionist, since "white collar jobs are becoming routine and repetitive." He argued:

> When an employee is on a third shift manning a multimillion dollar computer—and that is the only way they can justify the expense of the computer, to have three shifts—and the noise like a drill press, that white collar worker isn't going to think that he is going to become president of the company—at least not very quickly.[14]

The lack of opportunity for promotion may play an important role in determining whether clerks will join unions or not. But, again, there is little agreement on whether or not automation has resulted in a decline in promotion opportunities for office employees. A clerk who does routine work, however, does apparently find it more difficult to be promoted to the next level. This next level, which is made up of personnel whose experience and seniority gives them more skill and knowledge than the clerks, is growing smaller, a decline caused perhaps less directly by automation than by various office reorganization programs, such as the centralization of office work.

If observers have correctly assessed this trend, then why has Mills' prediction that the blockage of upward mobility will predispose clerks to unionism not been proven true? (It is not that white-collar people are happy about their opportunities to advance—in a 1963 Opinion Research Corporation survey 37 percent said their chances were poor; 33 percent said they were average, and only 25 percent thought they were good.) One reason is that companies have made use of certain safety valves. If only a limited number of opportunities for promotion are available, companies frequently favor the young male for the higher level positions or look outside the firm for new skilled employees, while allowing attrition to take care of the large number of female employees and older male workers. Management believes that both groups, but particularly women, are less likely than young men to push for unionism when they feel their upward mobility blocked. Management frequently expects that patience will be the female and the older male clerk's reward; that is, marriage and/or pregnancy will eliminate the girl from the work force, and retirement, perhaps at an earlier age, will do the same for the older male. Since so many clerical employees are female, and since, in general, women have not been as sympathetic to unionism as men, companies can afford to depend on their continued passive behavior despite lack of promotions—at least for the present.

Thus the character of the clerical work force provides a built-in safety valve that permits the job progression ladder to remain somewhat steady at least temporarily despite automation and lessens the pressures for unionism resulting from blocked upward mobility. On the other hand, some unions feel that current management promotion policies will bring more men into the clerical field, many of them coming from union families, and that they will be more receptive to unionism than the women who preceded them. However, the tremendous upsurge of male workers has yet to come. Meanwhile, the unions argue for fairer procedures in promotions or take the position of the head of the Office Employees Union that "union activity . . . is one of the best ways to get ahead."[15] In other words, modern-day Horatio Algers should first sign a union card.*

---

* Firms seek increased profit and productivity through other means than automation: reorganization of office work, for example, centralization of office work; subcontracting; the use of efficiency and time-and-motion experts; and company mergers. All of these have influenced the extent of white-collar unionism. Time-and-motion experts and company mergers have created some insecurity among clerks, and these fears have been turned to advantage by union organizers. Centralization, on the other hand, has had some negative results for unions. One of America's major companies has placed all of its computer operations in a few nonunionized centers. Many of the clerks now working in the

Job Insecurity

Automation, according to many union leaders, is supposed to raise a specter of unemployment that will frighten white-collar employees into unions. At the beginning of the 1960s, many unions asked clerks questions like these: (UAW) "Where will you go when the robot says, 'Get out! I'm taking over!'"; (OEIU, now OPEIU) "How long before my job is wiped out by The Machine?" The Office Employees predicted a loss of 4 million clerical jobs between 1960 and 1965, and in 1958, the International Union of Electrical Workers warned that salaried employees "are now becoming the first victims of automation, and the economic group most desperately in need of union solidarity and union programs. Without that solidarity and without organized labor's militant programs, hundreds of thousands of professional, technical and salaried workers are and will continue to be helpless to resist mass layoffs and unemployment."[16]

Labor's forecasts concerning unemployment have, however, proved false. In the ten years ending in 1968, unemployment for clerical and kindred employees reached a peak for one year of 4.8 percent. The nadir, however, was 2.9 percent, and unemployment had been at 3.2 percent or less from 1965 on. Moreover, manpower estimates for 1975 indicate that the greatest need will be for white-collar employees, particularly teachers, secretaries, stenographers, and sales personnel. It is possible, however, the unions were wrong only because they thought in terms of too short a time sequence. Perhaps they were deluded by the maxim that technological unemployment is a short-run phenomenon, while new jobs are created in the long run. These labor leaders consequently believed that automation would result in immediate job insecurity, and, as a result, increased demand for union membership. Although this maxim may have held true for the period following the industrial revolu-

---

main center had belonged to white-collar locals in their previous location. Up till now, the company has successfully kept the union out of the new computer centers through an extensive worker-personnel program: stock-saving plans, tandem increases, and so forth. Of course, management is running a risk here—with all of the clerks centralized in a few localities, if the union ever wins a bargaining election, it will represent the bulk of the company's clerical employees. And the union has by no means given up.

tion of the 1860s, it did not apply in the 1960s, when a number of factors cushioned clerical employees from the adverse effects of automation.

The first of these cushioning factors was a change in management philosophy. Company executives today no longer believe in treating employees as a commodity but rather tend to be committed to some form of social justice, with the result that many firms have not laid off redundant clerks. They have depended instead upon the A&P (attrition and pregnancy) approach to take care of the excess labor produced by the computer. Second, the unions themselves have played a role in protecting clerks. The unions have had clauses inserted into labor agreements that reduce the unemployment effects of technological change on the clerks they represent. One union, for example, has been pushing for a four-day week for clerks. Moreover, the unions' very existence causes management to be more cautious when it considers discharging clerks. Third, there is a social consensus favoring full employment, and it is matched by a general commitment to this goal on the part of the government. This has helped create an atmosphere in which clerks are kept employed even after the computer has made them surplus. Fourth, this decade has enjoyed general affluence, permitting management to carry the costs involved in maintaining extra workers. In addition, affluence has increased the demand for goods or services provided by clerks so that even with the increased productivity of the machines they used, the demand for their products has also grown markedly, thereby lessening the need to discharge clerks. Thus, in the last decade or so, nearly all banks have begun to use machines instead of people to process checks. In the absence of increased demand for checks and other bank services resulting from affluence, many bank employees would have been displaced by the machines. All these factors have thus far prevented automation from having the sharp, short-run unemployment effects predicted by the unions. But if the economy took a downturn, there might be a sharp rise in unemployment as surplus clerks were discharged and as clerical school graduates failed to find placement. Faced with reduced profits, management would no doubt cut costs, by discharging clerks, whatever the social consensus. Management would find this course particularly attractive since white-collar payrolls have risen as a total share of manufacturing payrolls and a cut there will surely result in marked economies. In addition, white-collar workers in general are not represented by unions that would protect them to some extent.

Thus, the unions failed to predict correctly the short-run implications of automation, mainly because they talked in terms of inevitable forces that they hoped would have immediate effects. But if they had dealt with the implications of automation on different levels, the unions might have been more successful, even in the short run.

One possibility relates to the employee's emotional reaction. In general, surveys indicate that white-collar employees seem to be less concerned about automation than other groups in the economy. Yet, some white-collar workers do have fears, however unjustified, about the effects of automation while others do not. We know, for example, that within the same company some nonmanual employees who are not directly affected by automation worry about it more than those who are directly affected. It is also clear that whatever the macroeffects of automation, there are microeffects. Some clerks do find the need for their skills diminished; some clerks do find their upward mobility blocked; some do have reason to fear for their job security; some are frightened by the threat of management's use of efficiency experts; others are concerned by the extent of subcontracting to computer centers. If instead of dreaming about the over-all effects of automation and how they might inevitably push clerks into unions (somewhat like the effect the backlash of the Great Depression or the impact of World Wars I and II had in pushing large numbers of blue-collar workers into labor organizations) unions had instead focused on clerks who feared or had been affected by automation, they might have found many likely candidates for union membership.*

As we have already mentioned, studies of automation's impact suggest that there are some long-term trends that could give unions cause to be cautiously optimistic about their future chances. But unionists must first recognize that the historical process takes time

---

* In fact, unions have even used automation in their organizing struggle. In one case, clerks mailed the IBM cards necessary for a company's operation to General Delivery and did not say where they were until the union had won its fight with management.

and that the formation of a white-collar identification with the working class, if it ever takes place, has to be a part of history. Professor E. P. Thompson's definition of class as "an historical phenomenon, unifying a number of disparate and seemingly unconnected events, both in the raw material of experience and in consciousness"[17] is appropriate in this context.

There are some trends that indicate that in the long run a salaried proletariat may emerge. These include some of the long-term implications of automation just discussed. The importance of these trends, however, cannot yet be judged. There surely is little, if any, evidence that the salaried proletariat is now in the process of creation since white-collar people still identify with the middle class. In any case, the time necessary to develop this group or working class consciousness has clearly not been adequate. Moreover, there has been no major event, such as a vast union drive, that might have served as a catalyst to create the sense of class consciousness.

Even the most optimistic trade unionist, therefore, should not place too much hope in developing class consciousness among white-collar employees. In fact, there are a number of indications that even as white-collar work becomes more like blue-collar work, or perhaps because of this trend, the clerks may more sharply identify with middle-class values or with management. As one observer put it, they feel that by joining a union "they will lose their middle-class status. To them, unions are dirty, noisy and lower class." In fact there are some studies of blue-collar union members who, when they switch to white-collar jobs (and a substantial number seem to be switching, according to one survey), relinquish their union membership.[18]

As white-collar employees "skid" downward, they, like many other such skidders, may actually become more conservative. The possibility exists that the white-collar employee, frightened by unemployment, degraded by a loss of skill, depressed by the lack of opportunity for upward mobility, may respond to the question, "Little Man, What Now?" as did the disillusioned and frustrated German middle class in the inflationary days of the 1920s. Alarmed by their fading prospects for the future, many members of the German middle class moved to the Right and helped support the burgeoning Nazi movement. Thus the unionization of clerks as a result of the claimed negative effects that flow from automation is by no means inevitable.

☐ Industrial Relations

The political, economic, and social milieu forms the base from which a labor movement may grow. But its growth takes place within the context of an industrial relations system. Such aspects of the system as the role of management, the policies of trade union leadership, the competition for power among unions, the position within the work environment of different workers, the relationships between unionized and nonunionized workers, and the collective bargaining agreements that are signed also help determine whether white-collar employees will join a union or not.

Management Policies

It is, of course, difficult to identify general managerial policies toward white-collar employees. There are too many companies and too few studies. However, one of the main reasons why unions have not grown in recent years is surely that personnel managers on the whole are far more sophisticated and that executives are willing to use these skills to prevent their clerks from joining labor organizations. Employers are also often willing to pay an economic price— giving the clerks the same or tandem increases in relation to unionized employees. Executives may have accepted the fact that their blue-collar workers will be represented by a business agent; they have not accepted the inevitability of this development on the part of their office employees.

In a survey of 137 companies for the American Management Association in 1963, the author found that most executives were convinced that their white-collar employees were not seeking the "benefits of union organization" because they were receiving these benefits and more from their firms without paying union dues. To make sure that this attitude continued, the companies reported that their policies were to:[19]

Pay good salaries. ("My unionized blue-collar workers never get a thing that is not passed on and more to my office employees—and without the latter having to pay union dues.")

Grant excellent fringe benefit coverage. ("Our aim is to gradually widen the fringe benefit gap in favor of white-collar employees.")

Provide channels for upward and downward communication. ("Through a good communications program the Company has sold its white-collar workers on the premise that there is nothing to be gained through third party intervention.")

Settle grievances. ("We provide adequate means for employees to air their gripes and complaints without fear of recrimination.")

Recognize individual differences. ("As long as white-collar workers are treated fairly and are recognized as individuals, I don't believe any specific steps are necessary to combat unionism.")

Ensure superior supervision. ("We carefully and completely educate supervisors to communicate the concept of fair, equal or better but different treatment of white-collar vs. blue-collar.")

Foster continued identification with management. ("A dedicated effort is being made to motivate all white-collar employees to identify themselves with corporate goals. We are trying to eliminate distinction among groups by moving toward unification of all corporate benefits.")

Provide job security. ("We try to give our white-collar people the same job security as guaranteed by a union contract.")

Permit upward mobility. ("We keep paths for promotion open so that white-collar people can [move toward] management freely. We reward real ability and performance with promotion as well as increased pay. Our white-collar people feel that they have a better chance to advance without a union.")

Give special treatment to white-collar employees. ("Our firm gives our white-collar people some special privileges—like social events with management—in order to add some prestige to white-collar positions.")

A 1968 survey of 143 senior executives in United States manufacturing corporations by the National Industrial Conference Board found that two-thirds of them feared that white-collar unionization would expand. To prevent this growth, the companies follow a number of policies that "reflect good management practice" rather than simply being "designed to thwart unionization." The policies include

> paying competitive salaries and offering fringe benefits in line with area practice, and matching or bettering bargaining unit compensation; fostering close personal relationships; making regular salary reviews, including cost-of-living reviews in some cases; offering stock options, profit sharing plans, and incentive compensation systems; maintaining good communications; treating employees as individuals; making employees feel they are part of management; attempting to achieve stable employment; establishing grievance procedures; training supervisors to be responsive to employee needs and complaints; and, in a few cases, using employee representation committees. A few companies report that they openly communicate to their white-collar employees that a union would be undesirable and not in their best interests.[20]

When asked why they felt white-collar unions would grow in the private sector, the executives gave the following reasons:

Unions will expend more effort in organizing office, sales, and professional employees since the blue collar sector offers diminishing organizing potential.

Unionism today appears more profitable to the white collar worker, particularly in light of recently negotiated settlements.

Unionism is becoming more respectable due to the increased unionization of government employees, professionals, and teachers.

Computers have created more routine and depersonalized white collar occupations which tend to be compatible with unionization.

The sociological bridge between white collar and blue collar workers is narrowing.

Unions are becoming more sophisticated in appeals to white collar groups.

White collar workers have less job security due to mergers.

There is a general trend to group identification, less to individual achievement.

The present labor laws and NLRB decisions are conducive to unionization.

White collar workers feel increasingly less able to influence their work environment and, like other groups in society, feel the need for more power.

Supervisors continue to make mistakes that lead to employee discontent.

The vast size of many companies has led to a loss of identity among white collar workers.

Those executives who did not expect white-collar unions to expand gave the following explanations:[21]

Management is doing a better job.

Unions do not understand the needs of the white collar employee.

White collar employees are independent and do not want unions.

The opportunity for and expectations of promotion to managerial positions make the case for unionism weaker.

Unions do not have enough organizers to unionize the growing white collar sector.

White collar workers are too intelligent to want union representation.

One respondent gives an "it depends" answer to the question of further unionization of white-collar workers: "White collar unionization indicates a failure on the part of management to communicate with their white collar employees and whether it increases or not depends upon the extent to which management develops proper communications programs with its white collar employees and listens to the needs and wants of this employment group."

Firms have taken specific steps to cope with the economic, political, and sociopsychological factors mentioned earlier. Some have even altered their organizational structure to create special sections dealing with salaried employees. On the other hand, the very growth in size of companies has made it harder for management to follow some of the policies it has enunciated. The nature of bureaucracy lessens the individual treatment afforded clerks. In addition, the bureaucratic system must function through supervisors, and a bad supervisor can destroy all of the effort of top management and bring a union into the office. Because individual bargaining is extremely difficult, if not impossible, to practice in a big firm, clerks may be forced to turn to group bargaining. Many managers remain convinced, however, that their policies will thwart white-collar unionism and that management will not repeat the mistakes that helped bring about blue-collar unionism in the 1930s. But the labor movement too has been developing policies that they hope will attract clerks into their fold, and they too have taken into account some of the factors that we have discussed.

Union Policies

Although many executives display confidence (perhaps complacence) concerning their relationships with their white-collar employees, those who are fearful, like those in the National Industrial Conference Board survey, worry most about the efforts being made by unions to attract clerks. Their fears may not be completely justified, however. First, unions have not been as active in organizing clerks as they claim. An early study indicates that 77 percent of clerks had never been approached by a union, and there is no indication that the unions have made any major commitment to an organizing drive among clerks in the years since then. In a 1963 survey, only 25 percent of the union leaders placed organizing white-collar people among the four or five goals and objectives to which their union would pay the most attention during the following five years. Organized labor has, in fact, experienced steady criticism, from both internal and external sources, for its failure to mount such an organizing drive.

Second, unions are not sure about the approach they should use with clerks. Some organizers think of clerks as part of the middle class and use one type of organizing method; others believe they are not too dissimilar from the working class and use methods that resemble those used to organize manual workers. When union leaders in 1963 were asked whether they thought that "the same appeals that have been successful in organizing blue collar workers also [would] be successful in organizing white collar workers," 29 percent said that they would be successful, 57 percent thought they would not; and the rest held no opinion. Clearly, then, the working class approach is the less popular.[22]

A statement by George Meany, head of the AFL-CIO, exemplifies the working class approach. In a meeting of unionists concerned with white-collar organizing, Meany told them that he would give them the same advice as he had given teachers in 1937:[23]

> I will give you some very good advice. Go over to Third Avenue and
> Fifty-Fourth Street, where you will find a sign in the window. It is the
> office of the Hod Carriers' Union. Tell them I sent you over. Ask them
> what they do for their members, and then you go and do the same
> thing. The problem that they have in securing working conditions and
> advancing wages and the welfare of their members is the same problem
> the teacher has when he or she goes home. The teachers have the
> same problem as the fellow who carries the hod, or digs the ditch
> or fixes the plumbing fixture.

The working class approach emphasizes that organizing clerks is not much different from organizing blue-collar workers. One should focus on sources of resentment, attack management for causing these problems, and emphasize the need for group activity and working class solidarity. "Nonunion white collar workers only pick up the crumbs from the bargaining table," announces a UAW leaflet, "since most managements subscribe to the theory that 'the squeaking wheels get the most grease.' And unorganized white collar workers do not dare to squeak even a little bit. The . . . loss of 34 percent pay status of the white collar worker . . . should be proof of the pudding—or of lack of pudding."

In the middle class approach, which appears to be more commonly used, the labor organizer conceives the white-collar person as different from a blue-collar one, and he will sometimes use words different from those associated with blue-collar workers so as not to frighten away the clerks. He calls the clerk an employee rather than a worker. Sometimes even the word union is dropped, and the organization is referred to as a guild or association. If it is called a union, however, the labor organization sets up a special room for the white-collar employee in the house of labor—special divisions, special bargaining committees. One nonmanual union even insisted that a contract refer to "district representatives" rather than shop stewards. If they can help it, many unions use a more innocuous name for strikes, a term deemed offensive to white-collar people. The organizer himself is different. He may be a she. He is frequently a white-collar worker who speaks and writes grammatically. With these qualifications, he will often use the personal approach of a door-to-door campaign in order to rid the clerk of his negative stereotypes concerning union officials.

A second aspect of the middle class approach involves reluctance to attack management, who are referred to as employers rather than bosses. Since unions frequently feel that clerks identify with their firms, they do not try to focus resentment against the companies but rather attack specific supervisors or managers. Sometimes the criticism of management is very gentle. One piece of organizing literature suggests that the demands of their jobs keep managers just too busy to pay all the attention they might want to the needs of their white-collar employees and that the union will thus ease the workload of management. The union representative may speak to management groups in an attempt to soften management's opposition to the clerks' organizing as well as show the clerks that this union speaks with, not against, managers. At times, such unions have been accused of organizing employers rather than clerks. Another argument, used by at least one union, contended that the clerks ought to sign a membership card because during a tour of the firm the company executives had told the labor leaders that if they worked in the office they too would join a union. Thus, the union suggested that white-collar workers emulate their managers and join. When the same union was engaged in organizing manual workers in the 1930s, it used to say that the president of the United States wanted blue-collar workers to join a union; the new tack is obviously a variation on an old theme.

In a related approach the unions argue that since companies join such organizations as the National Association of Manufacturers and use collective action, the clerks they employ should have the same option. Group decision making, the union claims, is "the very essence of our democratic way of life."

Some unions also claim that it is good business to join a labor organization. A UAW official, for example, argues that the union should recognize "loyalty to the company as a factor in organizing" and that "it's good business, not an act of disloyalty for an employee to protect his years of investment in a company by a contract." Similarly, when the Office Employees tried to organize clerks on Wall Street, it handed out membership cards that carried a stock certificate on one side. The text claimed that by the act of joining the clerks would be buying stocks in the union "redeemable in greater job security, better working conditions, overtime rates, sick leave and vacations, guaranteed bonuses and commissions, salary increases and health care." The same union has used a four-session course on investments, band concerts, and fashion shows to attract members.[24]

A third aspect of the middle class approach emphasizes snob appeal by making invidious comparisons with blue-collar workers. As mentioned earlier in the discussion of salary demands, a typical piece of organizing literature emphasizes that a janitor makes more than a clerk, that the clerk *obviously* should be making more, and that the only way for him to do so is through joining a labor organization. Moreover, labor attempts to refute the clerks' belief that joining a union results in a lowering of status. Thus, the Office Employees International Union changed its name to Office and Professional Employees International Union in 1965, in order, among other reasons, "to make our union more appealing to the unorganized." There are "lots of ways," says one union president, to "give a union the sweet smell of status." After all, declares organizing literature, Gregory Peck belongs to a union and, if that does not convince clerks that joining unions does not endanger their status, the literature also points out that England's Princess Margaret's husband belongs to a union. If the Earl of Snowden can join a union without any loss of status, why can't Dagwood? When a banker was quoted in *Newsweek* to the effect that union members could not be trusted with confidential papers, the head of the OPEIU responded, "does he [the banker] feel the same way about Bob Hope, Johnny Carson, Danny Thomas, Charlton Heston or Leonard Bernstein— all of whom, among other national and international celebrities— are proud to carry union cards? Or does he want the American public to believe that bank employees must remain second-class citizens?"[25]

The status approach helps explain why unions so vigorously support the drive to organize teachers and government employees. If these high status white-collar people join unions, the argument runs, then other white-collar people will follow suit. The appeal to desire for status also partially explains why white-collar unions are pushing to give supervisors the right to join unions. The unions recognize that these people are often the key to organizing clerks (as they have proved to be in other countries and in the past).

The problem of status is particularly important to female employees. Since women in 1967 constituted 54 percent of the "organizable" white-collar employees and nearly three-fourths of clerical employees, labor organizations are, therefore, trying to overcome the lack of receptivity females display toward appeals to sign a union card and to erode their pro-management proclivities. This campaign has included a number of facets: using female organizers; placing women in high positions in the unions; sponsoring fashion shows; publishing special organizing literature oriented toward a female audience; seeking special collective bargaining gains such as payment for baby sitters, promotion from within through job bidding open to women, seniority clauses protecting women in securing desired shift work, and job rights after maternity leaves; and by creating pressure for legislation beneficial to the working woman, such as tax benefits for child care and opposition to wage discrimination favoring males (partially to prevent lesser-paid women from replacing higher-paid males). Surveys indicate, however, that female clerks continue to be more favorable to management than males. Yet, management as well as union organizers must note with interest the items that women rank as "very important" more often than men. They are: "respect shown to employees, absence of favoritism, the kind of work they do, the 'atmosphere' at the company, the friendliness of fellow workers, the company's reputation in the community, [and] the amount of work expected of them"—items more concerned with status and style than with cents.[26]

But the fact that women are more and more participating in the labor force not just "until" marriage or "until" pregnancy but for the remainder of their working life may have a more important effect on changing the attitude of women toward labor organization than union tactics. But, in general, female commitment to the world of work remains less than that of males, as does female commitment to unions.

Whether they use a general approach that views clerks as middle class or as working class, the unions do frequently focus their organizing drives on specific issues: the need for fair procedures for promotion, better salaries, the impact of automation, unfair treatment, the need for grievance procedures, the importance of having a voice in the decision-making process, and a host of others. However, they have not as yet resolved the question of who should do the organizing of the clerks. A host of unions claim jurisdiction, and it would be not too much of an exaggeration to say that, for a time, unions appeared to be spending more time and energy fighting among themselves than in organizing the clerks.

Union Conflict

The union argument over jurisdiction in the organization of the clerks specifically and white-collar workers in general is not merely a power struggle. The dispute also concerns the kind of union that would be most effective in attracting clerks. In other countries the dispute has centered on whether there should be a separate federation of unions that organizes only white-collar employees or whether white-collar employees should belong to unions that are members of a federation that includes both blue-collar and white-collar unions. If the latter type of federation is chosen, a further dispute arises as to which union inside the federation should have jurisdiction over the clerks. In other words, should a white-collar union have sole jurisdiction or should an industrial union have the right to organize clerks within its own industrial jurisdiction? Perhaps unfortunately, the dispute in the United States, at least insofar as it has related to organizing clerks, has not focused on the first issue. Other countries have a separate federation of labor that has jurisdiction over white-collar employees wherever they work and in some, like Sweden, they have been extremely successful in organizing clerks. In the United States, independent single-company unions, which are not affiliated with the AFL-CIO or with any other federation, have been proportionately more successful than multicompany unions, which have tended to be affiliated with the AFL-CIO. (The UAW-Teamster alliance outside the AFL-CIO will be discussed later.) In 1961, 113,029 out of 452,463 (or one out of every four) members of independent unions were classified as white-collar as compared with one out of eight members in the multiplant unions. By 1967 the proportion of members in white-collar unions had gone up, reaching 32.6 percent (154,800 out of a total of 475,000) in the intrastate, single-employer unions.[27]

Drawing upon his studies of these independent unions, Professor Arthur Shostak suggests that they have certain features that make them attractive to white-collar employees: They are informal and permit "face-to-face relations"; they are "office-oriented," thereby protecting status; they are "employer-centered," thus reinforcing identification with management and dreams of upward mobility; they are conservative, which seems "natural to status-anxious, upwardly mobile middle class office employees, most of whom place a high value on respectability, appearance, and harmony"; and they are small, a quality that favors the individual while the multiplant unions favor big unions and big government.[28]

As mentioned earlier, however, the possibility that the independent unions constitute a potential base for organizing white-collar employees has not received much attention. Even when they are successful, the independent unions continue to be local, atomized operations. Still, they hold out definite promise. For example, the Office Employees has taken over a couple of independent unions in banking and used them as a base to try to organize other banks on a branch-by-branch basis. At its 1968 convention, the OPEIU also urged its organizers to contact the independent unions and try to convince them to join.

In addition to independent unions, there are those white-collar employees who are joining associations rather than unions, but this alternative, although important for professional white-collar employees like engineers and nurses, has less relevance for the clerk or the bookkeeper, whose ties with his fellow workers are not strong enough to bind them together in an association. Perhaps because such associations are mainly concerned with professionals and compete with unions for their allegiance, the AFL-CIO formed SPACE, the Council for Scientific, Professional and Cultural Employees, in

1967—indeed, this constituted one of the most important recent coordinated activities the federation has undertaken with respect to white-collar workers. SPACE is made up of a number of unions who plan to concentrate their joint efforts on professional and technical workers. In fact, recently SPACE began to discuss working with the independent associations. The lowly clerks, however, remain relatively ignored and little mention has been made of a special or separate white-collar federation or council which would include them.

Thus in the United States, rightly or wrongly, there has been little concern about the issues of independent unions or a separate white-collar federation. Instead the dispute has focused on which of the already existing unions should organize the clerks. In some aspects, the dispute between the white-collar organizations, led by the Office and Professional Employees International Union, and the industrial unions, led by the spokesmen in the Industrial Union Department of the AFL-CIO, has had a certain Alice-in-Wonderland quality. Each side has been vigorously arguing about who should organize but neither has had any real success in organizing. Their record of success is shown in Table 4. The fight has quieted

Table 4. Comparison of White-Collar Membership of American Trade Unions, 1961[a]–1966[b]
(in order of membership as of end of 1961)

Union	1961	1966	Percent Change	Rank in 1966
Retail Clerks International Association[d]	388,000	500,314	+28.9	1
American Federation of Musicians	269,000	227,238	−15.5	2
Brotherhood of Railway and Steamship Clerks	200,000	216,000	+8.0	3

[a] Benjamin Solomon and Robert K. Burns, "Unionization of White-Collar Employees—Extent, Potential, and Implications," *The Journal of Business of the University of Chicago* (April 1963), p. 146.
[b] Data for the year 1966 is from *Directory of National and International Labor Unions in the United States,* 1967, United States Department of Labor Bulletin No. 1596.
[c] The basic list of national and international unions is found in the Bureau of Labor Statistics *Directory of National and International Labor Unions in the United States and Canada,* 1961.
[d] All unions designated as White-Collar are in italics. All unions are members of the AFL-CIO except those marked (IND) which refers to independent unions not affiliated with the AFL-CIO.

Union[c]	1961	1966	Percent Change	Rank in 1966
Communications Workers of America	192,000	—[f, g]		
United Federation of Postal Clerks	140,000	—[f, g]		
National Association of Letter Carriers	138,000	0[m]		
United Steelworkers of America	130,000	—[f]		
International Brotherhood of Teamsters (IND)	88,000	—[f, g]		
American Federation of Teachers	70,000	125,000	+78.6	4
International Brotherhood of Electrical Workers	70,000	—[f, g]		
Office Employees' International Union[h]	65,000	70,000	+7.7	7
Retail, Wholesale, and Department Store Employees Union	64,000	—[f, g]		
American Federation of State, County, and Municipal Employees	63,000	—[f, g]		
American Federation of Government Employees	60,000	120,000	+100.0	5
Associated Actors and Artists of America	55,000	59,036	+7.3	8
The Order of Railroad Telegraphers[i]	53,000	44,550	−15.9	10
United Automobile Workers (IND[e])	50,000	56,108	+12.2	9
Building Service Employees' International Union[j]	50,000	6,970		
Alliance of Independent Telephone Unions (IND)	50,000	75,000	+50.0	6
National Rural Letter Carriers Association (IND)	38,500	0[m]		
National Postal Union (IND)	38,000	—[f, g]		
International Union of Electrical, Radio, and Machine Workers	32,500	16,000	−50.8	22
American Newspaper Guild	31,500	31,224	+0.9	11
The Commercial Telegraphers' Union[k]	31,000	22,612	−27.1	14
International Association of Machinists	30,000	25,085	−16.4	13
National Federation of Federal Employees (IND)	30,000	—[f, g]		
Amalgamated Meat Cutters and Butcher Workmen	28,200	7,061[m]	−75.0	
Amalgamated Clothing Workers	27,000	19,100	−27.3	18
National Association of Postal Supervisors (IND)	26,000	30,115	+15.8	12
Insurance Workers International Union	25,000	21,904	−12.4	16
International Air Line Pilots Association	14,800	16,184	+9.4	21

[e] United Autoworkers disaffiliated from the AFL-CIO in 1968.
[f] Data not reported.
[g] White-collar members believed to account for at least 5 percent of membership.
[h] Name changed to Office and Professional Employees International Union (AFL-CIO).
[i] Name of The Order of Railroad Telegraphers was changed to Transportation-Communications Employees Union in 1964.
[j] Name of Building Service Employees Union was changed to Service Employees International Union in May 1968.

Table 4. Cont.

Union[c]	1961	1966	Percent Change	Rank in 1966
National League of Postmasters of the United States (IND)	14,400	18,000	+25.0	19
American Federation of Technical Engineers	14,000	15,840	+13.1	23
National Alliance of Postal Employees (IND)[l]	12,600	22,200	+76.2	15
National Marine Engineers' Beneficial Association	11,000	11,000	0	18
International Organization of Masters, Mates, and Pilots	10,000	—[f, g]		
American Communications Association (IND)	8,000	merged in Feb. '67 with Teamsters		
Oil, Chemical & Atomic Workers International Union	7,600	16,533	+117.5	20
United Mine Workers of America (Dist. 50) (IND)	7,110	11,600	+63.2	24
Transport Workers Union of America	7,000	20,250	+189.3	17
United Electrical, Radio and Machine Workers of America (IND)	6,400	8,350	+30.5	24
Railway and Airline Supervisor Association	6,311	5,741	−9.0	26
National Broadcast Employees and Technicians	6,000	—[f, g]		
Theatrical Stage Employees and Moving Picture Machine Operators	5,000	6,216	+24.3	25
Railroad Yardmasters of America	4,500	—[f, g]		
International Chemical Workers Union (IND)	4,000	4,650	+16.3	27
American Train Dispatchers Association	3,500	3,718	+6.2	28
Directors Guild of America Incorporated (IND)	2,140	3,150	+47.2	29
International Union of Life Insurance Agents (IND)	2,000	1,900	−5.0	31
The National Association of Special Delivery Messengers	2,000	0[m]		
Writers Guild of America, West (IND)	1,868	2,443	+30.8	
Railroad Yardmasters of North America, Inc. (IND)	1,450	1,924	+32.7	30
Writers Guild of America, East (IND)	1,200	1,325	+10.4	
American Radio Association	1,000	1,000	0	
Technical Engineers Association (IND)	700	—[n]		
Airline Dispatchers Association	650	792	+21.8	

[k] Name of Commercial Telegraphers' Union changed to United Telegraph Workers, August 1, 1968.
[l] Name changed to National Alliance of Postal and Federal Employees.
[m] The dramatic change in white-collar membership is probably attributable to a difference in definition of "white collar" used by those reporting in the Solomon and Burns questionnaire and the BLS questionnaire. See Solomon and Burns, *supra*, p. 145 and BLS Bulletin No. 1596, *supra*, n. 1, p. 81, for further discussion.
[n] No longer meets the required interstate definition of a national union.

down in recent years: perhaps because some of the leading pro-
tagonists have died or left the labor movement; perhaps because the
fight seemed sterile; and perhaps because the dispute appeared to
be irrelevant to the primary goal of organizing itself. In fact,
however, the issue may well be crucial. Although a similar jurisdictional fight in the early 1930s might also have seemed sterile for a
while, it resulted in the birth of the CIO, which provided an
appropriate and welcome home for the semiskilled and unskilled
workers and thereby eventually forced the AFL also to extend its
hospitality to this group of workers.

To the OPEIU, the clerks are "psychologically much different
from manual workers" and do not want to be "tail on a manual-
workers' union kite." Henderson B. Douglas, the late director of
organization for the OPEIU, declared that:[29]

> The need for white-collar identification, greater emphasis on proper
> classification, promotional opportunities and understanding of the
> unique problems of clerical workers and their relationship to manage-
> ment, and promotional progression paths must be included in any
> program sponsored by a white-collar union if it is to be successful.
> Loss of identification in an industrial union, plus the historical failure of
> an industrial organization to recognize the ideals and aspirations of
> office and clerical crafts, have brought these industrial unions to a point
> where they are no longer an important factor in organizing white-collar
> workers.

The OPEIU would like to become the nucleus of a single big white-
collar union, one that encompasses not only the clerks in industry
and offices but also the American Federation of Technical Engineers. The latter has rejected OPEIU proposals for merger. The
industrial unions, however, deny the OPEIU's claim of jurisdiction
over clerks in industrial establishments although they acknowledge
the validity of OPEIU claims in such areas as banks, insurance companies, and Wall Street.

The industrial unions respond to OPEIU claims by stating that
clerks will benefit by joining an industrial union because the latter
possesses not only strength but also familiarity with the way top
management works. Furthermore, nonmanual employees work in
close proximity to manual workers in industry and thus are aware
of what the union has done for the manual workers. "Hourly or

Salaried—All Ford Employees Share Common Interests," declares UAW organizing literature. "We're All in the Same Boat," asserts an AFL-CIO throwaway. (Besides trying to convince the clerks of the importance of joint action, the industrial unions appeal to the production and maintenance workers, trying to enlist them in the drive to organize clerks since ". . . unorganized workers at your place of work could constitute a threat . . .")

Furthermore, because white-collar employees do not have the feeling of common craft that provides a tie between blue-collar workers that cuts across company lines, says the industrial unionist, the total resources of an industrial union must be brought to bear in order to back up the office employee in his struggle with big management. Therefore, the only way a clerk can come close to gathering enough strength to challenge corporate power is to join with the blue-collar industrial union in that same corporation. On the other hand, some white-collar workers who have joined blue-collar unions have protested that they are, at times, ignored in making policies since they are a minority in a predominantly manual-worker union. As a result, they have demanded, and often received, special powers in some of the industrial unions, such as the United Automobile Workers. Whatever the merits of the arguments of both groups, one thing is clear: Neither has been particularly successful in organizing clerks. The new Alliance for Labor Action, whose membership consists mainly of the Teamsters and the UAW, promises new organizing drives among clerks, particularly among those holding the lower-paid jobs in the white-collar field. It will be interesting to see if these blue-collar unions prove more successful than the white-collar unions or the other blue-collar unions in the AFL-CIO. In fact, one of the reasons that the UAW gave for leaving the AFL-CIO was the federation's failure to implement any real organizing drive while the UAW had undertaken a commitment of more "time, energy and resources" to white-collar organizing.[30]

The evidence provided by the results of elections and the figures concerning total white-collar union membership trends (already discussed) indicates that there is little immediate hope that there will be any marked union expansion among nonmanual employees. This prediction is particularly sound given the absence of any major activity to organize these people. A coordinated organizing drive, in which a number of unions work in concert in a given community, might be helpful. The unions have had minor successes with this method in some cities (Los Angeles and Boston, for example) and among such groups as public employees, but no great success has been reported among white-collar employees in the private sector. A second approach is to have unions cooperate in an organizing drive directed at one firm or a group of firms. Thus, the Office Employees and Retail Clerks have cooperated in department store organizing drives and the clerical union has been supported by the blue-collar unions in its activities at the shipyards. Both approaches have met with some success. In another form of cooperative activity, the OPEIU and the Teamsters signed a "no-raid" agreement in 1968. A third method is chain organizing. In this case, after an initial breakthrough in a company, the union tries to organize other white-collar units in the same company. The UAW has used this method at Chrysler but has not made the important initial breakthrough at Ford or General Motors. The Office Employees have been trying the same technique in the brokerage houses on Wall Street.

Although there appears to be no reason to anticipate any major breakthrough in organizing clerks, a small, steady expansion is not unlikely, given any kind of trade-union commitment. We have already discussed a number of factors that indicate that clerks are not adverse to some kind of representation in bargaining. In a 1963 Opinion Research Corporation (ORC) survey, when white-collar people were asked, "Do you feel an increasing need for representation in your dealings with management?" 40 percent said they did, while 53 percent said they did not. Of the males, 48 percent said they wanted some kind of representation, while 47 percent declared they did not. In May 1964, the ORC asked white-collar workers, "Do you think it's to the advantage of white collar employees such as office and clerical workers to join a union or to stay out of unions?" At this time, 47 percent said it was to their advantage to join (44 percent of the total public agreed). But the prounion sentiment apparently declined sharply because in May 1967 only 36 percent of the white-collar employees said it was to their advantage to join a union (now only 42 percent of the public agreed). Thus, after all the supposed trade-union effort to organize clerks, their interest in joining seems to have actually diminished.[31]

The important statistic to remember, however, is that more than one-third of the clerks surveyed in 1967 wanted some kind of representation. After all, only 28 percent of all workers in nonagricultural establishments are represented by unions. Clearly, there is some evidence that if a source of discontent exists, and if the discontented believe that a solution rests with organized group behavior, then the clerks may join bodies that are able to represent them, whether they are part of industrial unions, white-collar unions, independent locals, associations, or an independent federation of white-collar unions.

Surely, to secure white-collar members, organized labor must not only have a desire to organize clerks, but it must also do more actual organizing. Most white-collar employees have never been approached by a union. White-collar organizers often compare themselves to a group of men who admire an extremely attractive secretary and keep discussing what tactics they should use in order to get her to go out on a date with one of them. One day, they notice that a new male employee has taken her out, and they ask what methods he used to persuade her. His answer is simply, "I asked her."

Besides asking the clerks to join a union, labor organizers also need persistence and patience. In fact, one organizer believes that "Patience is the key to unionizing the white collar worker. We just have to wait until management, which is so content with itself and so sure of its relations with its white collar workers, makes a mistake—and we will be there always knocking at the door. Some manager will open it for us." Besides patience the labor movement needs a lot more knocking on doors. However, they must select the doors that are more likely to have behind them a number of white-collar people ready to listen. The sales pitches themselves must be developed after an investment of some thought and research, and so far research has been done more by management than by unions. (A leader of a labor organizing drive plaintively complained about the lack of research money, admitting, "We don't know all the answers. What makes a white-collar man tick? Is he different from somebody else? How come?") [32]

Some white-collar employees may indeed respond to union efforts by signing a union card. If enough do, their presence may alter the labor movement just as the inclusion of blue-collar workers changed the labor movement in the 1930s. Large numbers of white-collar workers joining unions is, of course, labor's hope, perhaps its last major one in the private sector if the union movement is to expand markedly.

NOTES

[1] "President's Report," *Proceedings* of the AFL-CIO's 4th Convention, 1961, Vol. 2, p. 4.

[2] Many of these figures come from an excellent paper delivered at the 1968 Labor Symposium, Wake Forest University, September 18–19, 1968, by H. M. Douty of the U.S. Bureau of Labor Statistics on "Employment Trends and White-Collar Employee Organizations in the United States."

[3] *White Collar* (January 1966).

[4] For an analysis of various theories of union growth, see Albert A. Blum, "Why Unions Grow," *Labor History,* 9 (Winter 1968), 39–72.

[5] *White Collar* (March 1966).

[6] Victor J. Sheifer, "White Collar Pay Supplements," *Monthly Labor Review,* 89 (May 1966), 496–502.

[7] Another indication of the narrowing of the gap is that the median annual wage increase in twenty metropolitan areas from 1953 to 1967 averaged 3.7 percent for male and female office clerical workers and 4.0 percent for skilled maintenance and unskilled plant males. See *Wages and Related Benefits: Part II, Metropolitan Areas, United States and Regional Summaries, 1966–1967,* U.S. Department of Labor, BLS Bulletin No. 1530–87, p. 74. See this report for trends in fringes also. For salary comparisons see the U.S. Department of Commerce's annual report, *Current Population Reports Series.*

[8] By permission of the publisher from AMA Research Study No. 63, *Management and the White-Collar Union,* by Albert A. Blum. © 1964 by the American Management Association, Inc.

[9] Solomon Barkin, *The Decline of the Labor Movement and What Can Be Done About It* (Santa Barbara, Calif.: Center for Study of Democratic Institutions, 1961), p. 69; Joseph A. Beirne, "A New Key to Organizing," *American Federationist,* 72 (February 1965), 21–22.

[10] "The Corporation and the Union," *Interviews on the American Character* (Santa Barbara, Calif.: Center for Study of Democratic Institutions, 1962), pp. 22–23.

[11] George Strauss, "White Collar Unions are Different!" *Harvard Business Review,* 32 (September–October 1954), 74.

[12] Joseph Shister, "The Logic of Union Growth," *Journal of Political Economy,* 61 (October 1953), 414–415; *White Collar* (November 1964).

[13] "White Collar Workers in Industry," *Summary Report of Staff Seminar,* Industrial Union Department, AFL-CIO, December 1–3, 1960, p. 4; for a general discussion of this issue, see Albert A. Blum, "Computers and Clerks," in Irene Taviss (ed.), *The Computer Impact* (Englewood Cliffs, N.J.: Prentice-Hall, 1970).

[14] C. Wright Mills, *White Collar* (New York: Oxford University Press, 1951), p. 307; *White Collar Report,* No. 638 (May 29, 1969), p. A9.

[15] *White Collar* (October 1966).

[16] *White Collar Report,* No. 213 (April 3, 1961), p. A4; *Proceedings* of the International Union of Electrical, Radio, and Machine Workers, Washington, D.C., 1958, p. 453.

[17] E. P. Thompson, *The Making of the English Working Class* (New York: Vintage Books, 1966), p. 9.

[18] Strauss, *op. cit.,* p. 73. See also Julius Retzler, *Automation and Industrial Labor* (New York: Random House, 1969); James L. Stern and David B. Johnson, *Blue- to White-Collar Job Mobility* (Madison: University of Wisconsin's Industrial Relations Research Institute, 1968).

[19] Blum, *Management and the White-Collar Union,* pp. 11–12.

[20] Edward R. Curtin and James K. Brown, "Labor Relations Today and Tomorrow," *The Conference Board Record,* 5 (August 1968), 46, 53.

[21] *Ibid.,* pp. 52–53.

[22] Opinion Research Corporation, *What's Troubling Labor Leadership?* (Princeton, N.J.: 1963), pp. A-2, 6.

[23] John W. Livingston, "The Answer for the White-Collar Workers," in *Labor Looks at the White-Collar Workers* (Washington, D.C.: AFL-CIO Industrial Union Department, 1957), p. 74.

[24] "A Personal Message to You From UAW President Walter Reuther," April 23, 1966; *White Collar Report,* No. 341 (September 19, 1963).

[25] *White Collar Report,* No. 523 (March 16, 1967) and No. 622 (February 6, 1969).

[26] Opinion Research Corporation, *The Union Drive for White-Collar Worker* (Princeton, N.J.: 1963), p. 21.

[27] Harry Cohany and James Neary, "Unaffiliated Local and Single-Employer Unions in the United States, 1961," *Monthly Labor Review* (September 1962), pp. 979–980. Data for 1967 obtained from personal interview with Harry Cohany, May 28, 1969.

[28] Arthur B. Shostak, *America's Forgotten Labor Organization: A Survey of the Role of the Single-Firm Independent Union in American Industry* (Princeton, N.J.: Industrial Relations Section, Princeton University, 1962), pp. 59–67.

[29] *White Collar* (October 1961); *White Collar Report,* No. 203 (January 23, 1961), p. C-1.

[30] *White Collar Report,* No. 584 (May 16, 1968).

[31] Opinion Research Corporation, "Current Union Demands: Who Speaks For Labor?" *Public Opinion Index Report to Management,* 25 (October 15, 1967), 7.

[32] *Fortune,* 65 (February 1962), 200.

THE RETAIL CLERKS
by MARTEN ESTEY*

Retail unionism has long been one of the most rapidly growing segments of the American labor movement, although it received little attention outside the industry until the mid-1950s.[1] Since then, however, retail unions have become the subject of widespread interest, and the Retail Clerks, the dominant union in the field, has been heralded as "one of the wonders of the contemporary trade union world."[2]

The current interest in retail unions in general, and the Retail Clerks in particular, stems from a combination of factors. The Clerks' record of almost unbroken membership growth, which was by no means extraordinary so long as total union membership was rising to successive new highs during the early 1950s, stood out in sharp contrast to the decline of membership of the labor movement as a whole that occurred between 1956 and 1964, when American unions altogether lost half a million members.

Furthermore, by 1968, when over-all union membership had recovered and risen to an all-time high, the Retail Clerks had not only passed the 500,000-member mark to become the eighth largest American union, but also ranked second only to the Teamsters in terms of absolute growth since 1956, having gained 252,000 members from 1956 to 1968, compared with the Teamsters' 387,000.[3]

This record is all the more notable because the union's membership has been carved out of the service sector of the economy, an area in which the achievements of unions have been generally unimpressive. Since it has been painfully evident to the leaders of the labor movement that the problems of organizing the service industries must be solved if the proportion of unionized employees in non-agricultural establishments is not to decline still further,

* Associate Professor of Industry, Wharton School, University of Pennsylvania. Portions of this article appeared in "The Grocery Clerks: Center of Retail Unionism," *Industrial Relations*, May 1968, pp. 249–261.

they tend to seize upon the achievements of the Retail Clerks in the hope that they will provide the key for unlocking the door to the organization of the service trades.

Indeed, the interest with which the growth of the Retail Clerks is observed by students and leaders of the labor movement alike has an even more specific basis—the belief that the Clerks may have found the formula for organizing the white-collar worker. There is a certain objective basis for this belief, since the Retail Clerks may well have the largest white-collar membership of any American union; in 1968, in fact, it classified its entire membership of 552,000 as white-collar workers. Whether or not we accept this classification, which assumes that grocery clerks are white-collar workers, the Retail Clerks' white-collar membership *is* large, and the Clerks' growth affords an important clue to white-collar union trends.

In any case, the rapid growth of the Clerks suggests that the continuing shift of the labor force from the goods-producing industries to the service industries may not necessarily be as great a barrier to union growth as has been feared and that instead the service industries may actually offer a vast potential for expansion and development of the labor movement in the United States.

It should be added that the success of the Retail Clerks in setting the pace for the organization of the service industries has not been lost on the leaders of the labor movement. An appropriate symbol of the Clerks' new-found status was the election of James Suffridge, then president of the Retail Clerks International Association, to fill a vacancy on the AFL-CIO Executive Council in 1957.

☐ The Beginnings of Retail Unionism

Like labor organizations in many other industries, the development of retail unions to significant size and impact has taken place within the past thirty years. Only since 1935 has labor organization been extended to hundreds of thousands of retail employees or become a significant factor in the economic calculations of employers in major segments of the retail trades.

But like many other labor organizations, the origins of retail unionism long antedate the Wagner Act and the New Deal. Of the major unions now active in the retail trades, the first to be established was the Retail Clerks, founded in 1890 as the Retail Clerks

National Protective Association, a title that aptly symbolized its cautious and limited program at that time. The appearance of the Clerks was shortly followed by the founding of the Butcher Workmen in 1897, and, significantly enough, by an immediate clash between the two unions over jurisdiction in grocery stores.

Although 1890 marks the birth of the first national labor organization for retail employees, the beginning of organized employee activity in the retail trades took place more than half a century earlier. Commons and Associates, in their *History of Labour in the United States,* record an apparent attempt by the retail grocery clerks of Philadelphia to win "early closing" in the summer of 1835.[4] From 1835 until the formation of the Retail Clerks (indeed, for a long time after the founding of the Retail Clerks) we find records of clerks uniting, on a local basis and in small towns as well as large ones, to seek "early closing," the reduction of hours by moving up store closing time, either daily or on weekends, usually as a short-run measure to give temporary relief from long hours during the hot summer months.

Whether or not these early closing societies were genuine trade unions is open to debate, for their objectives were perhaps as beneficial to the employers as to the employees, and indeed in some cases they were actively supported by employers. Furthermore, a major shortcoming of the early closing societies was their limited objective. Once it had been achieved, they generally had no further program, and whatever organization had been developed to achieve that goal tended to disintegrate. Perhaps even more serious, early closing could be maintained effectively only if consumers were willing to refrain from buying from stores that remained open after the appointed hour. Its success depended, therefore, not on the economic power of the clerks, but on consumer support and cooperation, which unfortunately was seldom forthcoming.

Regardless of their limited scope and objective, however, and regardless of their evidently ephemeral nature, the early closing societies gave retail employees experience in organizing for their mutual benefit. However archaic they now seem, they were the ancestors of today's retail unions. Indeed, even after they achieved a charter as a national union, the objectives of the Retail Clerks were for many years little broader than those of the early closing societies, and the same was true of the Butcher Workmen in their first few years.[5] Even today the problem of Sunday closing, which may be described as a modern manifestation of the early closing problem, still demands the attention of retail unions, particularly in small towns.

While the history of retail unionism is by no means fully explored, it may not be stretching the point too far to suggest that the turning point in retail union history coincides rather closely with the appearance of the chain store in the food industry soon after World War I. Until that time, the evidence is that retail unions concerned themselves largely with early closing.

The appearance of the chain store presented the retail unions with the opportunity for more ambitious programs along the lines of unions in the production industries. Although they were sometimes slow to take advantage of this fact, the evidence strongly suggests that it was the rise of the chain store, and the recognition of the possibilities it offered, that permitted the retail labor organizations to become unions in the full sense of the word. When, roughly a decade after the appearance of the chain store, retail unions received the added impetus of the Wagner Act (though its impact in retail trade was limited, as we shall see), the stage was set for the rapid growth that has characterized the past thirty-five years, during which the retail unions emerged as a significant force.

☐ The Unions Today

Although the Retail Clerks has the largest retail membership, it is far from having the retail trades to itself. There is vigorous competition for the membership of retail employees, with at least six international unions and an undetermined number of local independent unions claiming substantial membership among retail clerks.

The great majority of organized retail clerks are concentrated in three unions: the Retail Clerks International Association; the Amalgamated Meat Cutters and Butcher Workmen; and the Retail, Wholesale and Department Store Union. Next in importance, if not membership, is the Teamsters Union, which at present appears to have a relatively small membership among retail clerks. However, it has a substantial membership among warehousemen, stock clerks, and drivers, and plays an active and vital role in the retail labor relations picture. In addition, both the Amalgamated Clothing Workers and the Building Service Employees have enrolled small groups of retail clerks, although their role in the retail-union picture is best described as peripheral. Of the local independent unions, one of the largest and best known is the United Retail Workers, representing the Jewel Tea clerks in northern Illinois.

The task of ascertaining union membership trends and patterns in the retail trades is complicated by the fact that only one of the six unions active in the industry is a purely retail union. Close to half the total retail membership, in fact, is to be found in unions the bulk of whose jurisdiction and membership is outside the retail trades. It is thus difficult, and in some cases impossible, to get an accurate figure on their retail membership alone. Furthermore, although no two of these unions have identical jurisdictions in the retail trades, there is extensive overlapping among them, so that it is not unusual for employees in a single retail store to find two or three unions competing for their membership. In addition, the roster of unions interested in the retail trades tends to grow and change as retail stores experiment with providing an increasing variety of services, many of which previously fell within the jurisdiction of other unions. The recent trend of major department stores and discount houses, for example, to provide automobile repair services in conjunction with the sale of automobile parts and accessories has brought the Machinists into the retail-union picture, as the question has arisen as to whether employees in these repair shops "belong" to them or to the Retail Clerks. Similarly, the introduction of snack bars in supermarkets has brought the Hotel and Restaurant Workers, who look on snack bar employees as culinary workers, into competition with the Clerks, who often claim "wall-to-wall" jurisdiction in grocery stores.

The Retail Clerks

The Retail Clerks, with a reported 1968 membership of 552,000, is not only the largest retail union, but also the only union whose membership consists entirely of retail employees, primarily retail clerks. It has no jurisdictional interests outside the retail trades, and in 1968 it reported that 100 percent of its membership was drawn from the retail trades. *Within* the retail trades, it has not confined itself either to a particular branch of retailing or to particular occupational groups within the industry, although the bulk of its membership, in fact, is concentrated in food stores. It has perhaps the broadest *retail* jurisdiction of the six unions we will examine here.

In short, the Retail Clerks now comes close to being the industrial union of the retail trades. And it may well be that the growth of the Retail Clerks to its present size in part reflects the fact that of the six unions, it alone has really specialized in organizing retail employees and has not diverted its energies into other industries.

The Meat Cutters

Second in terms of retail membership is the Meat Cutters, which in 1968 claimed approximately 195,000 members in grocery stores and supermarkets. In contrast to the Retail Clerks, the Meat Cutters was originally primarily a craft union in the retail food industry, with a majority of its retail members being skilled meat cutters. However, it has long claimed jurisdiction over "all wage earners in any way connected with . . . retail markets,"[6] and has in many cases gone on to organize all retail clerks in a grocery store or supermarket. As a consequence, the Meat Cutters have long been the Retail Clerks' chief competitor for the membership of employees in the retail food industry.

The RWDSU

The smallest retail membership of the three major retail unions is the approximately 67,000 claimed in 1968 by the Retail, Wholesale and Department Store Union (RWDSU), founded in 1937 by a group of dissident Retail Clerks' locals in New York City and chartered by the CIO as the United Retail Employees of America. Like the Clerks, the RWDSU claims a broad jurisdiction within the retail trades; unlike them, it also claims a heterogeneous jurisdiction outside the industry, over "persons employed in and about retail, wholesale, department store, building service, bakery, confectionery and production establishments."[7] The RWDSU's retail membership appears to be concentrated in department stores and specialty stores, but unlike either the Meat Cutters or the Clerks, it is not a major factor in the retail food industry.

Clothing Workers

The Amalgamated Clothing Workers' (ACWA) membership among retail clerks is highly specialized, consisting chiefly of several local unions of men's and women's clothing salesmen, principally in New York, Detroit, and Los Angeles. Membership reports on these locals indicate that the total number of retail clerks who were members of the ACWA in 1968 was probably not more than 30,000.[8]

In 1948, the ACWA made a brief attempt at organizing the major New York City department stores, in connection with one of the periodic crises in its sister union, the RWDSU. The attempt proved abortive, however, and since then the ACWA's activity in the department store field has been generally limited to discount stores and smaller chain stores.

The Building Service Employees

The role of the Building Service Employees International Union (BSEIU) in organizing retail clerks is, if anything, even more limited than that of the ACWA. In 1944 and 1945, it acquired store-wide membership in several Chicago department stores (through a transfer from the Retail, Wholesale and Department Store Union), and in 1968 its members in these stores represented its total retail membership of approximately 10,000. While the Building Service Employees continue to express a fear that they may need to organize retail clerks to protect their basic building service jurisdiction from attack by the Retail Clerks,[9] they have so far not expanded their activities beyond this small nucleus in Chicago and are not a significant factor in the over-all retail labor relations picture.

The Teamsters

Of the six unions most active in the retail trades, the status of Teamsters is the most difficult to assess in quantitative terms. Their primary jurisdiction in the retail trades covers drivers and warehousemen, making the Teamsters a significant force, especially in grocery and supermarket warehouses. In the past several years they have sought national agreements covering drivers and warehousemen with a number of major chains. After securing national contracts with National Tea Company (1964) and Kroger (1966), the union announced its intention of gaining similar contracts with six other major food chains, beginning with A&P.[10] The Teamsters also represent some 18,000 employees in Montgomery Ward's warehouses, retail stores, and mail-order establishments. The Teamsters are reported to have 250,000 members in retail and wholesale trade combined,[11] of which we estimate that approximately 100,000 are retail employees.

□ Union Size and Growth

As the figures in Table 1 show, total union membership in the retail occupations in 1968 was approximately 950,000, of which well over half belonged to the Retail Clerks. Compared to the 500,000 retail union members reported in 1954,[12] this figure represents a substantial gain, both absolutely (450,000 members) and relatively (90 percent).

Table 1. Retail Membership by
Union, 1968

Union	Members
Retail Clerks	552,000
Meat Cutters	195,000
RWDSU	67,000
Teamsters	100,000*
Clothing Workers	30,000*
Building Service	10,000*
Total	954,000

* Estimated.

It is important to realize, however, that such rapid absolute and relative expansion in retail union membership is by no means unprecedented. The Retail Clerks, for example, has consistently grown at a faster rate than the labor movement as a whole for the past thirty-five years. Between 1933 and 1954, while total American union membership rose from 2.9 million to 16.6 million (BLS figures), or over 450 percent, the Clerks rose from a mere 5,000 to nearly 250,000, an increase of more than 4,800 percent, or more than ten times the *rate* of growth of all unions together. Between 1954 and 1968, the Clerks' increase of some 305,000 members, or nearly 125 percent, again outdistanced the 13 percent growth of the labor movement as a whole.

For whatever reason, no other union has come close to matching the Clerks' growth in the retail trades. The Meat Cutters, which rank second to the Clerks in terms of total retail membership, have grown much less rapidly. Their estimated retail membership rose from 120,000 in 1954 to 195,000 in 1968, a gain of 75,000 or 63 percent. The Retail, Wholesale and Department Store Union, in fact, reported a net loss in the retail trades of 13,000 members (from 80,000 in 1954 to 67,000 in 1968). Neither the Clothing Workers nor the Building Service Employees showed any significant gains in retail membership during this period. Indeed, it may well be that, next to the Clerks, the most substantial membership gains in the retail trades in the past decade have been won by the Teamsters Union; unfortunately, it is impossible to measure them.

We conclude, therefore, that the expansion of union membership in the retail trades has been primarily a function of the growth of the Retail Clerks. Furthermore, judging from past experience, it seems likely that in the immediate future, at least, the growth rate of retail union membership as a whole will be determined largely by the success or failure of the Clerks in maintaining their organizing momentum. Although their *rate* of growth has naturally slowed down, their long-run growth pattern suggests that the prospects for further substantial growth of the Retail Clerks (as well as of retail unionism as a whole) are favorable. This impressive growth record, in fact, has frequently led to predictions that the Retail Clerks are on their way to becoming the largest union in the country. Indeed, given the size of the retail trades, and the size of the labor force over which the Clerks claim jurisdiction, there is no question that they may be *potentially* the largest union.

One of the paradoxes of organized labor in the retail trades, however, is that the sheer size of the retail trades dwarfs even the most impressive union membership achievements. In July 1969, for example, there were 8.3 million employees on retail payrolls (not including those in eating and drinking places), of whom approximately 7.5 million were nonsupervisory employees.[13] In such a huge population, even a million union members (the approximate retail union membership in mid-1969) represents less than 15 percent of nonsupervisory workers, leaving the retail trades close to the bottom of the scale of industries ranked by degree of union organization.[14]

Furthermore, in spite of the notable growth of retail unions since 1954, the gain in union membership barely matched the absolute growth of the retail work force, with the result that there are as many nonunion retail employees today as there were fifteen years ago. In view of this situation, it seems likely that, barring a quantum jump in the growth rates of retail unions, the ratio of union members to the retail labor force will continue to rise only slowly, and will remain relatively low for many years to come.

Fortunately, the fact that they have organized only a minor fraction of their over-all industry has a less serious effect on collective bargaining for unions in the retail trades than it would have for unions in many of the goods-producing industries. The retail trades are primarily local market industries (although the mail-order houses and, increasingly, the department stores are important exceptions to this rule), and the area of competition is thus local rather than national.

The relevant area so far as the effectiveness of collective bargaining is concerned is the local market of a particular sector of retail trades (for example, grocery stores or department stores). The evidence is clear that in a number of major cities, the retail unions have succeeded in organizing the majority of workers in a particular branch of retailing. In these instances, they have unquestionably obtained the degree of local market control necessary for truly effective collective bargaining. In Los Angeles, for example, where the retail food industry is perhaps more highly unionized than anywhere else in the country, it is estimated that approximately 90 percent of all food store employees are union members—and it is doubtless no coincidence that their wages and fringe benefits are among the highest, if not *the* highest in the United States retail food industry.

The real problem that arises from the presence of vast numbers of unorganized workers in the retail trades is that it offers a constant and almost irresistible temptation to other unions to try their luck in the field, since there is clearly plenty of room to organize the unorganized, without running into the problem of simply transferring workers who are already organized from one union to another. In particular, their presence contributes to frequent jurisdictional squabbles between the Retail Clerks, which claims jurisdiction over *all* retail workers, and other unions active in the retail trades, which are inclined to regard unorganized workers as fair game, especially if their proximity tends to impede the progress of organized workers.

The Clerks and the Butchers have been engaged in an almost endless argument over jurisdiction in food stores for seventy years, while the Teamsters threatened to encroach upon the Clerks' territory as early as 1905. Similarly, the Retail, Wholesale and Department Store Union has had to guard against predatory moves by the International Longshoremen's and Warehousemen's Union (ILWU), besides preventing conflict between its own retail and warehouse locals.[15] Although the sheer size of the retail trades would seem to make it possible for various unions in the industry to stay out of each other's way, each of them naturally prefers the most rewarding targets, which, for reasons we will discuss later, are the chain food stores and the department stores. So the prospects for an early end to jurisdictional problems in the retail trades can only be described as slim.

□ Membership Distribution

Industrial Distribution

The distinguishing characteristic of retail unionism in the United States is its heavy concentration in retail food stores, and more particularly in the big food chains that play so large a role in food distribution. The evidence suggests, in fact, that food store employees constitute an outright majority of union members in the retail trades as a whole, as well as representing the largest bloc of members in the two largest retail unions, the Clerks and the Meat Cutters. Thus a recent report states that "although grocery employees are still the largest group in the (Clerks) union, they now (1967) make up only about 40 per cent of its membership."[16] As already noted, the Meat Cutters' retail membership of 195,000 consists entirely of food and grocery store employees. When we add the food employee membership of the Teamsters, the RWDSU, and the independent locals, it seems likely that a conservative estimate of union membership in food stores may be close to 500,000, or slightly over half the total retail union membership.

Although most of the growth in retail union membership since 1950 has been concentrated in the food sector of the retail trades,[17] it should be emphasized that the present heavy concentration of membership in the food industry is by no means a recent phenomenon. The Meat Cutters retail membership has been confined to food stores since before 1900. Over thirty years ago, the secretary-treasurer of the Retail Clerks acknowledged that grocery, food, fruit, and vegetable clerks had been the bulwark of the union since its founding in 1890. He estimated that they then (1938) constituted 63 percent of the union's membership.[18]

It is significant that grocery stores are the stronghold of retail unionism in Great Britain as well as in the United States. In a study made of retail unions in England in 1959, Robert Knight found that the core of their strength was in food distribution, particularly in chain stores.[19] Quite clearly, then, at least *some* of the basic factors that have contributed to the relatively great success of labor organization in the retail food trades are international in scope.

Food stores are the center of retail unionism not only in absolute numbers of members, but in relative terms as well. Nearly 40 percent of nonsupervisory employees in food stores were unionized in 1966,[20] compared with less than 15 percent in the retail trades as a whole.

It seems ironic, to say the least, that the Retail Clerks should have come to represent the great hope of the labor movement and that they should be thought of as the largest white-collar union, when at least 40 percent of the union's members are grocery clerks, whose activities can be described as "white-collar" work only by severely stretching the meaning of the term and which are, in fact, more nearly akin to those of the manual worker or semiskilled production worker than to those of the white-collar worker. Although we will see that this fact may contribute a great deal to the success of the retail unions in organizing the grocery clerks, it is a bit discouraging to those who hope that the Clerks have found the answer to the problems of white-collar unionization.

Indeed, the painful conclusion that the retail unions have not discovered the key to the white-collar unionization after all tends to be reinforced when we consider the state of the unions in the department stores, where we come perhaps the closest to finding the true white-collar employee of the retail trades. Although workers employed in department stores and discount houses make up the second largest bloc of retail union members, the situation in the department store field contrasts sharply with that in the grocery industry. With between 75,000 and 100,000 union members, department store employees represent only a small fraction of total retail union membership. Out of a nonsupervisory department store labor force of 1,145,500 in 1966,[21] union members represent less than one in ten employees in their field. Even a comparison of union wage scales in department stores and in grocery stores indicates that the grocery unions generally have made substantially greater economic gains for their members than have the department store unions.

Geographic Distribution

Like the labor movement as a whole, retail unionism is primarily an urban, even a metropolitan, phenomenon. Although the retail trades are so pervasive and widely dispersed that there are more retail stores in towns with less than 2,500 inhabitants than in cities of 500,000 or more, the cities (particularly the large ones), where there are large numbers of employees in each of the major branches of retail trades, offer unions economies of both scale and specialization in organizing and bargaining.

Accordingly, there is a fairly close correlation between city size and retail union membership. New York City has the largest retail union membership. There are an estimated 140,000 organized retail employees in the greater New York metropolitan area.[22] The Los Angeles–Long Beach area, with a total of perhaps 65,000–70,000 retail union members, ranks second, and Chicago, Philadelphia, Detroit, and San Francisco (the third through sixth largest metropolitan areas respectively) all have about 30,000 or more each. Together, these six cities account for over 300,000 retail union members, or a third of total retail union membership.

Similarly, if we note that the Boston–New York–Philadelphia–Baltimore–Washington megalopolis has perhaps 225,000 members altogether and that California has say 125,000 members, we can see that membership is concentrated in the great regional retail and population centers of the East and West coast. In 1967–68, for example, a BLS survey of plant workers (that is, nonoffice employees) covered by collective bargaining agreements in large and medium-sized retail stores in metropolitan areas showed that the degree of organization was 57 percent in the West, 47 percent in the Northeast, 41 percent in the North Central region, and 13 percent in the South.[23]

While the Boston–New York–Washington megalopolis undoubtedly has the largest number of retail union members, California continues to attract attention because, despite the fact that it is only Number Two in terms of numbers of members, the degree of organization there is generally the highest in the country, except in regard to department stores, where New York retains the lead. New York City's leading position in the department store field is dimmed somewhat by the fact that organization of the traditional department stores was virtually completed by 1950, and little headway has been made since. In fact, department store unions in and around New York have been trying to recoup the losses incurred when stores they had already organized had gone out of business, by focusing their efforts on the expanding discount store field.

When we look at individual unions, we also find interesting regional variations in their membership distributions. The Retail Clerks stronghold appears to be California, where the 95,000 union clerks represent just less than one-fifth of the union's total membership. On the other hand, the Clerks are relatively weak in New York City, where the Meat Cutters dominate the grocery field and the RWDSU and its affiliates represent the bulk of organized department store workers. Conversely, the Retail, Wholesale and Department Store Union, formerly a CIO union, which is relatively strong in New York City, has no significant membership on the West Coast, and is only lightly represented in the retail trades in the Midwest. This particular dichotomy, of course, is the historic reflection of the Retail Clerks' loss in 1935 of a group of New York City locals that became the core of the RWDSU, which eventually went on to build what has so far proved to be an impregnable position in New York City. For a variety of reasons, however, the RWDSU has never been able to expand its retail membership on a major scale outside the New York City area.

□ Obstacles to Unionization

In order to gain an adequate understanding of the patterns of union membership in the retail trades, both the unions' surprising strength in chain food stores and their limited success in other sectors of retailing, it is necessary to look first at some of the general obstacles that unions in the retail trades face. We will then discover (not surprisingly) that union strength has been achieved mostly in those areas where these obstacles are minimized, or where, in addition, there are certain special factors that tend to favor unions rather than to hinder them.

The general obstacles faced by unions in the retail trades are of two types—what we will call economic factors, or those that affect the cost of organizing in the retail trades, and what might be called socioeconomic factors, those that affect the worker's attitudes. Obviously, these two kinds of factors are interrelated, for the worker's attitudes toward union membership affect the cost of organizing him. For convenience, however, we will consider them separately.

Economic Obstacles

Perhaps the most serious economic obstacle facing retail union organizers is the economic geography of the retail trade, the almost atomistic dispersion of retail employees among literally hundreds of thousands of typically small establishments located in thousands of villages, towns, and cities throughout the country. Unlike the manufacturing industries, where large numbers of employees are often concentrated in large plants, 70 percent of all retail stores had five or less employees in 1963, and less than 1 percent (15,150 out of 1,708,000) had as many as fifty employees[24]—although this small group accounted for one-seventh of all employees! As a consequence, even if he is successful, an organizer can reach only a handful of workers in a visit to a typical retail store.

Coupled with the fact that the typical retail establishments are so small is the fact that they are so numerous. Today there are more than 1.2 million retail establishments with payrolls in the United States. Another 500,000 establishments have no paid employees; these are the classic "Mama and Papa" stores.[25] The problem of numbers is hardly reduced to manageable proportions by concentrating on one city at a time, as unions in such local market industries as retailing tend to do; in New York City alone there are over 100,000 retail establishments, and it is obviously an almost insurmountable task even to contact them, let alone organize them.

The large numbers of retail stores and their small size means that organizers must recruit new members on an almost individual basis and spend a disproportionate amount of their time going from one store to another. Measured in terms of worker contacts per hour or per day, the retail union organizer's productivity therefore tends to be low, and per capita organizing costs tend to be high.

Organizational gains, expensive at best, are rendered still more costly by the high labor turnover characteristic of the retail trades. Although no general labor turnover figures are published for the retail trades, the high ratios of short-time and part-time employees in the retail trades (particularly women) and the low skill requirements for many retail jobs are obvious sources of high turnover. In the absence of some form of union security, of course, high turnover forces unions to organize two or three workers in order to maintain a single membership. (With union security, new employees become members automatically.) As one retail organizer complained, "You've got to keep organizing day and night, but trying to keep up with turnover is just a mathematical impossibility. It's like pouring water into a sieve."[26]

For retail unions like the Clerks and the RWDSU, whose jurisdiction embraces literally millions of workers, the high unit costs of net increases in membership constitute a major obstacle to a significant degree of organization of the retail trades as a whole. These unions have been forced to specialize and to concentrate their energies where they can be most productive. And the obvious strategy is to concentrate on the largest group that is readily organizable—the food chain employees.

Once initial organization has been achieved, another economic problem confronts unions trying to bargain for retail employees. Although there are a variety of retail jobs that might be classified as skilled (for our purposes here, probably the most significant skilled group is the retail meat cutter) most retail clerks' jobs are relatively unskilled, and can be and often are handled by those with little or no previous experience. As a result the average retail employee can be easily replaced if necessary. Since the vast majority of retail stores have very few employees, it is often not much harder for an employer to replace his entire work force simultaneously than it is to replace one man. Under these circumstances, organized labor's traditional economic weapon, the strike, has little to recommend it, for the economic pressure that it brings to bear is minimal.

Yet without the ability to mount an effective strike collective bargaining performance tends to be hampered, and this in turn interferes with *new* organizing efforts, since it denies the retail union organizer of perhaps his most persuasive argument, a record of substantial bargaining achievements to prove that it pays to join the union.

To offset the disadvantage of the economic limitations imposed on them by the nature of the labor force and the structure of the industry, retail clerks unions have often sought other ways of applying economic pressure, including the boycott and the picket line. Such sanctions bring to bear the power of outside groups, whether consumers or other unions, in situations where the clerks are weak.[27]

Socioeconomic Obstacles

In addition to operating in a sector of the economy whose structure makes organizing costly, unions in the retail trades have had to live with the fact that in their jurisdiction there are at least four large groups of employees generally considered hard to organize— women, part-time employees, workers who anticipate either self-employment or advancement into the managerial ranks, and those whose employment in small establishments binds them closely to their employer.

In general, workers in the first three categories resist unionization because "organization is difficult, if not impossible, where individuals expect to work themselves out of the status of wage-earners, or where they expect to remain wage-earners but for a short time because of anticipated withdrawals from the labor market."[28] To those who have such short-run expectations, even the most promising and effective union performance may appear to be a poor investment. It seems likely, in fact, that no amount of polishing of labor's "image" or of following a "white-collar" rather than a "blue-collar" approach will have much effect on this problem, which is basically an economic one rather than a concern for status.

The problems these groups pose for the union organizer are, of course, not unique to the retail trades. They exist in every industry in which such workers are employed. The retail organizer's special problem, rather, arises because these hard-to-organize groups comprise such a large segment, both proportionately and numerically, of the retail labor force.

In 1967, there were over 3 million women in the retail trades (excluding those in eating and drinking establishments), and they made up more than 41 percent of all retail employees, as compared with only 27 percent in the highly unionized manufacturing industries.[29] Furthermore, the ratio of women to men in the retail trades has risen steadily (despite Michael Harrington's implication to the contrary[30]) to its present level from slightly more than 33 percent in 1939,[31] and seems likely to continue to rise. Furthermore, though the Retail Clerks claim over 250,000 women members, the statistical evidence is that women are nearly twice as hard to organize as men. In 1966, for example, less than 14 percent of the women in the civilian labor force were union members, as compared to 28 percent of the men.[32]

In addition, over 2 million workers, or more than 30 percent of all nonsupervisory retail employees, worked part-time (less than 35 hours a week) in 1966,[33] while only 13 percent of the total civilian labor force did so.[34] The retail trades, in fact, are one of the largest sources of part-time employment, accounting for almost a quarter of the part-time employees in the civilian labor force. To the concern of union officials, the part-time group also appears to be expanding; between 1948 and 1966 the proportion of part-time retail employees rose from 20 percent to 30 percent. Furthermore, a substantial increase in part-time employment, in which the retail trades will doubtless share, is predicted for the future.[35]

Another group, no less important because it cannot be measured in quantitative terms, consists of those for whom the American dream of becoming one's own boss is still strong enough to prejudice their attitude toward unions. In this connection, it is pertinent to note that the opportunities to become one's own boss, in the form of self-employment, are perhaps more numerous in the retail trades than in any other sector of the non-farm economy. In August 1969, for example, there were 1,171,000 self-employed workers in the retail trades, and these represented more than 48 percent of *all* self-employed non-farm workers.[36] Similar evidence is provided by business turn-over figures, which show that the retail trades still provide the most popular avenue of entrance into business. In 1962, for example, 168,000 new retail enterprises were launched, 40 percent of all new businesses in the United States that year.[37]

So long as the possibility of the "worker becoming boss soon" is still relatively high, the retail trades offer an almost classic modern example of Selig Perlman's description of the alternative to unionism, the chance to "escape into free and unregulated self-employment."[38] We infer, then, that the proportion of retail employees likely to be influenced by the prospects of self-employment is apt to be higher than in most other industries, and this, of course, works to the detriment of retail unions.

Finally, there are the factors that have long been a special barrier to the unionization of the small retail store—the daily contact between employer and employee and the absence of the significant differentials in both function and economic status that normally separate management and the worker. In this intimate, almost preindustrial environment, furthermore, a significant amount of individuality and lack of standardization exists, so that a union, with its strong pressures for standardization and uniformity, may actually threaten what is an important value to the worker. Whatever the explanation, the fact that, as recently as 1963, 70 percent of all retail establishments with payrolls had no more than five employees each suggests that so far as unionization is concerned, a vast area of the retail trades is rather barren ground, which can be cultivated, but only at relatively great expense and effort.

□ Food Chains: The Stronghold of Retail Unionism

Given this bleak and barren environment, in which so many factors, both psychological and economic, tend to impede rather than facilitate union growth, how can we explain the fact that one retail union, the Retail Clerks, has become the eighth largest American union, and that the several unions active in the retail trades have a combined retail membership of nearly 1,000,000?

The answer to this question lies in the diversity of the retail trades. Like the manufacturing industries, the retail trades are not a single, homogeneous industry, but include a great variety of highly differentiated types of industry, whose only common link in many cases is that they are engaged in the retail distribution, rather than in the production or transportation, of goods. Diversity, in fact, is the saving feature of the retail trades, so far as the unions are concerned. While there are vast areas of the retail trades in which the particular combination of the factors we have discussed virtually rules out unionism, in other segments where the variables are relatively favorable to their formation retail unions have flourished.

Since it is evident that unions have had by far the most success in the food sector of the retail trades, our problem becomes one of determining what factors have led to this result. While the factors favoring the unionization of grocery clerks are numerous and complex, central to any explanation of the concentration of membership in this area must be the nature of grocery clerks' work.

The Dirty White Collar

Unfortunately for those who hope that the success of the Retail Clerks may somehow contain the answer to the riddle of how to organize white-collar workers, perhaps the most important reason for union success in organizing grocery clerks is the fact that they are really not white-collar workers at all, at least in the accepted sense of the term. So far as the bulk of his duties are concerned, the grocery clerk probably has more in common with the manual worker or with the semiskilled production worker than with the white-collar worker.[39] As the reader doubtless knows from firsthand experience, the sales function, particularly in supermarkets, is minimal. Aside from answering occasional questions or putting produce into a bag, the grocery clerk seldom waits on customers. Most of his time is spent lifting, carrying, and moving boxes, cans, and produce—in short, performing manual labor. Indeed, his job may well be physically harder and dirtier than that of his fellow employee in the warehouse, whose tasks are likely to be much more highly mechanized. To put it colorfully, the grocery clerk's work gives him a dirty white collar.

But this very fact is an advantage for the union trying to organize him, for the grocery clerk has perhaps less psychological resistance to unionism than the true white-collar worker; the grocery clerk knows that he won't jeopardize his white-collar status by joining a union, because he doesn't have it to start with. The manual character of grocery clerking thus must be counted as a strongly favorable factor from the organizing standpoint.

Male Labor Force

Equally important in terms of union organizing is the fact that, as a direct consequence of the largely manual work in the grocery store, most grocery clerks (like manual workers everywhere) are men. Grocery stores and supermarkets, in fact, have remained a stronghold of male employment in the increasingly female field of retail trade. Men make up a much larger proportion of the work force in grocery stores than elsewhere in the retail trades. In 1966, nearly 70 percent of all grocery store employees were men, as compared with nearly 60 percent in the retail trades as a whole and barely 30 percent in department stores.[40]

Since the evidence indicates that in general men are nearly twice as easy to organize as women, the fact that the nature of the work tends to favor male employment in the grocery and supermarket is a great advantage to the union organizer and helps make his life easier (if somewhat less enjoyable) here than elsewhere in the retail trades.

It seems likely, in fact, that the manual work and the predominately male labor force that are distinguishing features of the retail grocery store are among the main reasons why unions have had markedly more success in *food* chain stores than in the 5-and-10 cent store chains (more accurately known as limited-price variety stores) or in drug chains, where the work involves less physical labor, and women, not men, constitute the bulk of the work force.

Limited Opportunities for Individual Advancement

Another feature of work life in the grocery store or supermarket is that it offers perhaps fewer opportunities for advancement through individual effort than are to be found elsewhere in the retail trades. The lack of advancement opportunities is due in part to the very flat organizational structure of the modern supermarket (and the supermarket chain as well). Unlike the department store, where the number of steps in the hierarchy is large, so that the chances for long-term advancement at a single store are relatively good, the supermarket has a very simple occupational structure and a very short occupational ladder. For example, in the 1970–71 agreement between Retail Clerks Local 770 and the Food Employers Council of Los Angeles, which represents the bulk of the food chains and supermarkets in that city, there are only four levels of jobs for union members—clerks' helpers, apprentices, experienced clerks, and department heads—and the level of experienced clerk, which is the second highest of the four, can be reached in a year. Should a man aspire to move up into management, there are only two levels of management open to him at the store level, assistant manager and manager, of which there is a contractual limit of one each per store. Opportunities for promotion within the single supermarket are thus narrowly circumscribed.

Because a chain of stores also tends to have an extremely flat organizational structure, the chances for advancement *beyond* the store level are also rather limited. The centralization of chain store management puts heavy odds against moving up from store manager to district or regional office, if only because it reduces the need for the skills and experience that working up through the occupational structure of the store is likely to provide. How clearly store managers themselves have recognized this situation is suggested by the fact that before the Taft-Hartley Act prohibited their inclusion in bargaining units established by the National Labor Relations Board they often not only joined the union, but were the leaders of the movement to organize as well.[41]

No Incentive Wages

The wage structure prevalent in the grocery store and supermarket field imposes another kind of limitation on economic advancement through individual effort. Although retail clerks and salesmen in department stores and other "dry goods" stores are often on some form of incentive compensation (such as salary plus commission) that gives them at least some degree of opportunity to relate individual effort and economic gain, as well as some control over income, the grocery clerk is customarily paid a straight hourly rate. As one expert put it, "The devil himself couldn't devise a workable incentive plan for the grocery industry." The grocery clerk, therefore, lacks either the opportunity for higher income that incentive compensation would afford, or the opportunities represented by a long and (possibly) promising occupational ladder. These circumstances create a situation in which the supermarket employee, perhaps more than workers elsewhere in the retail trades, may conclude that joining a union is the way to maximize his economic position and the most effective avenue to his economic advancement.

Homogeneous Labor Force

The simplicity of the occupational structure in the supermarket and the chain food store offers still further advantages to the union, both in organizing and in bargaining. Paradoxically, grocery clerks, although not a skilled group, resemble a craft in that they are an occupationally homogeneous group, whose members share a common work experience and common problems. Unlike department store clerks, whose unity is impaired by the fact that they deal with a variety of different products and their jobs may require any of a wide range of skills (and even of compensation methods), grocery clerks generally handle similar products and perform similar functions. Occupationally they are a unit, with a relatively great community of interests.

This homogeneity simplifies both organizing and bargaining, for solutions or proposed solutions that speak effectively to the needs of one group of grocery clerks are apt to fit the needs of many of them. The problem of bargaining *within* the union is also minimized because the relative uniformity of interests greatly reduces the complexity of the process of balancing the conflicting interests of different groups within the membership.

The Industrial Character of the Chain Store

The chain store and the supermarket also break down the personal relationships that have long been a barrier to the unionization of the small retail store. The ready and frequent contact between employer and employee, the absence of specialization of function, and the lack of significant economic differentials between employer and employee have all disappeared from the supermarket, particularly from the chain store. Here the employee finds himself working, not for the employer, but under the direction of a paid manager, who himself is often working under the supervision of a top management located in another city or state (the old absentee management issue!). The clerk performs no managerial functions (as he may in the small store) and the manager no clerk's work—indeed, the union contract is likely to prohibit it. The economic gap between the worker and top management is also quite evident. In short, the supermarket and the chain store have brought the industrial revolution to the retail trades. In so doing, they have gone far to create an environment more conducive to unionization than elsewhere in the retail trades, as is suggested by the fact that more than half of all grocery employees now work in stores with twenty or more employees each, and 46 percent work in chain stores.[42]

Economic Consequences of Size

The very size of the modern supermarket goes a long way toward overcoming two of the major economic problems that confront unions elsewhere in the retail trades, high organizing costs and lack of bargaining power.

By retail standards, supermarkets and chain store systems are large-scale business enterprises; a single modern supermarket may employ over one hundred people, while a major food chain often employs several thousand in a single city. This concentration of employees in large establishments permits unions to reach the largest number of employees with a given expenditure of effort, so that per capita organizing costs are probably lower here than elsewhere in the retail trades.

In addition, the centralized decision making that characterizes the chain store system of business organization greatly enhances the effectiveness, or productivity, of organizing by agreement with the employer (often described as organizing from the top down) rather than organizing the individual employee. Although organizing from the top down by putting pressure on the employer rather than by winning NLRB elections has been illegal since Taft-Hartley, its historic importance in opening the door to unionization of chain stores is undisputed. In his definitive study of *The Butcher Workmen,* David Brody has recounted in some detail how Patrick Gorman, for many years the leader of the Amalgamated Meat Cutters and Butcher Workmen, paved the way in the 1930s for the organization of such chains as Safeway, Kroger, National Tea, and A&P by going directly to the presidents of those companies and persuading them to agree, if not always to actively encourage unionization, at least not to oppose it.[43]

Today, union shop agreements with chain stores often provide not only for automatic extension of membership to new employees of existing stores in the bargaining unit, but also for *accretion,* the extension of the union shop to stores built or acquired in the future. In fact, most of the growth of Retail Clerks membership in chain grocery stores "until the early sixties" is reported to have been through accretion,[44] and is evidently related to the fact that between 1950 and 1958, 80 percent of the growth of major grocery chains was through the construction of new stores or through acquisitions.[45]

A second and perhaps even more important advantage to the union derives from the fact that in the chain store, to a greater extent than anywhere else in the retail trades, the union gains bargaining power through sheer force of numbers. Just as sheer numbers gave the semiskilled mass production workers the economic power to make industrial unionism effective, so the large numbers of clerks in a major grocery chain make their prompt and effective replacement virtually impossible in the event of a strike. Harrington reports that as early as 1944, James Suffridge, then head of the California State Council of Retail Clerks, forced Safeway to recognize the San Diego local by threatening a statewide strike of Safeway clerks, and concludes that this technique was "one of the most important" innovations that Suffridge brought to the International union when he became its head in 1944.[46]

The chain store, in short, by bringing large-scale business organization to the retail grocery field, has, however inadvertently, enhanced the economic power of the grocery clerks and enabled them to wield sufficient power on their own to be formidable opponents for even a major chain store system. Once they have reached this point, the impact of a grocery clerks' strike may be reinforced by the fact that not only are many of the commodities they handle perishable, but even more important, the *demand* for food is perishable; it cannot be deferred or postponed, and once it is past, it is gone forever. The retail food store may thus be particularly vulnerable to strikes.[47] On the other hand, the fact that Los Angeles supermarkets were able to operate with supervisory help in the face of a butchers' strike in late 1967 suggests that it is possible to mitigate the effects of grocery strikes.[48]

The economic power of unions in the chain store field appears to have been still further enhanced by the tendency of the major chains to centralize not only decision making, but the actual process of distribution as well. This centralization creates a critical bottleneck that may well make the chain store more vulnerable to interruption than the small independent grocer. Chain store distribution is often so centralized that a single chain store warehouse may supply 200 or more retail outlets with the great bulk of their merchandise, if not with everything they sell. Although this system has the advantage of cutting distribution costs, a work stoppage at the central warehouse (by Teamsters, not Clerks) is equivalent to shutting off the main artery supplying blood to the body. In November 1966, for example, a strike of only 300 Teamsters at the Safeway warehouse in Richmond, California, was reported to have idled 1,700 other employees and brought business to a standstill in 285 stores in Safeway's San Francisco division.[49]

Perhaps ironically, then, we are forced to conclude that the shift toward large-scale business methods and organization that has accompanied the chain store's growth in the grocery industry has enhanced the efficiency of the *unions* as well as that of management. If this conclusion is sound, retail unions can only look upon the continuing shift toward large-scale retailing as a welcome development.

Nucleus of Organization

One of the most crucial factors in the unionization of supermarkets and chain stores has been their almost universal employment of a group of skilled craftsmen, the retail meat cutters. Because of their skill, the meat cutters (along with other strategically located groups like drivers and warehousemen) have frequently provided the nucleus of organization, the focal point from which organization could spread to other employees. Once the meat cutters provided the entering wedge, the task of organizing the less skilled and less strategically located clerks, even into a different union, was greatly simplified.

The Amalgamated Meat Cutters and Butcher Workmen, indeed, tends to regard itself as indispensable to the organization of grocery clerks, asserting that "The history of the retail clerks organization will indicate that from the beginning, this group has followed the path blazed through the wilderness by the Amalgamated."[50] While it was by no means a hard and fast rule, the evidence is persuasive that, particularly in the major chains, and prior to the 1937 Supreme Court decision upholding the Wagner Act, the Meat Cutters generally *did* precede the Clerks in organizing chain store employees, and in so doing they accustomed both chain store management and chain store employees to unions. Indeed, the Clerks' complaint in 1936, that Safeway did business with "the organized meat cutters, the organized Teamsters and the organized building trades, but when it comes to the clerks, it's thumbs down on organization,"[51] clearly suggests that the clerks tended to be the last of the chain store employees to be organized.

Strategic Support

Skilled or strategically located workers have also played an important role in the unionization in supermarkets and chain stores by providing the clerks with economic support. This support has had particular value during the early stages of organization, before the clerks have built up the strength of numbers to be economically self-sufficient.[52]

Doubtless the most important strategic support has come from the Teamsters Union, whose drivers and warehousemen control the supplies upon which the continued operation of the retailers depends. The Teamsters thus wield the greatest economic power of any union in the retail trades, and their power, as we have noted, tends to be enhanced by the growing centralization characteristic of chain store systems. Strategic support of drivers and warehousemen, however, may have had a less important impact on the unionization of clerks in supermarkets and food chains than the presence of the Meat Cutters, if only because strategic support is more readily withheld in the not infrequent cases of friction between the Clerks and the Teamsters. Where it has been available, however, Teamster support has proved beneficial, not only to the Clerks, but also to the Meat Cutters, who, despite the advantage inherent in their skilled occupation, have not hesitated to turn to the Teamsters to further strengthen their position.[53]

Conversely, the failure of the Retail, Wholesale and Department Store Union to attain anything like the success the Clerks have enjoyed in the retail food industry may result from their inability to win this support. From the outset, in fact, the RWDSU was hampered, both in following the lead of the Meat Cutters and in winning the support of the Teamsters, by the fact that it was affiliated with the CIO, while both the Meat Cutters and the Teamsters were long-time members of the AFL.

Labor Law

Another factor in the singular success of retail unions in the food industry that has been almost entirely overlooked, at least in the admittedly limited literature on retail labor relations, is that labor law, like so many other elements in the retail environment, has had in practice a highly selective impact on the retail trades, favoring union activity in chain stores and department stores over the rest of the industry.

More as a result of administrative policies laid down by the NLRB than of the actual wording of the statutes themselves, the great majority of retail employees have been excluded from the protection of the National Labor Relations Act and the Taft-Hartley amendments, while employees and unions in chain stores and department stores have received effective coverage. While most unions basked in the sunshine of the National Labor Relations Act, the retail unions had to function in an area that remained largely in the shade.

Chain stores and major department stores were the first and, for a number of years, virtually the only kind of retail business over which the National Labor Relations Board would consistently take jurisdiction. As early as 1938 the Board found "no question" about the interstate character of a retail food chain that operated stores in New Jersey, Pennsylvania, and Maryland.[54] Indeed, since most major chains operate stores in more than one state, the Board's jurisdiction over them has seldom been challenged. Although some major department stores initially contended that theirs was a primarily local business, the courts consistently upheld the Board's view that their activities sufficiently affected commerce to subject them to the requirements of the act.

Aside from chain stores and department stores, however, the NLRB's policy for many years was to *waive* jurisdiction over the retail trades—not forfeit it, but waive it. This policy was based on the practical grounds that the effect on interstate commerce of labor disputes involving the small retail store (although legally demonstrable under a broad interpretation of interstate commerce) could hardly be considered significant. Therefore, small stores should be left alone, if only to conserve the Board's limited resources for more important cases.[55]

The result of this policy was that to a very significant degree the protection and encouragement given to union activity by the Wagner Act was unavailable to workers (and unions) in the retail trades in general. On the other hand, its early and continuous application to the chain store field obviously provided an immeasurable impetus to labor organization in that area. Indeed, although a number of other factors contributed to the superior accomplishments of unions in the chain store area, the differential application of federal labor policies in itself does much to explain the concentration of union membership among employees of the large food chains.

State Labor Relations Acts

To some extent, the great gap in legal protection of union activity in the retail trades resulting from the policies of the NLRB was filled by state labor relations acts, which covered unions active in intrastate industries. Although state labor relations laws are on the books in ten states, the New York State Labor Relations Act and the Pennsylvania Labor Relations Act, both passed in 1937, have probably had the most significance for retail unions, if only because they apply to areas that have the greatest concentration of retail employees in the country. It seems to be no coincidence that organization of retail employees in these two states developed early. Moreover, since these two state boards were handling department store cases five years before the courts had affirmed NLRB jurisdiction in that area, it seems hardly accidental that department store unionization, in particular, should be most highly developed in these two states. The availability of effective protection through these state laws also helps to explain the concentration of RWDSU retail membership and the union's relatively strong position in the department store field in New York state.

☐ Department Stores—The Next Union Goal

Soon after he succeeded James Suffridge as president of the Retail Clerks in July 1968, James Housewright established organizing of the traditional downtown department store as the "number one priority in 1969." As a first step in working toward that goal, he appointed a Department Store Committee.[56] At its first meeting, this committee selected nine cities as initial targets for a department store organizing drive.[57]

This display of union interest is understandable, for despite the fact that department store employees are the second largest bloc of retail union members, department stores have remained largely unorganized except for downtown stores in a few cities. In fact, in the past ten or fifteen years, a number of department stores that were organized in the 1939–1947 period—Wanamakers, Hearns, and Saks-34th Street in Manhattan; Namms and Loesers in Brooklyn; Snellenburgs and Frank and Seder in Philadelphia; the White House in San Francisco, and others—have gone out of business, with a consequent erosion of union membership.

Department stores also present a substantial target, which offers unions large numbers of potential members concentrated in by far the largest units in retailing. In 1963, for example, there were nearly a million paid employees in some 4,200 department stores, an average of nearly 230 employees per store.[58] As the task of unionization in the grocery chains approaches completion in some cities, retail unions begin to cast about for new avenues for expansion. Under the circumstances, department stores seem to fill the bill nicely.

However, although department stores appear at first glance to offer unions many of the same advantages of large-scale retailing found in the grocery field (including a rapid growth in chain store operations), some of the factors that have previously limited the ability of unions to organize them still remain, and these obstacles will continue to make union progress among department store employees more difficult than it has been among grocery clerks.

Traditionally, the nature of work in department stores has been substantially different from that in grocery stores. The most significant difference, perhaps, is that in the traditional department store the distinction between the selling and non-selling function still exists, and even relatively unskilled workers tend to specialize along these lines. By and large, the sales clerks, who wait on and deal directly with customers, are more nearly white-collar workers in the accepted sense of the term than semi-manual workers like the grocery clerks. Accordingly, the department store work force is largely female; almost 70 percent of all paid employees in department stores are women.[59] As a result, department stores present in concentrated form the problems unions generally face in attempting to organize women, as well as the problems involved in trying to overcome whatever resistance may stem from the white-collar aspects of their work. It is no accident, therefore, that it is the salespeople who have often constituted the major stumbling block to store-wide organization of department stores.

A second difficulty encountered by unions is that the department store has remained "a collection of small stores" under one roof, each differentiated from the others by skills, wage rates, and often methods of compensation as well. In short, almost the only economic factor uniting the employees in a department store is that they are working for the same employer; the ties of common occupation and common experience are to a large extent missing. To put it another way, the diversity of occupational requirements, skills, and employment experience that exists within a single department store tends to divide rather than unite the workers. Even if a union does succeed in becoming the bargaining representative, the problem of effectively representing the diverse interests of the different groups is generally more difficult to carry out effectively than it is in the case of the grocery clerks' unions.

Department stores also lack any group of employees who might *consistently* serve as an entering wedge for unions, as the meat cutters did in grocery stores. To be sure, department store drivers and warehousemen are frequently organized, usually by the Teamsters, whose economic leverage in the retail trades is well known. However, there is no group that could provide the nucleus of organization in the sales force itself. Although different groups, usually the skilled salespeople, such as the shoe clerks or appliance salesmen, have from time to time served as just such a nucleus, no one group has consistently paved the way.

Although the evidence is clear that when the clerks seek to organize, the initial support of the drivers and warehousemen may be crucial to their success, that vital support cannot be depended upon. Indeed, clerks' unions are as likely to encounter competition from the Teamsters as support. All in all, then, the task of organizing department store sales personnel appears considerably more difficult than it was in the grocery store.

The McClellan Committee hearings in 1957 tantalizingly suggested still another obstacle to organization of department stores. These hearings revealed that Nathan Shefferman, a labor relations consultant to a number of major department stores, had established a thriving business advising his clients on ways to prevent unionization.[60] How much Shefferman's advice interfered with unionization cannot be ascertained, of course, but it is likely that it affected unions adversely.

Discount Department Stores

Although the traditional department store continues to pose an organizing problem, the discount department store's rapid growth in the past few years has distinctly benefited the unions. The Retail Clerks recently reported that in the period 1963–1967 "the discount store industry has accounted for a great deal of our increased membership."[61]

Gains in organizing discount store employees have been attributed to the fact that "the employer-employee relationship is too new to have fostered loyalty to the employer."[62] A more fundamental explanation would seem to be that the discount store tends to bring more factory-like conditions to the department store, as the supermarket did to the grocery industry, mainly by minimizing, in some cases, even eliminating, the selling function. As Harrington notes, the discount store clerk has "little or no personal 'sales' contact with the customer,"[63] and is becoming increasingly a materials handler rather than a salesman. Further evidence that the traditional differences between selling and non-selling personnel are being modified by discount store practices comes from the NLRB, which found in a recent discount store case that "all store employees were unskilled, and working conditions, including wage rates, were the same for all store employees, both selling and non-selling."[64]

Finally, because the discount department store often includes a grocery department, or even a supermarket, it may be that the incorporation of grocery clerks into the discount store labor force will provide the nucleus for the organization of sales employees in the rest of the store. If so, one of the persistent problems in the organization of department store employees may be solved.

□ Conclusion

The patterns of union membership in the retail trades have been related to significant variations in the economic, sociological, and legal environment that exist in different sectors of the retail trades. Union success in organizing grocery stores, which employ the majority of retail union members, is attributed chiefly to the predominance of manual work and the prevalence of male employees; to the advantages inherent in the size and structure of chain stores and supermarkets; to the consistent presence of the Meat Cutters as a nucleus for organization and the strategic support of the Teamsters; and to the full and early coverage provided by the Wagner Act and Taft-Hartley.

In traditional department stores, union growth has been handicapped, despite some advantages of size and NLRB coverage, by the nature of work, the predominance of women, and the absence of a consistent nucleus for organization within the sales force. Discount department stores, on the other hand, have recently been the source of substantial membership gains.

We therefore suggest the following conclusions:

1. Grocery clerks will continue to be the center of retail unionism for some time to come.
2. The unionization of grocery clerks, which the unions view as a heartening sign that the service industries can be effectively organized, cannot be interpreted as a major union breakthrough into the white-collar occupations.
3. Department stores and nonfood stores may become important sources of future growth in retail union membership; this *would* represent a major achievement in white-collar unionization.

NOTES

[1] For early studies of this subject, see Marten S. Estey, "Patterns of Union Membership in the Retail Trades," *Industrial and Labor Relations Review,* 8 (July 1955), 557–564, and "The Strategic Alliance as a Factor in Union Growth," *Industrial and Labor Relations Review* 9 (October 1955), 41–53.

[2] Walter Galenson, in Michael Harrington, *The Retail Clerks* (New York: Wiley, 1962), p. v.

[3] See *Directory of National and International Unions in the United States 1969,* U.S. Bureau of Labor Statistics Bulletin No. 1665, and *Directory . . . 1957,* BLS Bulletin No. 1222, p. 11. Unless otherwise specified, all 1968 union membership data are from the 1969 *Directory.*

[4] John R. Commons, *et al., History of Labour in the United States* (New York: Macmillan, 1918), Vol. I, p. 390. As a matter of fact, closer examination of Commons' sources indicate that the event he reported was actually sponsored by employers rather than their clerks. See Marten S. Estey, "Early Closing: Employer-Initiated Origins of the Retail Labor Movement," *Labor History* (forthcoming).

[5] See David Brody, *The Butcher Workmen* (Cambridge, Mass.: Harvard University Press, 1964), p. 111.

[6] Amalgamated Meat Cutters and Butcher Workmen, *Constitution* (revised) 1944, p. 9.

[7] Retail, Wholesale and Department Store Union, *Constitution* (as amended) 1946, p. 4.

[8] Letter to author from Amalgamated Clothing Workers, April 28, 1967.

[9] See Building Service Employees International Union, *Convention Proceedings,* 1964, p. 313.

[10] See *Supermarket News,* January 9, 1967.

[11] *The New York Times,* July 10, 1966, p. 44.

[12] See Estey, "Patterns of Union Membership in the Retail Trades," *op. cit.,* p. 560.

[13] *Employment and Earnings,* U.S. Department of Labor, Bureau of Labor Statistics, 16 (September 1969), 59–60. Eating and drinking places are excluded because they are generally outside the jurisdiction of the retail unions, and because they were excluded from BLS data on retail trade prior to 1964.

[14] In 1966, the BLS placed "trade" (wholesale and retail trade combined) fifteenth among nineteen industries ranked by degree of union organization. See *Directory . . . 1967, op. cit.,* pp. 61–62.

[15] Estey, "The Strategic Alliance . . .," *op. cit.,* p. 51.

[16] See "A Union in Trade: The Retail Clerks," *Monthly Labor Review* (November 1967), p. III.

[17] See Ben Seligman, "Organizing Problems in Retailing," *Labor Today* (February–March, 1966), p. 7. Mr. Seligman, now Director of the University of Massachusetts Labor Relations and Research Center, was formerly Education and Research Director of the Retail Clerks.

[18] The Retail Clerks' *International Advocate,* July–August, 1938, p. 1.

[19] Robert E. L. Knight, "Unionism Among Retail Clerks in Postwar Britain," *Industrial and Labor Relations Review,* 14 (July 1961), 515–527.

[20] In 1966 food stores employed an average of 1,276,500 nonsupervisory employees. *Monthly Labor Review,* August 1967, p. 95.

[21] *Ibid.*

[22] Estimate courtesy of Division of Research and Statistics, Department of Labor, State of New York.

[23] See *Handbook of Labor Statistics 1969,* U. S. Bureau of Labor Statistics Bulletin No. 1630, p. 370.

[24] U. S. Bureau of the Census, *Census of Business, 1963, Retail Trade: United States Summary,* pp. 1–135.

[25] *Op. cit.,* pp. 1–8.

[26] See George G. Kirstein, *Stores and Unions* (New York: Fairchild, 1950), pp. 108–109.

[27] For a more complete analysis of this point, see Estey, "The Strategic Alliance . . .," *op. cit.*

[28] John T. Dunlop, "The Development of Labor Organization: A Theoretical Framework," in Richard A. Lester and Joseph Shister (eds.), *Insights into Labor Issues* (New York: Macmillan, 1948), p. 184.

[29] Bureau of Labor Statistics Bulletin No. 1312-6, *Employment and Earnings Statistics for the United States, 1909–1968,* pp. 2, 763.

[30] Harrington, *op. cit.,* p. 5.

[31] *Census of Business, 1939, Vol. I, Retail Trade,* p. 74.

[32] See *Directory . . . 1967, op. cit.,* pp. 55, 60. Labor force data from *Handbook . . . , op. cit.,* p. 27.

[33] *Handbook . . . , op. cit.,* p. 136.

[34] *Ibid.,* p. 57.

[35] *Manpower Report of the President,* 1965, p. 47. For a recent analysis of part-time employment in retail trade, see Rose N. Zeisel, "The Workweek for Production Workers in the Private Economy," *Survey of Current Business,* September 1969, pp. 23–24.

[36] *Employment and Earnings,* September 1969, *op. cit.,* p. 38.

[37] *Statistical Abstract,* 1964, p. 487.

[38] Selig Perlman, *A Theory of the Labor Movement* (New York: Augustus M. Kelley, 1948), p. 8.

[39] Everett M. Kassalow, "White Collar Unionism in the United States," in Adolf Sturmthal (ed.), *White Collar Unionism* (Urbana: University of Illinois Press, 1966), p. 342.

[40] BLS Bulletin No. 1312-6, *op. cit.,* pp. 768–771.

[41] Kassalow, *op. cit.,* p. 347.

[42] *Census of Business, 1963, op. cit.,* pp. 3-3, 4-4, and 4-5.

[43] Brody, *op. cit.,* pp. 130–139.

[44] "A Union in Trade . . . ," *loc. cit.*

[45] *Economic Inquiry into Food Marketing, Part I, Concentration and Integration in Retailing,* Staff Report to the Federal Trade Commission, Washington, 1960, p. 2.

[46] Harrington, *op. cit.,* pp. 13–14, 37–38.

[47] Herbert R. Northrup and Gordon Storholm, *Restrictive Labor Practices in the Supermarket Industry,* Industrial Research Unit Study No. 44 (Philadelphia: University of Pennsylvania Press, 1967), pp. 120–121.

[48] *Supermarket News,* November 27, 1967.

[49] *Supermarket News,* November 14, 1966.

[50] Amalgamated Meat Cutters and Butcher Workmen, *Proceedings, Seventeenth General Convention,* 1948, p. 53.

51 Retail Clerks *International Advocate,* November–December 1936, p. 1.

52 Estey, "The Strategic Alliance . . .," *op. cit.,* pp. 46–53.

53 Brody, *op. cit.,* pp. 135–136, 245–246.

54 See *Union Premier Food Stores,* 10 NLRB 370 (1938).

55 This section is based on the author's study, "Some Factors Influencing Labor Organization in the Retail Trades" (unpublished Ph.D. dissertation, Princeton University, 1952), pp. 99–110.

56 Retail Clerks *Advocate,* May 1969, p. 6.

57 See Retail Clerks *Advocate,* June 1969, pp. 18–19, and August 1969, p. 16.

58 *Census of Business, 1963, op. cit.,* pp. 1-7, 1-8.

59 BLS Bulletin No. 1312-6, *op. cit.,* p. 768.

60 *Investigation of Improper Activities in the Labor and Management Field,* Hearings before the Select Committee on Improper Activities in the Labor and Management Field. Eighty-fifth Congress, First Session, Vol. 5, p. 1579, and Vol. 16, p. 6570.

61 Retail Clerks *Advocate,* September 1967, p. 5.

62 "A Union in Trade . . .," *loc. cit.*

63 Harrington, *op. cit.,* p. 2.

64 *Thirty-first Annual Report, 1966,* National Labor Relations Board (Washington: 1967), p. 52.

ENGINEERS AND THEIR UNIONS

by JAMES W. KUHN*

Engineers began organizing in a few scattered locations across the country towards the end of World War II. At that time they had considerable success; their efforts did not arouse much controversy in the profession and they encountered almost no opposition from management. They organized in four of the largest aircraft companies on the West Coast and in eight of the nation's biggest electrical and electronic equipment firms. Smaller groups of engineers, chemists, and researchers employed by several different oil companies and by a few government agencies like the Tennessee Valley Authority also formed engineering unions.

□ From Success to Decline

By 1952 engineering unions were displaying a vitality in organizing and enjoying a success in attracting new members that seemed to promise that they would dominate the profession within another few years; in less than a decade they had enrolled nearly 10 percent of the nation's engineers. To prepare themselves for a concerted national effort to organize the remaining engineers the separate unions affiliated to form the Engineers and Scientists of America (ESA) with a national headquarters in Washington, D.C. ESA organizers immediately launched membership campaigns among engineers in companies still without unions. Various affiliated unions that had organized only one or a few plants of a particular company complemented the national effort by extending their representation of engineers throughout the company. The Council of Western Electric Technical Engineers, for example, expanded beyond the confines of the first two plants it had organ-

---

* Professor of Industrial Relations, Graduate School of Business, Columbia University.

ized in New Jersey by securing representational and bargaining rights in 1952 for the engineers in all Western Electric's plants throughout the country. In the next few years other ESA affiliates like the Engineers and Architects Association of Convair and the Association of Professional Engineering Personnel of RCA (now Association of Scientists and Professional Engineering Personnel) also organized new plants of their companies.

As the unions grew and spread some of the groups expressed a militancy for which managers and some of the engineers were hardly prepared. The Minneapolis Federation of Honeywell Engineers, backed by the Teamsters, won a two weeks' strike in 1950, and the Engineers Association of Arma (now Arma Division of AMBAC Industries) won large salary benefits and a union shop in 1951 through an organizing strike! At Western Electric engineers conducted a series of small walkouts in 1951 and 1956. The engineers struck again at Honeywell in 1955, at Arma in 1953 and 1955, at RCA in 1958 and again in 1960, and in 1960 at Convair. Some of the strikes were little more than brief demonstrations or one-day walkouts, but a number of them lasted for a week or more. The Arma engineers, for example, stayed out for ten weeks in 1955 in a major test of strength with management.

To many engineers within the new unions, strikes were a disconcerting tactic for "professionals" to use. Increasingly, officers and members became involved in a debate on the meaning of professionalism, although they did not focus on the issue of strikes, but rather on what they considered a more basic issue, the admission of technicians into a professional organization. By the mid-1950s the debate had deeply divided the ESA affiliates, embittering relationships among the union leaders. In 1956, ESA split apart; the unions whose membership included large numbers of technicians refused to follow the professional line adopted by the national organization and thus had no option but to leave. The Minneapolis Federation of Engineers, for example, opted to join the United Automobile Workers, but in a representational election in 1957 it was able to muster only a third of the votes of Honeywell's technicians and engineers and consequently lost its NLRB certification. Meanwhile the Council of Western Electric Professional Engineers, ESA's largest affiliate, began to weaken when it failed to secure a new collective bargaining agreement in 1955 after the old one expired.

Its failure enticed the Council into a representational election in 1960, which it lost. The Council's decertification was a death blow to ESA, which had seriously weakened itself by the purge of those affiliates that had enrolled technicians. The Council could no longer collect enough dues to maintain its organization and also help support the national organization; ESA dissolved, unable to secure enough revenue even to pay the salaries of its staff.

Two years later, in 1962, the third major engineering union in less than six years lost its representation rights when a majority of the engineering employees of Sperry Gyroscope rejected the Engineers Association, which had become part of the International Union of Electrical Workers. The following year, the Engineers and Architects Association lost its certification at two major plants of General Dynamics and the moribund Council of Western Electric Professional Employees lost a second representational election. RCA engineers at Burlington, Massachusetts, rejected the organizing efforts of the Association of Scientists and Professional Engineering Personnel; and an engineering group in a Westinghouse plant as well as one in a General Electric plant discontinued union representation.

Thus after a promising beginning, engineering unions rapidly wasted away. The largest remaining union is the Seattle Professional Engineering Employees Association, which represents about 10,000 engineers and enrolls about 60 percent of its bargaining unit. Smaller engineering unions have been able to maintain themselves in some of the plants of Lockheed, Douglas Aircraft, General Dynamics, RCA, Arma, and Westinghouse. With a few exceptions, they have managed to enroll only 20 to 30 percent of the engineers in the plants they represent. Even those unions that have attracted a larger proportion of members have not been able to extend their organization in recent years. Since companies tend to move work out of old locations and to expand their operations in new ones, the unions' inability to organize new plants has resulted in an erosion of their strength and a relative decline in their importance in already organized plants. Moreover, most of the engineering unions are merely existing. They carry on a low level of activities and have litte effect on management policy. Industrial relations officers in the aircraft companies, for example, consider the engineering unions to be merely minor annoyances and have no hesitation in expressing their contemptuous impatience with the organizations and their demands.

The recent poor showing of engineering unions suggests that the influences that once encouraged them have disappeared or diminished. Apparently changes in the engineers or in their circumstances have made unionization much less attractive to them now than it was fifteen to twenty years ago. Many officials and supporters of engineering unions blame the colleges and professional societies for the setbacks of the past decade. They charge that professors have indoctrinated their students with antiunion attitudes, which are then reinforced by the societies and employers. While engineering students in college have not usually been taught to appreciate unions and while the professional societies do disparage collective bargaining for professionals, it is likely that the content of the college courses and the societies' campaign are only contributing influences in the unions' decline. If unions offered services of worth to engineers who were dissatisfied with their conditions, they would be received more warmly. One union leader, the president of an engineering association on the West Coast, argued that engineers were quite capable of understanding their own self-interest; if they saw benefits in joining unions, they would join. "All I can say," he said, "is that when the customer doesn't buy your product, it is you and not he who is wrong. The leaders of these groups haven't given the engineers what they want."

Apparently the groups did offer what many engineers wanted in the ten years from 1947 to 1957, but in the years since then the engineering unions have not been able to provide a service attractive enough to allow them to grow or even to maintain themselves. An examination of the causes of organizational success in the last half of the forties and the conditions with which the unions have had to contend since the mid-fifties can help one understand both the early success and the more recent wasting away of the engineering unions.

□ Why Engineers Organized

Students of labor have suggested two reasons to explain why engineers organized when they did: First, declining relative pay and deteriorating work conditions led to discontent. Second, mass em-

ployment bureaucratized and degraded engineers, causing dissatisfaction and prompting an attempt to reestablish their standing and
self-respect. Writing when the engineering unions were at their
peak in 1955, James Bambrick and Albert Blum noted that though
the earnings of professional engineers had tripled since 1929, salary
differentials had declined markedly. While in 1929 engineers with
records of nine and twelve years' service received salaries 2.8 times
greater than beginners, in 1954 the ratio was but 1.9 times.[1]

A decade earlier Herbert Northrup had argued in the same vein,
but he believed that the roots of the engineers' discontent went
farther back, attributing them to the lingering effects of the Great
Depression and the wage changes of World War II. "Perhaps the
most important reasons for unionization of engineers and chemists
derive from the economic hardships they suffered during the depression of the 1930's."[2] He pointed out that approximately one-
third of all engineers experienced some unemployment between
1929 and 1934. Salary rates also declined during this period by 22 to
38 percent.[3]

Engineers, however, did not form unions in the thirties, when
unemployment was highest, or even in the early forties, when salary
differentials were narrowing. By the time they began to organize
unemployment in the engineering field had long since disappeared
and salaries had risen 50 or 60 percent above Depression levels.
Furthermore, by the time organizing began many of the engineers
were young men fresh from college or technical school who had
neither experienced the Depression as employees nor knew about
the older range of salaries.

The engineers who participated in organizing explained that the
new interest in unions resulted from discontent with work conditions. Undoubtedly some engineers were dissatisfied, but whether
discontent alone was strong enough to persuade many of them to
try collective bargaining as a remedy is open to question. The
complaints engineers brought to their unions do not in themselves
appear weighty enough to have persuaded them to organize. It is
more probable that the unions, once they had been formed, used
these complaints to provide additional reasons for their existence.
Overtime with no extra pay and punching time clocks were two
irritations frequently mentioned by engineers in interviews with the
author. One gave his opinion that:

> We may have felt put upon by the fact that factory people were getting
> overtime compensation in 1943–1945 and we were getting very meager
> benefits. It led us to consider organization. . . . We finally got
> paid for Saturdays just before the union election but still got no extra
> pay for overtime and incidental work. All of us were unhappy about it,
> but we weren't anxious to get an aggressive union or to support one.

Another engineer, who had been one of the first presidents of the
engineers' union in an electrical equipment company, said that lack
of overtime pay was unpopular in 1943 among his fellow workers,
too. They also complained because

> we had, for a long time, punch-in clocks and we had to punch them
> up until 1952 or 1954 [seven to nine years after the union was organized].
> We used to have some firings—in fact, quite a few in June and Decem-
> ber when men were easily weeded out [because new engineering
> graduates were available]. . . . At the end of the War [1945] we
> were not company lovers by any means, but we would have lived
> with the company and not organized.

One of the engineering unions sent out a questionnaire to all
members of its bargaining unit shortly after it had been certified in
1946, hoping to find out what areas of the engineers' concerns
needed attention. A quarter of the engineers returned the questionnaire and their summary answers hardly provided the officers with
many clues. Thirty-nine percent believed the company salary policy
was "good" and 40 percent that it was "fair." Only 15 percent said
it was "poor." Sixty-one percent replied that they had "an adequate
voice in job standards, schedules, etc." and 66 percent indicated
that the company used "wisdom and justice in making promotions."
While some engineers were not completely happy with their working conditions at the end of World War II, there is no indication
that they believed collective bargaining could bring improvements.
Whatever discontent they felt may have been only a correlate of
union organization, not a cause of it.

Dissatisfaction with mass employment, a second reason that has
been offered to explain the unionization of engineers, is also not
adequate to explain the timing and initial success of the unions.
Bambrick and Blum noted that by the late forties engineers were
hired by the hundreds and worked in plants with thousands of their
colleagues, and they concluded that many engineers no longer

enjoyed any personal relationship with their employer. Mass employment, they speculated, had broken down lines of communications so that engineers had no "appropriate means of resolving individual problems."[4] W. Lee Hansen asserted that "the rapid growth in the number and proportion of employed engineers in industry would alone be expected to open up possibilities for greater discontent."[5]

Although engineering staffs have grown enormously in the past twenty years, however, few companies counted their engineers by the thousands in the mid-forties and early fifties when organization began. Moreover, those companies that were organized did not employ large numbers of engineers. In 1945 RCA employed not quite 300 engineers; Minneapolis-Honeywell had about 200 engineers in 1946 and Sperry had only a few more. Arma employed about 300 engineers in 1951. Douglas Aircraft had but 654 engineers in 1948, while Lockheed and Boeing may have had 400 to 600 more. Since these firms and many others now employ thousands of engineers while engineering unions in general are stagnating, impersonal mass employment does not seem to have spurred the engineers to further organizing. At best, it must have been no more than a contributing cause of earlier union growth.

A curious feature of organization among the engineers is that it has generally followed a spotty pattern. Some of the largest engineering staffs did not form unions, some of the smaller ones did. Neither the size of the engineering department nor the location of the plant appeared to have been a factor in unionization. The engineers of Douglas Aircraft in the Los Angeles area formed a union, but those at neighboring North American Aviation did not; RCA's engineers in Camden organized, while Philco's engineers across the river in Philadelphia remained unorganized. Western Electric's engineers sought and gained a certified national bargaining unit; those at General Electric developed only local nonunion sounding boards. The engineers at the Whiting plant of Standard Oil of Indiana formed a union, but none were formed in the plants of Standard Oil of Ohio. The engineers of TVA formed a union; those of the Bonneville Power Administration did not.

□ Organizing to Avoid Organizing

The engineers' fear of being dragooned into blue-collar unions and the managers' preference that the engineers stay out of regular unions better explain the pattern of organization and its timing than any specific complaints the engineers may have had. As early as 1938 the Committee on Unionism of the American Society of Civil Engineers had suggested that the society should stand ready to help its members form their own collective bargaining agencies if and when they desired. To minimize the need for any collective action, however, whether by the engineers themselves or by outside unions, the committee further recommended that the society help engineers better their economic position.[6] The society ignored these suggestions at the time, but in the forties it began to pay more attention to the possibility that engineers would organize when unions began to make successful bids to enroll them. In a 1943 report that dealt with the spread of collective bargaining among engineers an officer of the American Society of Civil Engineers (ASCE) wrote: "There is no doubt that some employee engineers need help. There is no doubt that these employee engineers do not wish to turn to organized labor. There is no doubt that certain employee engineers needing help will have to join with others for group action."[7]

The help provided by the ASCE was to alert engineers to their legal right to protest against being included in a union with non-professional workers. The NLRB had long ruled that engineers could be incorporated in a bargaining unit with other workers only if a majority of the engineers themselves approved. By 1942 the aggressive and inclusive organizing drives of unions brought many appeals from managers for help in keeping "our engineers out of the unions." Engineers themselves asked, "How can we organize so as to bargain collectively in regard *our* employment conditions?" or "cannot the engineering societies establish procedures through which they could legally serve as a bargaining agency in the eyes of the law?"[8] Belatedly, the ASCE decided to encourage a new kind of engineering organization that could protect members of the profession from blue-collar unions. The society had discovered that acting merely as an occasional advocate for the engineers was not always sufficient when a nonprofessional union gained representational rights for the engineers at the Sunflower Ordnance Works in 1943.

The engineers had defined themselves as professionals and the ASCE had protested (but only at the last moment) their inclusion in the broader bargaining unit. The War Labor Board decided that the society had not shown a sustained interest in the engineers and that the engineers had not clearly considered themselves professionals. It had become obvious that if the professional societies hoped to defend the rights of engineers, they would have to act before a problem of representation arose, not after.

Later in 1943, therefore, the ASCE resolved to act boldly; it would forestall unionization of engineers by encouraging its members to form collective bargaining groups. It appropriated $50,000 for legal expenses and appointed four field representatives whose duties were to assist and advise engineering groups confronted with organizing drives by nonprofessional unions. Collective bargaining was clearly not the primary purpose of the "unions" the society hoped to establish. They were first of all defensive organizations, designed merely to serve as buffers against "subprofessional unions affiliated with organized labor."[9]

Only two organizations of much significance were established under the ASCE program. The Seattle section helped organize the Seattle Professional Engineering Employees Association (SPEEA) in early 1943. The association did little to recruit members, however, until 1945, when the Machinists, who had already organized Boeing's production workers, announced a drive to enroll the rest of the company's employees. In a certification election held the next year SPEEA received a majority vote of 81 percent of the eligible engineers. In the meantime the Los Angeles section of the ASCE had established the Southern California Professional Engineering Association. In consent elections in 1945 this association won representational rights for engineers of the Douglas Aircraft Company and later for engineers of the Southern California Gas Company.

Perhaps more important than the direct results of the ASCE's program was its indirect influence. The fact that the oldest, most prestigious professional engineering society was helping engineers to organize for collective bargaining to stave off nonprofessional unionization encouraged a number of managements to follow suit. Many engineers and managers had reservations about the need for collective bargaining for engineers, but they did not actively oppose the ASCE program. They saw it as the lesser of two evils.

In accordance with the policy of the ASCE, the Engineers and Architects Association (EAA), a southern California professional organization founded in 1894, formed its own bargaining organization for the engineers and secured representational rights in order to head off an attempt by an AFL technicians union to organize the engineers at Lockheed in 1943. The company did not oppose the EAA efforts. According to engineers active in the organizational drive, the company even encouraged an industrial relations staff-man to resign his post and take an organizing position with the EAA. He helped recruit engineers in Lockheed and in other plants in the Los Angeles area.

The story of organization in other companies in the Midwest and on the East Coast was similar to that on the West Coast. At Sperry Gyroscope, RCA, Arma, IT&T, and other companies the engineers formed their own organization when they felt themselves threatened by nonprofessional unions. The companies seldom welcomed the engineers' organizations, but neither did they actively oppose them. The experience of an engineer who helped found the organization in his company is typical:

> We were trying to keep out the CIO and we organized [the association].
> . . . The organizing committee went to the company for advice and
> asked, "What do we do now?" The head of industrial relations at
> that time took us under his wing. He led us to believe that we would
> have to organize formally, but we wouldn't be a union in the usual
> sense. We had to go through the motions, but we didn't need to get in
> a sweat about it.

In this case the new engineering association selected a lawyer from a firm that handled company affairs as well. In other cases, the company helped the engineers less directly. Supervisors simply passed the word along that membership in the organization was desirable, and officers of the struggling engineering organizations were allowed plenty of company time at full pay to work on organizing affairs.

Not all engineering employers were willing to tolerate, let alone abet, the organization of engineers. Employers whose engineers were not threatened by blue-collar unions or those who felt that such a threat was exaggerated believed that the ASCE policy of encouraging engineering unions was wrong. An industrial relations official of one company that has had no engineering union has explained why the engineers have never organized in the company for which he works.

> In 1946 the engineers saw themselves being enveloped by the UAW-type unions and no way out. They didn't organize here because we have a pretty strong industrial relations section. . . . We've always been against white-collar unions. Any of them is a luxury we can do without. Why should we have a white collar union to put in our good policies? . . . When we discover any union activity we use every way we have available within the law to stop it. There would be no stone unturned.

This company has a reputation among engineers throughout the industry that fits the words of the official: "You don't talk unions and stay with . . . [this company] very long."

This company has been active in the National Society of Professional Engineers and the Engineers Joint Council. It and other companies have "persuaded" the professional engineering societies to drop their former sponsorship and encouragement of collective bargaining among engineers. The societies now argue for commitment to a professionalism that excludes any kind of collective bargaining. By stressing the differences between professionals and workers and by urging managements to emphasize and respect those differences, they have tried to make defensive engineering unions unnecessary. Consequently, though the professional societies nurtured and encouraged the engineering unions in the late forties, by 1952, they bitterly opposed them; and company opposition to the organization of engineers after the early fifties became firm and unyielding.

In summary, most of the engineers who organized essentially backed into collective bargaining; they were encouraged by the professional societies and tolerated by some managements. Their aim was to flee unionization and to avoid inclusion in blue-collar unions. In a sense they organized before their time. Before a sizable minority, let alone a majority, had become dissatisfied with individual bargaining, engineers in a dozen or so plants across the country found themselves possessing the means to carry on activities that they did not completely understand and for which they had little use. That such associations should survive or display much vitality after the immediate reason for organizing had disappeared would be surprising. One labor expert predicted in 1946 that these unions would be short lived exactly because they had no continuing purpose beyond that of defense.[10]

A few unions have succumbed, as already noted, but usually only after bitterly fought decertification elections that were costly to both sides. Union sources estimated that Western Electric spent "close to $4,000,000 in its intense [year-long] campaign to persuade the professionals to vote against representation [in 1960],"[11] and the engineering organization was bankrupted. Furthermore, a sizable minority of the engineers have supported the unions even when they lost certification. At Western Electric, as at Minneapolis-Honeywell, 40 percent of the engineers voted for their union. At Sperry an even larger proportion (47 percent) supported the union. Some officials of Sperry and Western Electric privately expressed disappointment at the large number of engineers who still supported collective bargaining. Though they are a minority, a sizable number of engineers continue to look with favor upon unions after once having been members. Although neither the engineering unions nor their competitors show any signs of being able to launch organizing drives in the near future, the decertification votes did indicate that, for many engineers, the unions begun in the mid-forties to protect professionals against "unions" possessed either the promise or realization of other services too valuable to dismiss.

In plants where engineering unions continue to exist, a sizable minority of engineers, somewhere between 20 and 50 percent, maintain membership. Typically about a third of the engineers belong to the union. The proportion declines when a company wins a big government contract and hires a large number of new, young engineers, and it rises when a company slashes salaries across the board, as Douglas did in 1960, or when a company loses a contract and has to lay off hundreds of engineers, as Boeing did in 1963 when Dyna-Soar was canceled. Apparently, the unions provide something that this minority of engineers values, though the unions' original purpose of warding off blue-collar organizing has long since been fulfilled.

☐ The Unions as a Hedge Against an Uncertain Future

Engineering unions may have continued to exist merely out of inertia; once they were established, enough members may have paid their dues out of habit to support the limited activities the unions carried on. As long as management did not actively oppose them, the unions could maintain their routine. However, inertial existence could not have sustained the unions in the face of the rapid expansion in engineering staffs. If they had merely maintained their original membership, they would have shrunk nearly into invisibility.

Between 1950 and 1965, the number of engineers increased greatly in those plants in which the engineers were organized. For example, the unions enrolled two or more times as many members as they had before at Boeing, three times as many at Arma and Convair, and four times as many at RCA. To maintain even a 30 percent membership the unions had to enroll new members at the same rate as the number of eligible engineers increased.

Furthermore, the engineering unions lose many of their officers and most active members to management. The rapid growth of engineering departments has required an even greater increase in the number of supervisors. Union officers, who are experienced in handling wage problems, familiar with the organization of the company, and used to dealing with people, make likely candidates for managerial positions. Officers are also reluctant to stay away from their engineering work too long, and thus they seldom serve more than a few years. The prestige of office is not great, and engineering skills and knowledge become obsolete quickly if they are not constantly updated. The result is that the engineering unions probably have had to recruit proportionally more new leaders and activists than production workers' unions.

Obviously, in those plants where unions are available, a sizable number of engineers have continued to find something about engineering unions attractive. Although it is only a minority, this group grows in absolute numbers as the engineering work force expands. Why have engineers continued to join the unions long after the original causes of organization have disappeared? According to those active in the unions, engineers join to improve their economic position, a reason that suggests that the engineering unions have improved or expect to improve the engineers' pay and fringe benefits. Managers suggest that the engineers with the poorest salaries expect to gain the most from collective bargaining and are the strongest union supporters.

Neither suggestion had much validity in the eight major engineering unions studied. If there is any relationship between salary level and union membership within the thirteen plants that were examined for this study, it is direct rather than inverse since engineers with the higher salaries tended to join unions proportionately more than did lower-paid engineers. Furthermore, the labor market, the location of the firm, and the kind of engineering work performed probably influence salary levels more than the petty efforts of the few scattered engineering unions. The largest engineering union, SPEEA, which represents Boeing's engineers, hardly demonstrates much ability to push up salaries. In 1963 it complained that the Boeing engineers' average salary was 10.5 percent below the national average.[12] That people join unions for economic improvement is a reasonable assertation and may in part be true, but it does little to explain the pattern of union membership among engineers.

More sophisticated explanations suggest that one needs to analyze the conditions and circumstances of particular groups of engineers within a firm. A negotiator for an aircraft company reported that the structural design engineers were the most likely to join a union because:

They are so closely geared to production that they do not have the freedom that the more technical engineering groups have. Many times in the design process supervision may have to make changes and the engineers are never told the reason why. This kind of engineer is a frustrated man because he does not know what was wrong with his original work. Then, too, the structures and design departments are larger than the rest. They work in large rooms with hundreds of them together.

Engineers in that and other plants made similar comments.

In Design you'll find that bays of 500–800 engineers are jammed so tight that if you had a fire in there, 180 of them would be killed. That's why they join; they're fed up with being treated like cattle.

In another plant a supervisor explained why the engineers in Airborne Systems joined:

> It's a service type of work and certainly not creative. They prove, not initiate; they just sit and check figures. How can they ever meet a customer or aspire to join management? They can't and they join [the union].

These statements may express *some* of the reasons engineers join unions, but they do not explain why engineers in other groups in similar circumstances in the same plants show higher or lower proportions of membership. Engineers and union officials have suggested that an examination of such characteristics of engineers as race, religion, the kind of school attended, wartime experience, geographical location, previous union experience, family economic level would help explain the pattern of membership among engineers in a plant. These characteristics may help explain why engineers accept or reject a union, but a study of such data as were available in a number of plants showed no correlation between any of these personal characteristics and membership. However, because the data were not complete, no definite conclusions can be drawn.

An examination of other data related to the engineers in the plants studied showed some correlation with membership. (See Table 1.) The middle and higher salary grades or ranks generally showed a higher percentage of members than the lower ones. Since higher ranking engineers usually are older and have had longer tenure, membership is thus also higher among the more senior men. This was the case in four of the six plants for which data were available. In the other two plants, O and S, however, there was no positive relationship between length of tenure or labor grade and union membership. The companies in both cases had been expanding their engineering force rapidly, hiring men from outside to fill the higher positions. In plant S, for example, the number of engineers had nearly doubled in the previous year because the firm had received a big long-term missile contract. Men were both hired away from other companies and transferred from other divisions of the firm. Thus men who had short as well as long tenure with the firm were mixed together in the same grade. In plants E and L, employment had been stable or declining somewhat; in plants C and M,

Table 1. Membership in Engineering Unions by Salary Grade in the Early 1960s

Salary Grade	Number of Engineers	% Members
Plant C		
4 (highest)	166	82
3	459	80
2	512	76
1	202	53
Total	1,379	75
Plant E		
11 (highest)	79	88
8	207	69
6	8	25
5	85	76
4	161	56
2	4	25
1	220	53
Total	764	64
Plant O		
10 (highest)	98	8
8	29	3
7	564	26
6	64	28
5	149	50
4	509	28
3	96	20
2	67	21
1	308	16
Total	2,040	58
Plant M		
4 (highest)	160	79
3	358	70
2	237	77
1	163	70
Total	918	76
Plant L		
11 (highest)	8	50
8	78	59
6	6	17
5	67	34

Salary Grade	Number of Engineers	% Members
4	69	39
2	1	0
1	86	32
Total	315	41
Plant S		
12 (highest)	1	0
11	65	42
8	302	40
6	1	0
5	146	53
4	433	48
2	36	33
1	1,065	40
Total	2,049	43

SOURCE: Confidential employment records of the companies.

hiring had been proceeding at a fairly rapid rate. Out of necessity the company had hired men at higher grades, though its usual policy was to bring engineers in at the lowest rank and promote them. The proportion of union members therefore was more closely related to tenure in this company than to salary grade (Table 1).

Added support for the conclusion that engineers who hold longer tenure and have higher salaries tend to join unions is found in a survey made of engineers in still another company. The company had increased the number of its engineers by almost 20 percent in the three years immediately preceding the survey. The need for expert engineers had been so great that the company had to hire many in at high grades. The outcome was a dilution of the strength of union membership in those grades (see Table 2), resulting in a relatively higher percentage membership in the lower grades. Membership in the union increased with length of tenure, however, except in the case of those few engineers (less of 3 percent of the total), in grades 8–11, who had been with the company since before 1945. (See Table 3.)

The observations of union officials and engineers lend some additional support to the possibility that length of tenure is an important determinant of membership. A long-time member and former

Table 2. Membership in Federation of
Minneapolis Honeywell Engineers by
Labor Grade, 1957*

Professional Engineers Labor Grade	% Members
12	27
11	39
10	38
9	48
8	49

* Based on survey made by the Federation of Minneapolis Honeywell Engineers. There were 596 returns out of 2,200 total engineering personnel, professional and technical.

Table 3. Membership in Federation of Minneapolis
Honeywell Engineers by Labor Grade and
Hiring Date, 1957*

Professional Engineers Labor Grade	% Hired Before 1940–45	% Hired 1946–51	% Hired 1952–54	% Hired 1955–57
12	36	27	18	18
11	8	55	20	17
10	14	36	21	29
9	4	29	34	33
8	11	35	23	31

* Based on a survey made by the Federation of Minneapolis Honeywell Engineers. There were 596 returns out of 2,200 total engineering personnel, professional and technical.

officer said, "When a new man comes in he's leery of unions and he's probably resistant to the idea of joining. It takes time in the absence of campaigning to get them to change their minds." Other observers pointed out that new engineers often fear membership might hurt their chances for promotions to management or for advancement in classification. Even if they have no fear of unions, they still may see no need of them. A former officer of a decertified union commented that:

It was the younger engineers—new hires—who didn't belong. The starting rate is good for a B.S. He's apt to be single, in his early twenties and with low expenses. The first few years he gets quarterly increases and he's riding a breeze. He thinks it is going to go on forever.

Therefore, while an engineer who hires into a noisy design bay crowded with hundreds of drawing boards may be more tempted to join a union than one who joins a small computer department in spacious, quiet quarters, his tendency to join is probably more significantly influenced by his length of service than by the size and work conditions of engineering groups.

The relationship of tenure to membership may also partially explain another characteristic of the members of engineering unions. The results of a survey of engineers in one Midwestern engineering firm showed that membership declined as the amount of college education increased. (See Table 4.) Even more striking,

Table 4. Membership in Federation of Minneapolis Honeywell Engineers by Education, 1957*

Education	% Membership
No college	69
Some college	66
First degree	57
Graduate degree	46
Other	55

* Based on a survey made by the Federation of Minneapolis Honeywell Engineers. There were 596 returns out of 2,200 total engineering personnel, professional and technical.

when compared with engineers with no college, more than three times as large a proportion of the graduate degree engineers were very much opposed to the union and only half as many of the graduate engineers were active members who attended meetings. Management and union officials in other plants generally agreed that graduate engineers were not as active in or as committed to unions as the nongraduates. Managers frequently dismissed their engineering union as merely a collection of "insecure men without degrees."

However, such data as are available suggest that the higher proportion of nongraduates in the unions may reflect their longer tenure rather than their schooling. Companies used to upgrade technicians to engineering rank more than they do today. Only forty percent of the engineers in one West Coast aircraft company had degrees in 1952; by 1959 two-thirds had them. All of the air-craft companies studied showed a similar trend. Of their recent hires as many as 90 percent or more were graduates. Consequently, nongraduate engineers have, on the average, a longer employment tenure than graduate engineers. Thus the differential membership might be expected on the basis of the difference in tenure alone.

Although graduate engineers may be less disposed to join unions than nongraduate engineers, comparisons over time and between different firms suggest that possession of a college degree does not have a particularly important influence upon membership. Despite the growing numbers of graduate engineers in the bargaining units, the proportion of union members who are graduate engineers has not declined for any of the existing unions. Since the unions attract about the same proportion of members from among the engineering personnel today as they did earlier, recently graduated engineers must find unions as attractive as recently hired nongraduate engineers. An example of this tendency is provided by one electronics firm in which 75 percent to 85 percent of the engineers take out union membership. Ninety-five percent of the firm's engineers are graduates, since the company has never hired engineers without degrees and only a few technicians have been promoted to engineering positions. Nevertheless, union membership is and always has been high, maintaining a proportion higher even than that of the company's production workers' union.

Influences other than those related to length of tenure no doubt affect engineers' willingness to join unions, since there is no fixed relationship between tenure and membership in different companies or even in different plants of the same company. Yet tenure appears to be a general and widespread determinant of membership: the longer the engineer's tenure, the greater his tendency to belong.

Why should engineers display a greater interest in unions as their tenure increases? Mere passage of time itself is not a likely causal agent. Engineers in interviews and union officers in their publications particularly stressed three problems for which collective bargaining might offer solutions. Although these problems involve issues of importance to all engineers, they are of acute concern to engineers who have been employed for some time in a particular line of engineering.

The problem that receives the most attention is salary progression. No other unionists in the nation subject their salary data to so many modes of analysis as do engineers. They use the full resources of their mathematical competence to detail the time correlates of their pay. Beyond their continuous interest in merit increases, which will be discussed, engineers develop a concern with their salary growth curve, which is the rate of salary increase over beginning pay. For almost all engineers, the curve rises rapidly for the first five to eight years and then begins to flatten out. Since the competitive market for new engineers has tended to push up starting salaries, the engineers who have been in service longer fear that if the salary curve does not move up, the differential between their pay and that of beginners will decline. A few of the outstanding engineers may find their salaries continuing a rapid rise, but most engineers do not. Unable to secure a raise in their own individual pay, they find somewhat appealing the use of collective bargaining to raise the pay of their whole salary group.

Reinforcing the longer-tenured engineers' interest in the circumstances of the group as well as their own individual situations is a second problem, the narrowing of opportunities for advancement and promotion as time passes. As one engineer with twenty years' service in an aircraft company remarked:

You're always in danger of reaching a level and getting pegged. Suppose you start in hydraulics and you get tagged. You work in the same area and though you may be working on different planes, you're probably doing pretty much the same work on all projects. Outside of some catastrophe you stay there. It's to the company's advantage of course and you get more efficient by concentrating in that one area. But you stay at the same level. You don't necessarily get stuck there because of your capabilities but [rather] because you're tagged as that level an engineer. If you're lucky and don't get pegged you'll reach a higher level of capability and of course, your salary levels off the same but higher up.

The chances of being promoted into management also decrease markedly after the first five to eight years of employment. The Council of Western Electric Technical Engineers estimated that an "engineer's chances of advancing to the first level of supervision [or beyond] at Western Electric is 1 in 10 if he is under 35. The chances for older men to break into supervising ranks are 3 in

100."[13] When asked if such an estimate was reasonable, most personnel and industrial relations managers agreed it was. If an engineer is not spotted as likely supervisory material quite early in his career and promoted to a first level soon thereafter, the odds are much against him moving into management at all. Thus his opportunity to move ahead by demonstration of his individual performance is blocked. In contrast to his earlier situation where room for individual initiative and rewards appeared ample, collective action and group benefits begin to seem more worthwhile to the engineer as his term of employment lengthens.

The third problem that tends to attract longer-tenured engineers to group or union activities is the shadowy but alarming threat of skill obsolescence. The technologies that require the greatest number of engineers are changing rapidly. A man whose training and specialization are in aircraft design, for example, may find little demand for his skills in the day of the missile. An engineer who is an expert in the problems of the electrical circuiting of fifteen years ago may be poorly equipped to exploit the opportunities of microcircuiting and optical masers today.

An industrial relations official observed that:

> The older and more senior engineers are often disturbed at the lack of attention and consideration they get in the new promotions and advancements within the company. But to be truthful, I think that the new engineers are more valuable than the older men. . . . In aircraft and missiles we have new materials and problems not even thought of previously. The engineers have got to keep up to date or the field will rush by them.

A second-level supervisor employed for ten years by an aircraft company commented that:

> I felt from the very first that the engineering here is done by the young men, that is, those of less than five years experience. . . . If we should ever have a sizable layoff, a lot of older guys will be laid off. The older men have been out of school for a while, like me, and we're out of touch with the newer techniques of engineering. We have the contacts in the company and know how to get things organized, but we're not needed for the engineering work.

A 1956 survey of the attitudes of an engineering union's members also suggests that the older the engineer, the more attractive collective bargaining looks to him. In this case, the older engineers also tended to be men with longer tenure; though the company had recently hired a number of older engineers, few, if any, had joined the union. The proportion of members who wanted some collective voice in job transfers rose from a little over a quarter of the youngest engineers to just over half of the oldest. The oldest members tended to look with more approval upon contractual regulation of the merit system than did the youngest, the proportion rising from 29 percent to 44 percent. While three-fourths of the youngest members believed that seniority ought not to be considered in keeping an engineer on a job, only half of the oldest felt that it should be disregarded. (See Table 5.)

Over the past thirty years, first one group of engineers and then another has risen to the top. The president of one union, a specialist engineer who has since become an engineering consultant, described the changes in the aircraft-aerospace industry:

> First there was the vital science of learning how to hold an aircraft together. That focused attention on the structures department. During the War [World War II] and immediately afterwards that was the big and important area of engineering. Those guys were on top. Then the emphasis changed and aerodynamics became the important area. How do you make these things fly faster and higher? The boys who could provide the answers and analysis came to the top. But not for long; now we have a complete different change. Missiles are the problem now and it is the electronics engineer who decides whether the equipment is going to be successful or a failure. These shifts are important because different people bubble up at different times. No group has an assured place. You may be getting the glory one day and the next you're on the fringes. You start out on a project and ride it up, copping all the valuable jobs and exciting challenges. Then the changes come and you wind up you don't know where.

Another engineer who had been a union officer explained the longer-service engineers' interest in unions this way:

> I think that they are mostly more security conscious. You've reached your position and salary in good part because you've been around rather than because of outstanding ability—at least for some. Just how useful will you be to the company from now on you wonder.

While some engineers may join unions in the hope that the organization can provide some added protection from technological

Table 5. Member Attitudes Toward Company and Union, By Age.*
Total Sample: 569 out of 936 members

| Age | N | Percent Response† | | |
		Agree	Undecided	Disagree
1. The Company should consult with the Federation on job transfers.				
25 & below	(37)	27	19	54
26–30	(176)	28	18	55
31–35	(201)	33	16	50
36–40	(92)	39	16	45
41 & above	(62)	51	18	31
2. The Company's use of the merit system should be regulated by contract.				
25 & below	(37)	29	32	38
26–30	(176)	30	20	50
31–35	(201)	35	13	51
36–40	(92)	32	15	51
41 & above	(62)	44	19	37
3. The best man should be kept on the job regardless of seniority.				
25 & over	(37)	75	16	8
26–30	(176)	74	11	16
31–35	(201)	71	11	17
36–40	(92)	73	17	10
41 & above	(62)	51	21	28

* Taken from Tables 4, 12, and 21, Technical Appendix, *Report of Findings on Attitudes, Communications, and Participation,* The Minneapolis Federation of Honeywell Engineers, August 1956. Survey conducted and report prepared by Industrial Relations Center, University of Minnesota.
† Percentages do not add up to 100 in all cases due to rounding.

change, there is no evidence to suggest that many are convinced that the union can have much effect. However, membership is not expensive and as long as it does not entail involvement in unpleasant activities like strikes, it represents a kind of low-grade insurance. None of the unions has developed any program to help the engineers solve the problem of obsolescent skills. Each man finds the responsibility to be his own. As one engineer remarked, "We'll all operate barber shops if we don't keep up with the changes in technology and knowledge in our field." Depending on their own efforts more than on group activities to protect their jobs, engineers probably have enrolled in university extension classes and night courses and in company-sponsored schools at a faster rate than they have joined the unions.

Apparently the engineering unions offer just enough hope of doing something to solve these wage and skill problems to induce a sizable minority of engineers to take out membership. One may well conclude as did the slightly cynical head of one union:

> The engineers are not too much impressed by their engineering organization. . . . There is no imperative need for organization for most of them. At best we are only improving a rather satisfactory situation. The plus that we're able to give the engineers is small and thus they tolerate only a small incremental burden imposed by the union.

In general this conclusion is sound. Engineers across the country have shown little enthusiasm for collective bargaining. They backed into it in the first place because they were trying to avoid unionization by others, and what appreciation they do muster for it tends to come late, if at all. There are, however, several places where engineers developed strong, militant organizations that carried on the full range of the usual union activities. Their vitality and their attractiveness to their engineers indicated that their members saw them as more than a possible insurance against future troubles. These few unions appealed strongly to their engineers because they were able to provide immediately helpful services. The next section will discuss why a few unions were able to develop such services while most did not.

□ How to Bargain Collectively Without Really Trying

Because they had been pushed into organizing by their fear of blue-collar unions in the forties and early fifties, engineers did not expect much from collective bargaining. They knew little about it, believed that it held no particular promise, and feared that it would have an adverse effect upon their traditional view of themselves as professionals. For the engineers, collective bargaining was an accompaniment of organization, a necessary but not welcome part of the strategy to forestall "outside" unionism.

A few engineers hoped that it might be used, not for vulgar, unprofessional purposes, but to provide a louder voice for engineers in the companies for which they worked. They believed that collective bargaining might call managers' attention to the engineers' recent complaints and growing dissatisfactions, particularly those concerning the deterioration of the engineers' status symbolized by the time clock that many of them had to punch and the narrowing salary differential between new hires and engineers of experience. Through collective bargaining they would seek remedies to only a few limited problems, however; they would approach management reasonably and conservatively. Above all, they were determined to avoid the emotionalism, radicalism, and militancy that they identified with the common practice of collective bargaining. The president of Convair's Engineers and Architects Association described the engineers' view of collective bargaining in terms that had wide currency among engineering unions. "Our practices are always based on a rational approach with facts and moral suasion as our strength. Conducting our affairs in a dignified but resolute manner is our tenor."[14]

Those who joined an engineering union or "association" usually expected collective bargaining to supplement, rather than to supplant, individual efforts. Typical of the attitude of many engineers toward collective bargaining was that expressed by the Southern California Professional Engineering Association: "This Association shall preserve and strengthen an individual's opportunity to bargain for himself in those matters where individual bargaining is most practical."[15] The president of another engineering association expressed similar sentiments: "We encourage individual bargaining even if it tends to divorce the engineers from us because that's the kind of organization we are."

Because they generally eschew any comprehensive collective bargaining, or at least refrain from exploring its potential, the engineering associations have tended to keep the scope of collective action narrow and its value unemphasized. They negotiate labor agreements periodically and these agreements include the provisions covering wages, hours, welfare benefits and work conditions that are usually found in any union agreement. Some unions also have added provisions covering matters of peculiar relevance to engineering work such as flight and travel pay, "hardship" assignments, absences or leaves for professional reasons, and patent rights.

Though the list of provisions appears comprehensive, in practice it is not. The engineers have sought only minimum standards. Collective action simply provides a floor upon which individuals may bargain for further gains. Thus, the vice-president of the Southern California Professional Engineers Association declared in 1962:

> When engineers are employed in large numbers by an organization, there must be a set of *minimum standards* expressed. With today's labor laws these minimums can be expressed in a contract with a certified Engineering Association. No other type of organization can perform that function, although some have tried.[16]

The provisions in agreements are general, allowing considerable scope for individual adjustment of the actual terms as they apply to engineers in different work groups and job categories. The association negotiators bargain over the limits to salary ranges, for example, but each engineer must negotiate his specific merit increases himself. Thus individual gains secured by moving up within a salary range may be more important than any increase in the limits. The provisions for layoffs, transfers, promotions, and overtime also allow management great flexibility and require individual engineers to bargain on their own.

The over-all impression gained by engineers—members and non-members alike—is that their union's collective bargaining has little relevance to them, since the decisions vital to their pay and work circumstances are influenced more by their own actions than by those of the group. A member of one of the largest engineering associations on the West Coast explained that, "our organization brings our problems before the company so that they realize our problems and do not forget us," but he also admitted that, "salary and transfers are individual problems and so you do not take those to the association. They do not affect it at all. . . . Most salary increases come from merit increases and we get these by bargaining ourselves. It's bargaining on an individual level and has nothing to do with the association." The head of an association of electronic and communication engineers saw his organization's collective bargaining in much the same way:

> We bargain only for the broad outlines and let the individuals fill in the details. It is like school. The professors present a curriculum but the

students can choose what courses they want to suit their purposes. They also get the opportunity to strive for A's or B's or C's in grades. We are trying to control only the broadest aspects of standards—like the doctors. They negotiate with each patient for their fee but within the over-all limits set by their professional body.

One may question the validity of analogies with professor-student and doctor-patient relationships, but for engineers the point is clear. At best collective bargaining provides common minimums, leaving a wide area in which to exercise individual initiative.

Not only do engineering associations restrict the scope of their periodic negotiations, but they also limit their daily services at the place of work. The emphasis is again on individual, not collective, action. Departmental representatives seldom perform any organizational work at the place of work other than passing out membership applications to new engineers. Most of them are not at all sure that handling grievances and discussing the application and administration of the agreement are appropriate. In an article on discharges and layoffs officers of the Southern California Professional Engineering Association as much as told their members not to expect any help from the association. They point out that discharges are usually for poor performance, but

if the engineer is honestly doubtful about having performed poorly, then it is possible that SCPEA can help him . . . but it must be recognized that once an engineer's supervisor has decided that he can operate his section productively without that particular engineer, then the problem of reversing that decision is extremely difficult. . . . To look for an arbiter to prove that his supervisor's decision is wrong is a useless endeavor. . . . An engineer's whole future . . . depends on his supervisor's opinion of him. At the first sign that his supervisor rates him below his own evaluation, and this difference is not resolved, an engineer simply must *transfer* to some other supervisor.[17]

When the associations hold such an attitude towards grievances, it is not surprising to hear a departmental representative plead impotence in dealing with problems brought to him by engineers that involve interpretation of the agreement. "I can't interpret the contract," he said. "A lawyer has to do that. I need legal counsel whenever I look at the contract." A member of the executive board of one association also indicated the absence of collective activity at the place of work when he sourly commented on a new, proposed budget: "It seems to me that all we have here are negotiations every couple of years and then a slack season of twenty months in which we do nothing. I don't know why we need such a high budget to do nothing." In fact, "nothing" is a fairly apt description of what the engineering associations do for their members on a day-to-day basis. There are a few perennial complaints that the officers are always bringing up—distant, muddy parking lots, dirty lunch rooms, or locked lunchroom doors. Managers and even the engineers consider such complaints something of a long-standing joke, though newly elected officers sometimes take them more seriously.

By the standards of nonprofessional unions, grievance activity is conspicuous by its absence among engineering associations. An official of a union that represented 2,000 to 3,000 engineers in a communications company plant could recall only one grievance. It had come up seven years earlier. The company had originally offered the union representatives fifteen hours a year per plant for grievance work. Since the time was never used, however, both parties agreed to drop it from the agreement. In a missile plant where about 2,000 engineers are employed, an industrial relations manager reported, "We have very few grievances. We had a few back in 1957 when we first started and then had a layoff. We got five grievances out of that. But in the past five years we haven't received more than 10." The union in another aerospace company that had grown from 4,000 to 10,000 engineers in thirteen years had brought one grievance to arbitration and no association officers knew of or could remember any other grievances.[18]

□ The Opportunities for Individual Bargaining

Some observers have explained the engineers' lack of daily "shop" activity and restricted form of collective bargaining as a reflection of a quixotic individualism[19] or of professional biases against unions.[20] Such explanations give too little credit to the engineers' sense of self-interest. If individual bargaining provides benefits equal to or surpassing those that can be obtained from collective bargaining employees may wisely choose to bargain individually. Only the assumption that collective is always superior to individual bargaining would suggest that engineers' heavy reliance on individual effort is misplaced.

For fifteen years or more engineers have had plenty of opportunities for successful individual bargaining. The ever-growing demand for engineers, the swift changes and constant upheavals in company engineering projects, and the fluid, shifting managerial organization in which engineers work have made individual bargaining possible and in many cases desirable as well.

Once hired, engineers do not find themselves entering well-established organizations with fixed work groups and carefully drawn procedures. In the electronic, communications, aerospace, and aircraft companies, change, upheaval, sudden cancellation, new developments, unexpected breakthroughs, and intermittent expansion of staffs are normal accompaniments of the work situation. While some jobs have disappeared and others have shrunk in importance, for a majority of engineers, the net effect of all the changes has been the creation of a plenitude of opportunities. A man may lose ground if he has been working on a project such as the eventually cancelled B-70 chemical bomber, Skybolt, or Dyna-Soar, but many more have ridden high on such projects as the F-111 (TFX), Saturn, and Apollo, advancing in rank and pay while being challenged by new and exciting engineering problems.

Besides confronting engineers with an ever-changing array of opportunities that they can exploit as individuals, rapid expansion of engineering forces has led companies to promote men of relatively little tenure or experience to supervisory posts. Such promotions fulfill the hopes of engineers, if not always those of top management. Managers often choose their engineering supervisors for their technical qualifications, rather than their competence in directing men effectively and efficiently. Lacking sophistication in the art of managerial persuasion, the new supervisors may be more vulnerable to the importunity of subordinates than men trained especially for supervisory posts. Inexperienced in administration and leadership, they often find the performance record of their sections or departments particularly dependent upon the cooperation of those they lead.[21]

A supervisor who is in charge of a team of good engineers is usually reluctant to let any member of the team leave, either by transferring within the company or by quitting to take a job elsewhere. Men of equal or better ability may be available in a company, but with projects and work in a state of constant flux, they are not easy to locate. Unwilling to lose engineers with whom they have worked successfully and whose work has been instrumental in building up the supervisor's own record, a supervisor tends to bid for the man who can afford to "look around." He may offer a higher merit rating, a raise, or a better job position. If the first supervisor cannot offer any extra benefits, another in a second group may be able to provide some. If an engineer becomes too dissatisfied with his lack of progress or feels he is unappreciated, he can leave the company with fair assurance of another job in another engineering firm. Not all engineers can or are willing to go so far, but for large numbers of them, some degree of individual bargaining power is available. Engineers and supervisors interviewed were almost unanimous in their conviction that deals and "dickering" are major ingredients in the managing of engineers. Bargaining between individual engineers and supervisors appears to be so common that its cause must be basic and widespread. This cause appears to be the mode of management in firms that employ large numbers of engineers.

Typically an engineering firm permits a supervisor to exercise his own judgment in treating subordinates, imposing but few limiting rules and providing even less guidance. This is particularly true in the area of merit rating and performance reviews; supervisors are asked to consider each engineer individually, but they are given only complicated forms or vague standards by which to rate them. Instead of setting forth clear standards, the firms ask one supervisor to second guess another. Whatever the rank of the supervisors, it is their personal, frequently inexperienced judgments, rather than over-all rules or guides, that direct their decisions regarding transfers, promotions, merit rating, salary raises, job assignments, and layoffs. Of course, budgets, office space, and contract specifications limit their decisions. The over-all number of engineers, their total salaries, and the general kind of work that will be performed is fixed higher in management echelons than the supervisors in the engineering department. Within these broad and sometimes flexible limits, however, even first-line supervisors may exercise authority over engineering careers with latitude and even autonomy.

Engineers seldom work under supervisors who wield sole, direct line authority. Many engineering firms have adopted a dual form of supervision by combining the project and systems forms of organization.[22] Engineers specializing in particular functional areas are under the administrative direction of project supervisors who coordinate the over-all development of a project, be it an aircraft, a missile, or a communications network. Engineers can thus specialize in particular technical areas, which increases their efficiency, yet still be used flexibly because they can work on a variety of large complex projects over time. If projects are small, a systems group may even work on more than one at the same time.

The constant shifting of systems groups from one project to another seldom allows engineers to become familiar enough with formal channels of communications and authority to use them regularly or efficiently. The pressures for speed in clearing up difficulties and the problems of coordinating highly interdependent systems designs put a premium on informal relations. Thus, engineers often find opportunities to approach both higher and lower supervisors, technical as well as administrative. As a chief engineer in a plant making aerospace equipment said: "In this business the organization of the groups is not real hard and firm. A man can't really get out of bounds in this sort of organization. The engineers and lead men and supervisors feel pretty free to handle things their own way within limits and to work out problems among themselves."

The informality and loose procedural arrangements, combined with the diffusion of authority within engineering departments, provides a fertile ground in which individual bargaining can flourish. As they angle for other positions and assignments, many engineers are encouraged to play off one supervisor against another; led to question ratings that are often subjective, poorly informed, or hasty; and tempted to call their work to the attention of higher level superiors. Consequently engineers and their supervisors spend a considerable amount of time and effort in their individual negotiations, politicking, and dickering.

Engineers engage in these activities willingly, not because employers insist or because they have no other alternative. Only a minority of the engineers show any interest in restricting the use of individual bargaining. Some complain that this method is seldom equitable and that it is merely a way for supervisors to reward apple-polishers and friends. A few are convinced that it favors the "politicians" and "squeaky wheels" rather than men of merit and real engineering skill. Among the engineers interviewed, including members of engineering unions, however, such complaints and criticism were held to be invalid for the most part. They felt that friendships or pull might help a man to get a position, but that he had to prove himself an able, fully capable engineer to hold it. The standards for judging engineering work are not precise, and the measurement of an engineer's worth is not easy, but engineers insist that the differences between a good engineer and one who is merely competent or between a competent engineer and a poor one are clear enough. They argue that all concerned can usually reach some consensus in their relative ratings of each other.

Furthermore, the requirements of most engineering work are sufficiently demanding that men need not do work that is beneath their capabilities forever. However misused they may feel, many engineers believe they enjoy much better opportunities to work up to the limits of their abilities and to demonstrate their worth in fairly unmistakable ways to their colleagues and supervisors than most blue-collar workers, for example. Not every engineer gains when he bargains for himself, of course, and merit is not always rewarded, but on the whole the system works tolerably well. Very few engineers, even those who are union members, see any need for collective bargaining to supplant individual bargaining over such things as transfers, promotions, complaints, and job assignments. A survey of the attitudes of members of the Minneapolis Federation of Honeywell Engineers in 1956 indicated that a small proportion of the engineers were dissatisfied with their individual bargaining over job transfers, distribution of overtime, merit rating, and layoffs. About a third wanted the federation to have more say, through collective bargaining, about transfers and merit ratings; about the same number doubted that the company gave full credit to the individual engineer. Only about one out of six members believed that the company unfairly distributed overtime or that it should lay off men according to seniority, a standard for which a number of engineering unions have bargained. The data indicate that about half the members were not anxious to extend the scope of collective bargaining. (See Table 6.)

A survey of both member and nonmember engineers was made a

Table 6. Member Attitudes Toward Company and Union.*
Total Sample: 569 out of 936 Members

	Percent Response†		
	Agree	Undecided	Disagree
The Company should consult with the Federation on job transfers.	34	17	49
The distribution of overtime is now handled fairly.	64	19	16
The Company's use of the merit system should be regulated by the contract.	34	18	49
I get full credit for the work I do for the Company.	47	19	34
I think that the best man should be kept on the job regardless of seniority.	70	14	16

* *Report of Findings on Attitudes, Communications and Participation,* The Minneapolis Federation of Honeywell Engineers, August 1956, p. 8. Survey conducted and report prepared by Industrial Relations Center, University of Minnesota.
† Percentages do not add to 100 in all cases due to rounding.

year later (1957) after they and the technicians rejected affiliation with the United Auto Workers and also voted to decertify the federation. Forty percent of the engineers who responded indicated a belief that the union had a desirable effect upon their relationship with management; 60 percent said it had an undesirable effect. Of the engineers who gave an opinion, 54 percent said that they enjoyed their present position because of individual merit and professional achievement. Three out of five also indicated their individualism by claiming they could and did solve their work problems in the company for themselves. These surveys suggest that most of the Honeywell engineers did not perceive much need for union help in protecting and advancing their job interests.

Since by and large the engineering unions have displayed a similar lack of eagerness to extend collective bargaining beyond the common minimums of their labor agreements, one might assume that the unions are serving those they represent very well. The low membership figures of most of the unions do not substantiate such an assumption, however. Since typically no more than 30 percent to 50 percent of the engineers in the few organized plants have taken out membership, the engineering unions have hardly proven themselves successes in the past fifteen years. They have continued to exist and they have grown as their potential membership expanded, but they have not been able to generate much excitement or many expectations among engineers.

□ Bargaining in Spite of Themselves

Plentiful, easy-to-get jobs, an ample supply of defense dollars for wages, and constant change in the exact nature of the work do not in themselves preclude more substantive collective bargaining than most of the engineering unions have been able to provide. These conditions can, as they do in the case of blue-collar unions, favor successful collective bargaining. The organizational structure within which the bargaining is carried on can be far more crucial to the success of collective bargaining, however. Two engineering unions whose experiences have been quite different from those examined previously demonstrate the validity of this observation.

These unions have been strikingly different from the engineering unions already described. First, they have had the support of a much larger proportion of the engineers in their bargaining units. One has a voluntary membership of about 80 percent; the other enjoyed nearly 100 percent membership under a union shop. In the latter case, since only about one in ten of the engineers in the highest salary grade "escaped" when they were permitted to withdraw from the union, voluntary membership would probably be in the 80 to 90 percent range, even without the union shop. Second, the two unions provided a different kind of service for their members. Collective bargaining has been for them a continuous process, not just negotiation of a labor agreement from time to time; it has been the daily administration, adjudication, and grievance bargaining that makes up a full, comprehensive service. Third, both have used strikes as a bargaining tactic with some effectiveness, without injury to themselves.

Although such activities were very different from those of a typical engineering union, these unions were not otherwise unusual. Their members, who were employed on aerospace projects of the Defense Department and also engaged in the manufacture of commercial electronic and communications equipment, performed the same kind of work as the members of other unions. The companies employing the members are large and have greatly expanded their engineering departments since the unions were formed. Like the typical engineering union, each of these two active unions was at first encouraged by management in order to forestall unionization by production unions. They also resembled the typical engineering union in that their membership was either mixed or consisted exclusively of professionals. One of the unions limited membership to professionals (usually engineers with an engineering or similar degree) and the other included both professionals and technicians. In short, although the two unions quite clearly acted differently from the typical engineering union, the reasons for the differences are not obvious.

The fact that engineers have established two such strong, active unions embarrassed the immediate managers as well as the leaders of other engineering unions. The support engineers gave the two unions and the services the unions provided in return belied assertions of general management and professional engineering groups that engineers do not want, cannot use, and will overwhelmingly reject collective bargaining. The success of these unions also showed up the leadership and accomplishments of the other engineering unions to poor advantage.

The two active unions developed under company and managerial conditions so dissimilar that they might be characterized as polar. Yet the kind of services they developed and the type of activities they carried on were much the same. An examination of the influences that persuaded or constrained managers and engineers to develop regular, comprehensive collective bargaining under such contrasting circumstances provides further understanding of the requirements for developing collective bargaining for professionals and for employees generally.

The most striking difference between the two active unions and their quiescent fellows lies in the use they make of the grievance procedure. In the active unions, grievance work, in its wider sense of daily bargaining, makes up the bulk of union activity and keeps union officials perpetually occupied. Yet the organizers and leaders of the two active unions never specifically directed their efforts to the development of the grievance procedure. In fact, management was more responsible for the grievance process of the first active union to be organized, than the engineers. These engineers organized in 1945, in the hope of avoiding inclusion in a technicians' union. They planned only

> to create a consultative board that could represent them in discussions with management. It was envisioned that these groups would serve as a 'sounding board'—without becoming involved in the complications of formal 'unionism.' Exploratory conferences with Company representatives, however, quickly dispelled any thoughts of this type of idealized relationship—since the Company indicated that it could not (or would not) deal with an organization of engineers unless it was officially accredited . . . as a legal bargaining unit.[23]

The engineers devised a rather sketchy kind of grievance procedure that would have differed little from the informal methods of bringing complaints to one's supervisor that were then in use. The company rejected such a procedure as inadequate and proposed instead the kind of detailed grievance system commonly found in most industrial union agreements. Grievances were defined; time limits were set for processing; a hierarchy of hiring levels was established; and the method of record-keeping was set forth. Company officials not only insisted upon a grievance system but also formalized work rules, job standards, and administrative procedures. For example, they began programs of job analysis, job evaluation, and merit rating for engineers and other salaried employees. Any disagreement with the rating could be made a grievance. As negotiations continued, the engineers brought to management's attention a number of discrepancies in salaries. All were adjusted to the benefit of the engineers. Other such favorable adjustments led the engineers to experiment further with their new grievance procedure. In the succeeding years the volume of grievance work grew, becoming the main reason for the union's existence. Active members performed their apprenticeship for higher offices as grievance committeemen, and all engineers learned that the union could help an individual who had a question or complaint about the way rules were enforced and standards applied.

Although there was some skepticism at first, both management and the engineers gradually became familiar with the grievance procedure. Handling and processing grievances became as accepted a part of daily work as the shop activities of union officers. The large number of engineers who were newly hired each year as the company expanded its engineering department eight times over in a fifteen-year period quickly and readily took out membership. The union conducted no membership drives and has always used a soft-sell approach on new hires. No explicit propaganda was needed to gain acceptance of the union by the engineers and management; the growing use of the grievance services was sufficient. Joining the union became the thing to do; voluntary membership has averaged 80 to 85 percent of all eligible engineers.

The grievance work carried on by management and union has not eliminated individual bargaining by engineers. All of the parties gave examples of men who, on their own, sought transfers to promising projects, negotiated with supervisors for additional jobs and interesting problems, arranged special leaves, holidays, and vacation schedules, and even "dickered" over merit ratings. Engineers negotiate most of the adjustments of the merit rating reports themselves, but the grievance procedure provides a backstop and support for the engineer's own efforts. The advice and aid of grievance representatives supplement, but do not supplant, the judgment and initiative of the individual.

In encouraging the use of regular procedures and in helping to delineate a role for the engineering union in daily administration, the company has not been a "patsy." Company officials accept unions and collective bargaining, but they do not readily accede to union demands. Agreement on the first negotiations was reached only after federal mediators intervened to prevent a strike. Since organizing in the mid-forties, the engineers have struck twice to support their demands and have met with indifferent success. The company has agreed to arbitration, but several times the union has had to resort to lengthy court proceedings to settle arbitration cases. The salary ranges, hours, fringe benefits, and conditions of work are not significantly higher or better than in other companies employing large numbers of engineers. The competitive limits of the labor market and company product markets have precluded any great variation from industry standards.

The gains and benefits that have accrued to the engineers as a result of the union's activities and that apparently have proved attractive to them are not markedly noticeable to an outsider. The major advantages seem to be, according to the engineers, assurance of fairness and equity in their treatment by the company and the knowledge that their views and opinions may reach those who make those company policies that affect their work lives. Although they are given a respectful hearing, however, the grievances through which the engineers make known their views and opinions seldom cause any major change in policies.

The company whose engineers organized the second active union was not stable, well established, or soundly administered. Until World War II it was a small engineering firm that made special equipment for the Navy. The two founders ran the company out of their hats, in a paternalistic and highly personal way. Personnel policy was chaotic, subject to change any time a new idea or a new adviser caught the fancy of the two men. When the war ended and the number of military contracts began to fall off, the company nearly foundered. A larger company took over control and appointed new managers, but the old policy—or lack of policy—continued. The company's recovery began when it obtained Defense Department contracts to develop special technical equipment.

As the company prospered, the engineers and workers languished. The swift inflation during the early months of the Korean War eroded salaries and the absence of any coherent personnel and managerial policy produced confusion and inequities. The engineers became especially unhappy when the company agreed to grant them only a $6 across-the-board weekly increase, giving no consideration to rank or merit. At the same time the company agreed to an increase of $14 a week for its newly organized production workers. When the American Federation of Technical Employees and the International Union of Electrical Workers attempted to enroll the engineers late in 1950, management encouraged the engineers to form their own union. Disgruntled as they were, they needed little encouragement. In early 1951, they began their first negotiations.

The engineers negotiated with managers who had been with the company less than a year and who left a few months after the first agreement was signed. In general, the engineers got whatever they asked for, and they asked for a lot, because they had combed a variety of union agreements to find items that looked worthwhile. Among the items they asked for were a full grievance procedure, arbitration, and ample pay for union officers and committeemen who investigated grievances or attended grievance hearings.

During the next several years, as the engineers learned how to run a union, the company suffered from managerial instability and a lack of continuity in management policy. One group of managers followed another as the parent company sought men who could control production and costs by establishing some administrative order in the organization. The managers often found themselves in embarrassing positions. One manager, for example, suggested to a conference of engineers some changes in a particular personnel policy. An officer of the engineering union pointed out that under an interpretation agreed to earlier the change was not possible. "Well, which one of my seven predecessors did that?" he exploded. "It's a damned hard job figuring out what went on here before."

The manager had reason to be exasperated, but he was not accurate. It was not difficult to find out what had gone on in the company; one only needed to ask the union leaders. They knew company policy well, because they had devised most of it and they had administered it for a longer time than any manager. In this company the engineering union performed many of the personnel activities usually carried on by managers in other firms. The union, not management, has been responsible for most of the procedures through which personnel policies and work standards are established and enforced. By assuming this responsibility the union created an important role for itself in the company, which made it an indispensable aid to the engineers.

The union participates in many activities other than grievance handling. Jointly with management it worked out job descriptions for technicians. It helps administer the filling of all engineering vacancies since engineers have the right to bid for vacant positions on the basis of seniority if they are qualified. It reviews all personnel policies and suggests changes that are sometimes adopted by management. The union also examines all salary data and salary changes with the aid of electronic computers, and it often makes analyses that are more detailed, careful, and revealing than those of the company. The union is so active and so perceptive in many of its criticisms of management that managers have at times fallen back upon an argument that hardly enhances their prestige—the right to mismanage.

In both unions the engineers of longer tenure (five to eight or more years) are the most active participants, and it is they who make up the highest proportion of membership. The second union enjoys a union shop so, of course, all engineers must pay dues. The engineers who have shorter tenures are more apt to complain about the required membership than are the more senior men. In this respect, the union is like the quiescent unions, though a far larger share of engineers in each tenure group has joined the organization.

☐ Conclusion

The two active engineering unions discussed here developed their activities and began offering their services within two quite different kinds of situations. In one case the environment was highly structured and rules and regulations established by central authority governed employee-employer relationships; in the other, relationships were chaotic, disorganized, and irregular. In response to the first situation the union was molded into an organization that provided daily grievance services at the place of work and the union representatives were encouraged to challenge the original work rules and regulations and to insist upon a role in modifying them or establishing new ones. The second situation offered the union leaders the opportunity to become the company's personnel "managers" and the primary rule-making body within the plant. In both cases collective bargaining either demonstrated its superiority to individual bargaining or proved to be a valuable supplement to such bargaining as individual engineers could conduct.

The quiescent engineering unions have neither been required to develop continued, on-the-job services for engineers nor have they been presented the opportunity to provide them. The employing organizations tend to operate with a loosely defined and only partly bureaucratized management structure, which allows considerable scope for individual bargaining. The rapid increase in employment of engineers and the resulting growth of engineering departments have (or seem to have) made collective bargaining unnecessary. Despite the absence of collective bargaining, starting salaries and wage increases in the early years of employment have gone up at a satisfying rate. Expanding engineering staffs have offered the realization as well as the promise of promotion to managerial positions for large numbers of young engineers; the rapid changes in engineering projects have continually provided opportunities for engineers to seek out on their own better positions, work groups, or job advantages.

The analysis of engineering unions presented here suggests that the future of unionism and collective bargaining among engineers will not be bright as long as the structure of management and ample opportunities in the profession allow individual engineers to gain reasonably satisfying rewards from their own bargaining. However, should firms find that the rewards that they have been able to offer engineers cannot be maintained, or that they cannot continue to fulfill as large a share of their promises in the future, unionization could spread rapidly. If for economic or other reasons, managements are forced to tighten control over their professional engineering employees or if loss of defense contracts should demoralize management and produce chaotic, completely unregulated conditions of work, collective bargaining for engineers could spread as it is now spreading among other white-collar employees such as teachers and nurses; it might even become as common as it is for musicians, actors, and airline pilots.

NOTES

[1] James J. Bambrick and Albert A. Blum, National Industrial Conference Board, *Unionization Among American Engineers,* Studies in Personnel Policy, No. 155, 1956, p. 4.

[2] Herbert R. Northrup, *Unionization of Professional Engineers and Chemists* (New York: Industrial Relations Counselors, 1946) , p. 4.

[3] Bureau of Labor Statistics, *Employment Outlook,* 1949, Table 18, p. 63.

[4] Bambrick and Blum, *op. cit.,* p. 7.

[5] W. Lee Hansen, "Professional Engineers: Salary Structure Problems," *Industrial Relations,* 2 (May 1963) , 34.

[6] Northrup, *op. cit.,* p. 6.

[7] Howard F. Peckworth, *The Engineer and Collective Bargaining* (New York: American Society of Civil Engineers, 1943) , p. 32.

[8] "Collective Bargaining—A Historical Review," *Civil Engineering,* 14 (1944) , 311.

9 See M. E. McIver, H. A. Wagner and M. P. McGirr, *Technologists' Stake in the Wagner Act* (Chicago: American Association of Engineers, 1944), p. 102.

10 Northrup, *op. cit.,* p. 18.

11 Association of Professional Engineering Personnel *Newsletter,* May 11, 1960.

12 *Northwest Professional Engineer,* December 1963, p. 18.

13 *San Diego Engineer* (a publication of the Engineers and Architects Association of Corvair), October 1957, p. 5.

14 "The President's Roster," *The San Diego Engineer,* December 1958, p. 13.

15 "SCPEA's Policies," *1960–62 Handbook, Professional* (Los Angeles: SCPEA, 1961), p. 8. SCPEA has members in the Douglas Aircraft Company and the Southern California Gas Company.

16 *Southern California Professional Engineer,* August 1962, p. 11. Italics added.

17 *Southern California Professional Engineer,* October–November 1957, pp. 5–6.

18 Richard Walton also found little evidence of much grievance activity among the engineering unions. See *The Impact of the Professional Engineering Union* (Boston: Graduate School of Business Administration, Harvard University, 1961), p. 311.

19 Bernard Goldstein, "The Perspective of Unionized Professionals," *Social Forces* (May 1959), pp. 324–325.

20 Jack Barbash, "Unionizing the Professional Worker," *Industrial Relations Conference,* University of Pennsylvania, November 18, 1960, pp. 6–7.

21 See also Walton, *op. cit.,* pp. 333–334, where he discusses the balance of forces that produces bargaining between engineers and supervisors.

22 E. S. Arndt and others, *Engineering Manpower: How to Improve Its Productivity,* 3rd ed. (Boston: Graduate School of Business Administration, Harvard University, 1957), p. 11.

23 Quoted from a union handbook that gives the history of the organization.

TEACHERS AND COLLECTIVE NEGOTIATIONS

by WESLEY A. WILDMAN*

Public elementary and secondary education in the United States is a vast, complex, and highly diversified enterprise. During the 1967–1968 school year, approximately 44 million students attended public elementary and high schools in the United States.† The students were distributed among approximately 100,000 different school facilities in nearly 20,000 separate operating school districts, each with its own governing board of lay citizens from the local community. Teachers employed to educate the youth of the land in the public school system numbered over 1.8 million.

Of course, a good deal of concentration exists in the larger cities and the huge urban areas of the country, and there is much diversity in the size of districts; for instance, less than 4 percent of the operating school districts in the United States enroll more than half of the pupils in the country, while 2 percent of the school systems employ over 40 percent of the nation's teachers.

Each of the fifty states has its own laws governing the activities of the school systems within its boundaries, its own regulations concerning the certification and hiring of teachers, and so on. In recent

* Industrial Relations Center, the University of Chicago. Many of the observations on the results and impact of bargaining in the schools contained in this article are drawn from a comprehensive study of teacher negotiations made from 1964 to 1968 and sponsored jointly by the U.S. Office of Education and the University of Chicago, and directed by the author. I want to give very special recognition to Charles R. Perry, now of the University of Pennsylvania, who served as associate director of the USOE–UC project, and was responsible for much of the work that generated many of the findings contained in what follows. Finally, thanks are due to the Charles A. Jones Publishing Company for kind permission to borrow from *The Impact of Negotiations in Public Education: The Evidence from the Schools* by Charles R. Perry and Wesley A. Wildman (1970), the introductory material which appears here on the history of teacher organizations and the negotiations movement in the United States.
† While not insignificant in size, the private schools of the country are dwarfed by the public system; in 1967–1968, approximately 7 million pupils attended nonpublic elementary and high schools in the U.S.

years, various federal government laws and regulations have also had an increasingly important impact on the operation of the locally controlled public schools.

The methods of financing the public schools and the dollar amounts expended per pupil vary widely from community to community and from state to state. A total of $31 billion was spent on public grade and high school education during the 1967–1968 school year; per pupil expenditures varied from a high of $982 per pupil in New York State to a low of $346 per child in Mississippi. Average teacher salaries varied from a high of nearly $9,444 per year in Alaska to a low of $4,611 in Mississippi.

It is in this context of extreme complexity, variability, and a relatively high degree of decentralization, then, that we will discuss the most dramatic recent development in public education in the United States—the increasingly militant effort of teachers to seek recognition and more powerful roles in policy formulation and administrative decision making through the medium of "collective bargaining" or "professional negotiations" in local school districts.

Collective negotiations in the schools in the United States is almost wholly a post–World War II phenomenon. Indeed, most significant bargaining relationships between teacher organizations and boards of education have developed since 1960. The major teacher organizations in this country, namely the National Education Association (NEA) and its important state affiliates, and the American Federation of Teachers (AFT) and its locals, have, of course, been in existence for many years. However, while more than occasionally concerned during their long histories with teacher welfare, they have not—until recently—sought power for the improvement of the lot of teachers through local school district negotiations.

□ The NEA and the State Associations

In 1857, a small group of sixty superintendents, principals, and college presidents and professors met in Philadelphia, at the call of ten state education associations, to form a national teachers association, which later became the National Education Association.* The

* The name of the organization was first the National Teacher's Association. In 1870, two previously independent national associations of superintendents and

future hardly looked promising; a number of similar efforts to organize educators nationally had foundered on the shoals of regionalization or diversity of interest. The task of the new organization, as the charter members saw it, was "professional," and its purpose was "to elevate the character and advance the interests of the teaching profession and to promote the cause of popular education in the U.S."[1] In the nineteenth century, few classroom teachers belonged to the national association or its forerunners, and the problem of teacher welfare was left largely unarticulated. Occasionally, a committee on salaries or teacher tenure was appointed at conventions, but it was not until after 1900 that the work done by such groups had any significant impact on the educational scene.

The first state association of teachers and school officials was formed in 1845 in Massachusetts, and by 1910 every state and territory except Delaware and Tennessee had a functioning group. However, in 1907 only 14 percent of the nation's eligible teachers were enrolled in state associations. The traditional goal of the early associations was usually stated to be "professional improvement"—in practice an essentially noneconomic concept. By 1910, though, nearly half of the state associations had conducted investigations in their jurisdictions on teacher salaries, tenure, and pensions, and had taken some affirmative action, primarily through lobbying, to enhance the status of the classroom teacher. The results were variable, but the evidence indicates that at least some of the state groups did play an important role in influencing legislation during this period.

Meanwhile, prior to 1900, the National Education Association (never enrolling as many members directly as the state associations) was developing a traditional "professional" philosophy that considered teaching as work done "primarily for public service and secondarily for earning [one's] living."[2] If teaching, in this view, was an expression of "unselfish social service,"[3] money matters tended to be considered, in the words of a superintendent speaking before an NEA convention, "beneath the dignity of the association."[4] It was generally expected that salary increases and welfare

---

normal schools joined to become departments within the association, and the name was changed to the National Educational Association. In 1906–1907, the name became the National Education Association.

benefits would be extended by a grateful public in appreciation of increased professional effort.

The first tangible evidence of significant NEA concern for the "meat and potatoes" aspects of teacher welfare was the appointment and funding in 1903 of a Committee on Teachers' Salaries, Pensions and Tenure. The establishment of the committee was largely the result of goading by two leaders of the Chicago Teachers Federation, Catharine Goggin and Margaret Haley. The Committee's detailed report was made in 1905, serving as a model and fund of information that stimulated city and state organizations to conduct their own investigations and engage in more intensive lobbying activities on behalf of teacher welfare. The 1905 report was to represent the full extent of NEA "welfare activity" for many years.

In 1912, the Classroom Teachers Department was formed within the National Education Association. It held its first meeting in 1914, and immediately expressed interest in matters of welfare and teacher participation in school management. Classroom teachers' desires were echoed in NEA resolutions, but the association commanded few instrumentalities for achievement of any stated goals. In 1906, a convention speaker noted, ". . . we shall resort to no trade union methods. We shall continue to present our claims with dignity and moderation. . . ."[5] By 1918, though, Joseph Swain, an NEA past president, was emboldened to remark: "But suppose the nation cannot be made to see its duty. Then there is only one other way: that teachers by concerted action and the application of the principles of collective bargaining must compel the nation to wake up."[6] This statement, softened by Swain himself when he opined that collective bargaining would not be necessary because he was confident the American people would face up to their educational problem without such a drastic stimulus, was, and remained for many decades, the high watermark of even implied NEA enthusiasm for collective bargaining.

By 1923, the state associations had enrolled nearly 62 percent of the nation's teachers. During the twenties, many of them hired full-time executive secretaries and substantially broadened their legislative lobbying activities. However, while gains were made in a number of states, over-all achievements in the welfare areas (except in regard to pensions) were less than spectacular.[7]

To the present day, the state associations have continued to grow in membership and influence. Although they offer a wide range of membership services, the emphasis in most states is still on lobbying; in many instances the impact of the state associations on teacher welfare and other educational legislation has been immense. Indeed, in some states the state education association has traditionally been the most powerful single entity in the educational complex. With the advent of collective bargaining, new powers and responsibilities have accrued to the state associations, particularly in those states with legislation calling for negotiations between teachers and school boards (for example, Michigan and Connecticut).

Spurred by AFT successes (the AFT gained more members in the three-year period from 1917 to 1919 than the NEA had in fifty), the NEA in 1917 formed the Commission of the National Emergency in Education to promote NEA membership and to fight the growing affiliation of teachers with organized labor. As a result of a drive which began in 1918, the NEA by 1931 had enrolled 220,000 members. However, the depression took its toll, and by 1936 membership had fallen to 165,000. The 1931 level was not reached again until 1943.

During this period, NEA consciousness of problems of teacher welfare was developing rapidly. In 1936, Willard Givens, NEA executive secretary, wrote to signal the change in outlook:

> The association is determined to exert every effort its resources will permit in behalf of the economic and professional welfare of teachers. . . . Only through increasingly effective organization of the profession in local, state and national areas can teachers achieve the rewards and the security which are justifiably theirs.[8]

Indeed, throughout the twenties and thirties, through organizational changes, the establishment of the Research Division, the Division of Teacher Welfare, and so on, the NEA moved in increasingly effective ways to serve the educational community in general and to support activities in behalf of classroom teacher welfare and other interests on local, state, and national levels. The NEA today, of course, with its multitudinous research and lobbying activities and its numerous separate subject matter departments, is the preeminent teacher organization in the country, enrolling over 1 million members.

☐ Early City Organizations

At the turn of the century, several factors, including low salaries, the increasing availability of "respectable" alternative occupations for the predominantly female teacher labor force, a "popular contempt for a lightly rewarded occupation," and dissatisfaction with working conditions that gave rise to the "factory hand" analogy between teachers and rank-and-file industrial employees, led to significant unified protest activity by organizations of teachers in the larger cities. Chicago, often referred to as the "birthplace" of teacher unionism, provided perhaps the best example. These city associations were undoubtedly, for at least the first two decades of this century, the most important single medium through which teachers fought most directly to improve their welfare and the schools generally. For the most part, the city associations were led by women who, inspired by the feminist movement (and a desire for pay equal to men), fought assiduously against tax-dodging and arbitrary and capricious funding by school boards. The associations were often quite active politically and occasionally joined in sporadic and short-lived affiliation with organized labor in their localities. City association leaders employed such methods as lobbying for appropriate local and state legislation, arousing public opinion through all available forms of publicity including petitions, rallies, handbills, and so on, and the policing of tax rolls and payments (particularly by corporations) through the courts.

☐ The American Federation of Teachers

The first recorded affiliation of any teacher group with organized labor took place in San Antonio in 1902. Later that year teachers in Chicago affiliated with the Chicago Federation of Labor to gain some visibility and support in the battle against tax-dodging and for higher salaries. In 1916, the AFT, boasting eight locals, was chartered by the parent American Federation of Labor. The union's immediate successes somewhat exceeded expectations, and by 1920 membership stood at over 10,000. (At this point, we might note, the memberships of the AFT and of the NEA were almost equal.) Bad times lay immediately ahead, however, and the decade of the twenties was marked by declining membership and a struggle for existence. Throughout the twenties, the AFT was often on the defensive, fighting for its life. There were a number of reasons for the problems that beset the AFT during this period. First, there was the reluctance of many teachers (which persists today) to identify with the predominantly blue-collar "working class" labor movement. Furthermore, public opinion, particularly following the Boston police strike of 1921, was strongly opposed to "unionism" among public employees, and the whole phenomenon was considered to border on the anarchistic. Also, tangible opposition by boards of education, in the form, for instance, of "yellow dog" contracts, was widespread.

During the depression, the AFT again gained membership strength, and various AFT locals in the large cities were active in lobbying and pressuring, with some success, against board of education retrenchments occasioned by the economic decline. In the late thirties, some direct "negotiations" confrontations on specific issues between AFT locals and boards took place. By 1938, the AFT had enrolled 29,000 members. However, the federation was soon weakened when various communist locals were "purged" by the leadership. NEA membership climbed to 195,000 by 1938.

Predominant concern for essentially economic issues candidly marked AFT activities during this period. Since its inception, however, the union has also been assiduous in its defense of teacher civil liberties and academic freedom in specific cases. Perhaps the greatest tribute to this aspect of the AFT's activity was paid by Donald DuShane, later a president of the NEA: "The most fearless and effective work [in defense of academic freedom] has been done by the AFT. Their example and the principles for which they have fought have had a very stimulating effect upon the non-unionized federations and unorganized teacher members of the NEA and of state associations."[9]

While occasional historical references (emanating mostly from New York) concerning the feasibility for teachers of collective bargaining procedures and practices can be found in AFT literature, the organization took no fixed policy position on the subject until well after World War II, and bargaining, as we know it today, was not implemented in AFT locals. Indeed, until the 1950s, the AFT formally disavowed the strike as an appropriate weapon for teachers.

Today, with a membership of 150,000 (predominantly in the large cities), the AFT is an organization of significantly increasing power and influence which represents teachers in negotiating relationships in a majority of our major cities. With its increased size and wealth, the AFT has begun to modify its image as an organization which is interested only in teacher welfare by supporting an increased publication program, underwriting at least a modest research activity, and intensifying legislative activity on behalf of higher aid for education generally.

□ Postwar Developments (1945–1967)

During the period immediately following World War II, two of the first local collective bargaining relationships in schools appeared. In Norwalk, Connecticut, an association of teachers achieved formal recognition as the official bargaining agent for teachers in that system as the result of a 1946 strike, and the Pawtucket, Rhode Island Teachers Alliance (AFT Local No. 930) successfully forced the board of education to negotiate on its proposal for salary increases after a strike. In 1947, the first representation election among teachers was held in a Chicago suburb. Initially requested by the AFT, the election was conducted by the Illinois Department of Labor with the consent of the board of education and resulted in a victory for the AFT local.

Though both the AFT and the NEA had long supported teacher participation in determining school policies, neither organization at this time supported the establishment of formal collective negotiations at the local level as a matter of national policy. By 1947, however, both organizations began to shift ground. The NEA Executive Committee declared: "Group action is essential today. The former practice where teachers individually bargained with the superintendent of schools or the board of education for their salaries is largely past."[10] Later that year, at the NEA convention, a resolution was passed recommending that "each member seek salary adjustment in a professional way through group action." The AFT sought similar action: "Methods whereby various groups may participate in policy formation must be devised. Procedures which will permit successful democratic participation must be perfected."[11]

Competition for membership between the two organizations, which characterizes much present AFT-NEA rivalry, was largely absent from the immediate postwar period. In 1945 direct membership in the NEA was nearly 331,000, while AFT members totaled only 31,000. Between 1945 and 1948, both grew by about one third, so that by 1949 the NEA had over 427,000 members, and the AFT had more than 41,000. In the 1950s the NEA far outstripped the AFT in membership growth. The NEA's membership grew by 57 percent, from nearly 454,000 in 1950 to almost 714,000 in 1960. The AFT grew only 43 percent for a total membership of 59,181 in 1960.

During the 1950s the AFT committed itself to collective bargaining and resolved to "assist and support locals in establishing collective bargaining procedures" by collecting and distributing public-employee agreements and AFT bargaining agreements to locals.[12] The union achieved written agreements in a number of districts, including Pawtucket, Rhode Island, and established several new collective bargaining relationships, including those in East St. Louis, Illinois, and Gary, Indiana.

The 1960s were years of intensive organizational rivalry between the NEA and the AFT. In 1961 the United Federation of Teachers (AFT Local No. 2) won representation rights for New York City schools. This victory was achieved against a hastily organized NEA-supported coalition of teacher organizations and represented the first situation in which the NEA, as a national organization, faced the AFT in a highly visible test of strength. In 1962 the AFT acquired membership in the Industrial Union Department of the AFL-CIO and began receiving financial aid in its organizing efforts. In 1962 Walter Reuther spoke at the AFT convention and called for a 1 million-member AFT.[13]

The New York City AFT victory set the NEA in motion. At its 1962 Denver convention the following resolutions marked the NEA's official entry into collective negotiations and the development of the concept of "professional negotiations":

The National Education Association insists on the right of professional association, through democratically selected representatives using professional channels, to participate with boards of education in determination of policies of common concern including salary and other conditions for professional service.

The Association believes that procedures should be established which provide an orderly method for professional education associations and boards of education to reach mutually satisfactory agreements.[14]

Almost immediately thereafter, two of the first NEA professional-negotiations agreements appeared in Denver and Champaign, Illinois. To counter the AFT's organizational drive, the NEA created the Urban Project to strengthen its position in the cities, where NEA affiliates faced strongest competition from the AFT.

Today, competition between the NEA and the AFT occurs at local, state, and national levels. The major burden of the competition in the context of collective negotiations, however, is being carried by local and state organizations rather than by the national parent bodies.

At the local level, representation elections have occurred at a significant rate over the past few years and will undoubtedly continue under the impetus of state legislation granting bargaining rights to public school teachers.[15] The AFT has won the majority of contested representation elections both in and outside the larger cities, and the number of teachers covered by election victories favors the AFT. However, the NEA currently represents more teachers under exclusive recognition clauses (which grant collective negotiation status to one organization) partially, at least, because the association has been unilaterally designated as representative by school boards in many systems where there is no AFT competition.

During the 1967–1968 school year, approximately 900,000 teachers in the United States were working under a total of about 2,200 "agreements" (at minimum, some form of written acknowledgment of the existence and recognition of a teacher organization in the district).[16] However, much of this coverage was under "recognition only" or "recognition plus negotiation procedures" type memoranda or "agreements" with school boards by NEA state association affiliates. More significantly, however, an estimated 300,000 teachers are presently covered by some 600 *substantive, bilateral, signed contracts* with boards of education which contain salary schedules, grievance procedures, and clauses covering all manner of so-called "working conditions" and, perhaps, "professional" matters. In this all-important category, the AFT's coverage is probably at least half of the 300,000 total, resulting from the fact that the NEA (and its state affiliates) have great strength throughout most of the country outside of the larger cities, while the AFT holds exclusive representational rights for teachers in such major metropolises as New York, Philadelphia, Detroit, Cleveland, Boston, Chicago, Washington, and Baltimore. The AFT's potentially greater strength in the larger districts has reduced significantly the differential between the two organizations in terms of number of teachers represented in "hard" bargaining relationships that result in comprehensive, bargained agreements. What strengths the NEA does have in terms of formal negotiation relationships lies primarily in those states where it was strong enough (even in this case, usually outside the larger cities) to take advantage of state legislation providing for teacher bargaining (for instance, Michigan, Wisconsin, Connecticut, etc.).

□ Why the New Militancy?

Why has the so-called "new militancy" and aggressive drive for organization and local district bargaining suddenly emerged in the 1960s? The "causes" are numerous and diverse; we will mention only a few:

1. First, of course, teachers simply desire more money and benefits, "a bigger share of the pie," which, they have just recently discovered, collective negotiations can deliver. Teachers want more money for themselves and (a concern often shared with school boards) more money for education generally.

2. The percentage of males in the teaching force is increasing, and teachers of both sexes are better trained and prepared than ever before. Also, turnover among teachers is moderately decreasing. The great disparity in years of formal preparation that used to exist between rank-and-file teachers and administrators is no longer much in evidence. Many teachers are, without question, becoming increasingly "professionalized" in terms of training and career commitment, and they want a larger voice in determining exactly how they will be allowed to go about the job of teaching.

3. In many school systems, teachers also want a voice in formulating the rules and policies of the bureaucracy that controls their work lives. In addition, in many districts teachers evidently feel that

they need some way of protesting allegedly discriminatory application of the rules and policies that control their day-to-day existence, a desire they hold in common with blue-collar workers in private industry.

4. Legislation that grants bargaining rights to teachers is, of course, both a crucial cause and an effect of the new teacher militancy.

5. Quite important also is the NEA-AFT rivalry, intensified by the desire of the larger labor movement to organize the white-collar workers of this country.

6. The monumental problems of the big-city school system are quite important as one traces the genesis of the movement for bargaining among teachers in the United States. The drive really began, after all, in the early 1960s in New York City, where teacher dissatisfaction is (or at least was) simply much greater than in small-town, rural, or suburban systems. The AFT successes in New York spurred the NEA to begin acting like a union in many localities. Of course, the process is, to a certain extent, now self-sustaining.

7. Last, but not necessarily least, is the fact that we seem to be living in what one commentator has characterized as "an age of political activism, in which collective action, demonstrations, and thrusts for power are both fashionable and effective."[17] The drive for teacher power undoubtedly derives strength from this cultural context.

☐ Emerging Legal Doctrine

The emergence of collective negotiations in education is part and parcel of the struggle for recognition and the right to organize and to bargain among public employees in general. The rapid changes in the laws relating to the rights of teachers and other public employees to organize and negotiate have played a critical role in the shaping and development of bargaining in the public sector in recent years.

By late 1969, twenty-three states had statutes relating directly to collective negotiations or "discussion" in the schools. In some jurisdictions, teacher bargaining is provided for in separate legislation; in others, teachers are included with other employees under legislation relating to the rights of municipal employees generally. In four of these twenty-three states,* the laws relating to interaction between teachers and school boards are quite rudimentary in form. In addition, they are "permissive" in that they provide only that a board of education may or may not, *at its discretion,* undertake to recognize and negotiate or open discussions with teachers or a representative teacher organization. In the remaining nineteen states,† the negotiating laws are "mandatory" in that they provide that boards of education or their representatives *must,* if the teachers or their organization so request, discuss, negotiate, "meet and confer," or whatever, according to the dictates of the statute.

There is also much teacher "bargaining" or "negotiating," some of it quite formal, in states that have as yet no specific legislation on the subject.

In most states, teachers, as well as other public employees, now have the right to join together in organizations of their own choosing. Although (except for states with recent statutes) the crucial majority privilege of exclusive representational status is not available to public employees as a matter of right, the concept of majority, exclusive representation has been voluntarily extended in practice to public-employee organizations by many public employing agencies, including school boards, across the country. Quite recently (in what is still a minority view) courts in several states have given approval to voluntary adoption by boards of education of schemes calling for elections and the designation of exclusive representatives, of negotiations, and even of the signing of formal bilateral collective labor agreements.[18]

In most jurisdictions, regardless of whether or not they have statutes specifically authorizing bargaining by public employees, the union shop and union security clauses generally have not been sanctioned in public employment negotiating agreements. They are often prohibited on the ground that requiring union membership as a condition of employment is irrelevant to or inconsistent with the concept of merit. In a recent significant development, how-

---

* Alaska, Florida, New Hampshire, Texas.
† California, Connecticut, Delaware, Maine, Maryland, Massachusetts, Michigan, Minnesota, Nebraska, Nevada, New Jersey, New York, North Dakota, Oregon, Rhode Island, South Dakota, Vermont, Washington, Wisconsin.

ever, the Michigan Labor Mediation Board has held that a request for an "agency shop" clause* is a mandatory subject for bargaining in public employment under Michigan's public employee bargaining law, and, thus, that inclusion of such a clause in a contract between an employee organization and a public employer is legal in that state.[19] A number of "agency shop" clauses have already been included in agreements between boards and, most frequently, affiliates of the education association in Michigan. The problem of reconciling the "agency shop" with the tenure act, which guarantees continuing employment, has not been resolved.

The doctrine of illegal delegation of authority—which has been so potent in forestalling bargaining in the public service and in denying to public employers the right to negotiate binding collective agreements with employee groups—is under attack in both theory and practice. In addition to the new statutes, the courts increasingly (in what is still a minority position, however) declare such contracts valid on the grounds that most governmental agencies (school boards included) have implied authority, pursuant to the statutes under which they operate, to conduct their business in the most effective and efficient manner possible and that that authority extends to the right to collectively contract for the terms and conditions on which labor is to be supplied.

Agreements in public employment to submit disputes to binding arbitration often meet the same objection—illegal delegation of governmental authority—as does the signing of a collective contract. However, a number of recent court cases (particularly in states with statutes) have progressively relaxed the prohibition against binding arbitration in governmental operations. Public agencies in a number of states now have the right to agree to submit to arbitration grievances over the interpretation or application of the collective agreement. It is not likely, though, that submission of the basic terms and conditions of the collective agreement to binding arbitration will be widely permitted or practiced in the foreseeable future.

With the exception of Vermont, both the federal government and

---

* A typical "agency shop" clause provides that while the employees in the bargaining unit do not necessarily have to belong to the bargaining representative organization, all employees must at least pay a sum equal to the organization's dues (to support cost of representational activities) or lose their jobs.

the states, through statutes and virtually unanimous court decisions, prohibit strikes by public employees.* This situation is likely to continue in a majority of jurisdictions, despite growing support for the position that at least certain categories of public employees (for example, those serving in "nonessential" areas) should be allowed to strike under some circumstances (for example, where the public employer is guilty of "bad faith" bargaining or refuses to accept a fact-finder's recommendations). The related problems of effective prohibition of strikes in the public sector and the fashioning of strike alternatives for the equitable settlement of bargaining impasses remain, of course, the critical unresolved issues relating to bargaining in the schools and in public employment in general.

☐ Teacher Organizations and the Variability of Response

In any assessment of local school district teacher collective activity in the United States, there is a tendency to draw conclusions and make projections from those districts practicing relatively formal, adversary, conflict-and-compromise-oriented negotiations; this, after all, is where the "drama" and "action" are most intriguing and visible. However, it must be noted that the procedures, processes, and even basic assumptions underlying interaction between school boards and teachers or their organizations are anything but homogeneous and uniform in the United States.

Many of the organizations vying for teacher allegiance in this country have somewhat differing views regarding the applicability to the schools of adversary procedures based on the assumption of

---

* It might be noted, parenthetically, that a recent important Michigan Supreme Court case refused to sanction the virtually automatic issuance of an injunction in a teacher strike. Holding the Michigan public employee antistrike law valid ("the sovereignty may not deny to its employees the right to strike") the court nonetheless ruled that "the only showing made to the Chancellor was that if an injunction did not issue, the districts' schools would not open, staffed by teachers, on the dates scheduled for such opening. We hold such showing insufficient to have justified the exercise of the plenary power of equity by the force of injunction." (*School District for the City of Holland Education Association et al.*, Michigan Supreme Court, reported in 239 Government Employee Relations Report D-1.)

conflict of interest. Many National Education Association local and state affiliates, for example, manifest a deep-seated analytical or philosophical ambivalence and uncertainty regarding the applicability to schools of the basic assumptions of conflict and power that form in essence the theoretical and practical underpinning of collective bargaining. They are not so sure about the inevitable inherency, nature, and depth of conflict in the schools, are somewhat uncomfortable using the rhetoric of power and opposed interests to discuss the relationship of one segment of the educational fraternity vis-à-vis another, and are instinctively wary of collective bargaining as a suitable method for structuring the leader-led relationship within a school system.

For instance, it is the considered view of some NEA state affiliates that adversary procedures that employ any significant number of the key elements of industrial bargaining and that assume the existence of conflict are not appropriate for most school systems. In this view, the well-ordered school system with a sophisticated superintendent and reasonable board does not manifest significant degrees of conflict. With all of the facts on the table and discussion taking place in an atmosphere of free communication, the result will be consensus, agreement, and problem-solving to the mutual benefit or advantage of all concerned, without the necessity for compromise, concessions, or conflict. Proponents of this position maintain that to make essentially adversary procedures available to school systems in any given state by legislation will result in the employment of these procedures out of competitive necessity in many instances where their use is unwarranted. The procedures will then tend to become self-confirming in practice; that is, they will result in the creation of unnecessary and dysfunctional conflict between administrators and teachers. The adoption of adversary procedures and the threat of the use of power may be necessary, in this view, only occasionally in those districts that have pathologically unreasonable or intractable administrations and boards. State legislation, if any, should be limited to requiring boards and administrators to communicate on an ongoing basis with teacher groups. In addition, it should leave wide leeway for flexibility and experimentation in the forms and procedures of interaction to be utilized by individual school districts as they respond to their own unique sets of circumstances. In sum, this position alleges that problem-solving and consensus within the united profession and general amicability in relations with boards of education is much more frequently the reality of modern school life than conflict and compromise between and among teacher groups, boards, and administrations. The so-called "professional negotiations" statutes in California, Minnesota, Oregon, and Washington best reflect this position.

On the other hand, a quite different stance within the NEA family—one that perhaps initially reflected adaptation to circumstances more than willing espousal—is illustrated by the ability of the Wisconsin and Michigan education associations, for instance, to utilize and compete successfully under laws in those states that permit the public sector, including school districts, to employ most of the salient features of industrial collective bargaining. Experience in these states has proved that while a state association may be reluctant to do so at the outset, it is evidently able, when circumstances demand, to adapt the organization's philosophy to activities comprising what is essentially private sector bargaining.

The position of the American Federation of Teachers is quite uniform and somewhat easier to characterize. The AFT accepts as a given the existence of significant conflict in the schools, declares that the teachers need power to wield in that conflict, and sees collective bargaining on the industrial model as the appropriate means for gaining the power and handling the conflict. The AFT fully supports the Wisconsin and Michigan type of legislation, which makes available to teachers most of the key elements of bargaining as practiced in industry.

Underscoring these varying philosophic orientations is the significant, practical difference of opinion between the organizations on the question of whether or not administrative personnel should be included in the local teacher negotiating unit.

The AFT's position is clear—the exclusion of administrative personnel from classroom teacher organizations and bargaining units is preferred. This position is based on the private industry or conflict of interest model of supervisor-supervised relationships. The supervisor who bears the responsibility for carrying out the programs, policies, and decisions of the organization is empowered to dispense rewards and to apply sanctions, that is, hire, rate, discipline, and discharge. It is basically this power over rewards and the status difference it implies that provides the bases for a conflict of interest between supervised and supervisor.

The practical effect of this conflict is an unwillingness on the part of labor organizations to include supervisors within their membership, as this would make the conflict of interest an intraorganizational problem. The existence of this conflict also implies that management is reluctant to see supervisors included in a broader bargaining unit, lest membership in such a unit lessen their willingness or ability to distribute rewards and exercise sanctions in the interests of maximum progress toward organizational goals.

The NEA's position is not definitive, although many of its affiliates still favor inclusion of administrators in the local unit for negotiating purposes; their claim is that inherent conflict between administrators and teachers in many school districts is minimal, that any existing problems can be solved intraorganizationally, and that collective negotiations and the profession generally will be strengthened by keeping administrators and teachers in the same unit.

Among many experts in private sector industrial relations and within the union movement in education, it has become almost a test of one's devotion to the principle of "true" collective bargaining in education to subscribe to the idea of teacher-only units, free from all administrator influence or domination. The issue is, though, somewhat complex. If teacher organizations are truly interested in changing significantly the pattern of lay control of education in this country or in diminishing the power of administrators and placing the relationship of administrators to teachers on a truly collegial basis, one might expect that a prime tactic would be the early absorption of the administrative hierarchy into the more numerous and potentially powerful teacher group. There are indications that school boards however would much prefer, if they must have collective bargaining at all, to have it modeled on the traditional pattern with their administrative staff left wholly intact and out of the "rank and file" organization. The boards perceive that a greater threat to their traditional role lies in the all-inclusive bargaining unit approach.

There are indications that interaction between teachers (usually in conjunction with administrators) and boards in those states, for instance, whose laws call for proportional representation of teacher and other groups through an employee council, has less of a conflict orientation, and is marked by much less visible, substantive "hard bargaining" than is the case in those states whose laws more closely approximate the private sector model. But why? Is it because poten-tial or actual conflict over means and ends among boards, adminis-trators, and teachers is actually minimal in the majority of school districts, which, to date, have found it satisfactory to work with a council, or with some similar system not directly based on assump-tions of conflict of interest? Or must the employee council and similar "facts and consensus" oriented "professional" approaches to school board-teacher interaction be viewed as a sort of unstable halfway house between no interaction (wholly unilateral board decision-making and control) on the one hand and hard, adversary, collective bargaining on the other?

As we have seen, it has been argued that intense organizational rivalry and uncritical adoption of the private sector model of bar-gaining, based as it is on the assumption of conflict of interest, may actually produce dysfunctional conflict and make it self-sustaining. On the other hand, investigations in the "employee council" states indicate that the council system and accompanying practices and procedures (which distinguish interaction in these states from "bar-gaining" in states working under essentially private sector type legislation) prevent the formulation and articulation of conflict, and thus fail to result in compromise and concession-oriented negotiation by fragmenting power and making it difficult for teach-ers to achieve consensus on specific issues. Committees, for instance, usually consider a vast range of subject matter (much broader than that normally touched upon by teachers in districts that are en-gaged in formal negotiations) and often seem to have little ulti-mate impact. The committees' inability to focus conflict is not necessarily a result of the fact that agreement is reached or that there is a meeting of the minds between teachers and administrators on these committees. Frequently, the committee deliberations seem to end in a stalemate and have little substantive impact on adminis-trative decision making.

We will now examine briefly the impact of negotiations in American education on the money issues, the working conditions of teachers, and "policy" and professional matters.

□ The Money Issues

Experience indicates that collective bargaining and the threat or exercise of teacher group power that underlies it have had at least a short-run impact on both the *level* and the *structure* of teacher compensation. In most of the districts studied in the U.S. Office of Education-University of Chicago (USOE-UC) research in 1964–1968 one, and usually both, of the following phenomena were observed: (1) an increase in the absolute and relative size of the total resources allocated to teacher compensation within the district budget; (2) an increase in the absolute and relative size of yearly service increments and differentials for academic training beyond the B.A. degree.

The threat or exercise of power by teachers produced the following changes in the fiscal framework of salary negotiations: (1) at least a short-run increase in the willingness of the state or the local community to support public education; (2) an increase in the willingness of boards of education to reallocate available resources *from* other anticipated uses *to* teacher compensation. The practical effect of these changes was to enhance the priority given to teacher compensation in the formulation of school district budgets and, thereby, to end the traditional practice of making salary determination on a residual basis. The immediate result of this change in the system of salary determination was a marked increase in average teacher compensation.

The changes observed in the *structure* of teacher compensation can be traced to the impact of teacher power on the definition of need-to-pay utilized by boards of education. Specifically, the threat or exercise of power by teachers forced boards of education to consider more heavily the desires and satisfaction of teachers in the allocation of resources available for teacher compensation. The practical effect of this change was to add equity, as defined through the political processes within the teacher organization, to efficiency, as defined by the labor market, as the basis for decisions regarding the structure of teacher compensation. The immediate result of this change was a marked increase in the relative compensation of those teachers who were most active in supporting the teacher organization—generally, the teachers who had been in service longer and particularly those in the secondary schools where a master's degree was required or strongly preferred.

Thus, while it is clear that negotiations in many school districts have been responsible for short-run economic gains to teachers that are considerably in excess of what would have been forthcoming in the absence of collective pressure, a number of factors indicate that the rate of gain in salaries may well diminish in the future.

1. First, increasing numbers of public employees are bargaining on the municipal and state levels. The pressure generated by these employees at city hall and in the state legislature for their "fair share" of the tax dollar will probably force those public officials responsible for over-all governmental budget decision-making and planning to place the needs of the educational enterprise into perspective. They are therefore likely to resist, to a greater degree than has been the case in very recent years, the insistent pressure of teachers and their organizations for very large salary increases.

2. There is no hard evidence as yet that the exercise of teacher power has changed the basic attitude of the tax-paying public toward the appropriate levels of total community support for the educational enterprise. There *is* some evidence, though, that, increasingly, taxpayer and legislative resistance may mount in the face of board and teacher demands for ever-larger school budgets that continually increase as a proportion of total state and local governmental expenditures.

3. The opportunities, grasped initially as a result of bargaining pressure, for reallocation of funds within the school budget to increase the economic gain of teachers through higher salaries and fringe benefits have tended to diminish in succeeding negotiations.

4. Finally, as bargaining experience is accumulated, as basic unresolved policy issues are settled with regard, for instance, to the strike and impasse problems, and as the often chaotic nature of school negotiations (which would seem, as far as "power balance" is concerned, to favor teachers and their organizations more often than not) become more "settled" and "rationalized," gains in the economic realm are likely to level off and be less spectacular.

As boards of education and the public at large learn to live with and perhaps even occasionally "break" a teacher strike, and as counterbalances to teacher power begin to develop in the form of power exercised by other employee groups in government and in the form of local voter and legislative resistance, will the impact of the new teacher militancy be blunted, countered, and absorbed without the need for the state government to take control? Or, will chaos and the triumph of strong, relatively large, "essential" public service groups over weaker ones through the undisciplined, coercive exercise of strike power force the state, in order to counter the effectiveness of employee groups, to arrogate unto itself, centrally, all significant decision-making power?

Assuming that teachers and other groups of public employees continue to strike, and strike successfully, the state may find it desirable and necessary to centralize decision-making on salaries and other important aspects of the employment relationship. If, for instance, large school districts in a state are able to strike success- fully at the expense of smaller ones, and if the large, powerful organizations of public employees working in relatively essential services are able, through the exercise of strike power, to starve the less vital and less visible functions of government, state legislatures may have to directly assume the role of bargaining agent on the employer's side. The purpose of such a move would be twofold: (1) Within education, to achieve a parity among all districts of all sizes within the state, and, (2) For the entire governmental enterprise, to achieve parity among teachers and all other employees in the government service.

If it is decided as a matter of public policy not to prevent or at least adequately control public employee strikes, chaos in budget making and other aspects of the conduct of government may result, making centralization of vital governmental decision-making in- evitable.[20] While strikes would not necessarily be prevented by such centralization of decision-making, at least there would be only a single agent in each field of employment to be dealt with and the probability of the whipsawing of the legislature might be reduced.

All the evidence on this point from the big city school districts engaged in bargaining is not yet in, and their relationships to their state legislatures are anything but stable. In one of our large cities, for example, the first round of negotiations forced an increase in the state aid formula. The second time around, the legislature is indicating that it may refuse to provide more funds to "bail out" the board of education's salary "deal," which forced the board into a debt position. The threatened strike, if it ensues, will clearly be against the legislature, not the school board. In another major city, the first significant round of negotiations actually resulted, in effect, in bargaining at the eleventh hour with the legislature. In direct communication with legislative leaders, it was agreed to trade off money for a promise that the school week would not be shortened. In the second round of negotiations (in this case, the governor and the legislature adamantly refused to take action) the district committed itself to going deeply into the red to underwrite an impressive salary schedule agreement. We might also note, parenthetically, that going into the red in another of our large cities provided more than a little of the motivation for the board to file suit against the state asking for "equalization" of state aid so as to provide for equality of educational achievement and results.*

In all probability, the pace at which teacher bargaining will force legislatures to begin rationalizing the state budget-making process and centralizing control will be a function of the effectiveness of the strike, or, conversely, the extent to which public policy successfully prevents strikes.

□ Working Conditions

Collective negotiations in the schools have had a significant impact on many of the myriad rules and regulations governing the day-to-day working life of the American teacher.

The length of the school year, although it is frequently controlled by law, has become an issue in negotiations in a number of systems. In one large city, for instance, the teacher organization was ultimately successful in negotiating the elimination of an entire week from the school calendar. In a number of systems negotiation has been responsible for shortening the school day. In some contracts the precise number of clock hours a teacher is expected to be in the school and on duty is specified. In other districts the teacher organization has been content to gain a negotiated guarantee that the present school day will not be lengthened unless required by law.

---

* The new, so-called "equalization" suits will ultimately force a legislative response in the direction of an overhaul of state aid formulas and a closer scrutiny of local school district operations generally, which may well strengthen tendencies toward centralization of decision making.

Utilizing the power generated by collective negotiations to effect further significant reductions in the school day and/or the school year could conceivably have a negative impact on community support for the schools. However, there are formidable legal and practical limits to any significant curtailment of the school year or the school day, and it seems doubtful that any long-run trend in this direction will be established through negotiations. Negotiated gains made in this area to date have been largely at the expense of "slack" in systems in which schedules were already well above the maximum set by the law or above the average for districts in a given area. Certainly, negotiation has been utilized to gain the elaboration of precise rules delimiting the school day, and these rules have had some impact on the principals' flexibility in this area; the teachers claim that they have gained because the rules allow them to know precisely what the system's day-to-day demand on their time will be.

In some districts, negotiations have reduced the teachers' class load, both in terms of the number of classes teachers have to meet per day or per week, and in terms of the number of preparations for which each teacher is responsible in a given semester or school year.

In many systems, negotiations have been instrumental in gaining for teachers duty-free lunch period programs and additional preparation and planning periods in both elementary and high school. Often, contracts will provide for the gradual phasing in, over a period of years, of complete and adequate schedules of preparation periods. In other cases, commitments for provision of additional planning and lunch periods are made subject to the availability of funds, extra personnel, and so on. In some systems, teacher organizations have claimed, successfully, that when, because of the absence or shortage of regular teachers, a teacher is given an extra class assignment or had her load increased in some manner, she should receive either additional pay or compensatory time off. Alternatively, when the demand for extra pay has been rejected, the board of education has sometimes agreed to provisions calling for overloads to be distributed equally among the staff.

With regard to the number of hours per week teachers must actually meet with students, it would seem that, with the possible exception of compensatory educational programs and "difficult" schools, a practical lower limit will ultimately be reached that will not be subject to further significant reduction. The substitution of planning or preparation and unassigned periods for actual classroom teaching or "administrative duty" periods, could, of course, have a positive effect on the quality of classroom activities and the "professionalization" of teachers in general; however, any increase in class achievement deriving from this shift in the use of teacher time is not likely to become visible for some time (if ever) and will be exceedingly difficult to measure.

In systems where teachers have gained additional free, nonteaching time through negotiated agreement, there has been conflict between boards and administrations on the one hand and teacher organizations on the other as to the use of these unassigned or preparation periods. The teacher feels that this time is fully under his control, while the principal or the board may feel that some demands or limitations should be placed on its use; charges and countercharges abound as to "professional" uses to which teachers are or are not putting their newly won free time. When more free teacher time is provided by the hiring of additional paraprofessional personnel, the implications for the budget are, of course, measurable and obvious. In some of those systems in which free (nonteaching) time has had to be squeezed out of existing schedules and available personnel, there is strong evidence that day-to-day and week-to-week scheduling of facilities and personnel time has been rationalized and made somewhat more efficient.

Although much of what appears on the subject in contracts between teacher organizations and boards reflects preexisting policy, there is no question but that teachers have used the power generated by collective bargaining to exercise control over the length of time spent working outside of the regularly scheduled school day as well as to gain extra compensation for it. For instance, after-school meetings held by the principal or administrative personnel may be limited in terms of both duration and frequency. Similarly, in some contracts, time out of the regular teaching schedule has been provided for parent teacher conferences. Furthermore, in many districts, limitation of and pay for extracurricular activities has received much attention in negotiations. In some systems, a weekly maximum has been set for "expected" extracurricular services. In others, a certain number of extracurricular "functions" per year at which attendance will be expected is specified. The collective agreement will sometimes provide extra hourly pay for all time spent on extracurricular activities beyond a specified maximum.

The push in negotiations for extra pay or compensatory time for overload or extracontractual duties or for equalized rotation of such "additional" chores has forced a further tightening of schedule-making procedures and, once again, has had a significant impact on the discretion and flexibility that can be exercised by the local school principal. The principal has also been affected in those school districts where every judgment made concerning the deployment of teacher aides or claims that might be made on a teacher's "free" time is subject to question through a grievance and arbitration procedure. It has thus far been impossible to measure whether or not subjecting extracurricular activities to specific rule-making via negotiations has significantly reduced the amount of time spent by teachers on such activities.

In a number of systems, one of the major accomplishments of negotiations, from the teacher's point of view, has been relief from having to perform a variety of clerical and other chores (milk distribution, supervision of playgrounds, cafeterias, sidewalks, corridors, and buses, money collection, scoring of standardized tests, book distribution, register-keeping, etc.) not directly related to the instructional function. In a number of systems, although there is often a mutual commitment in negotiations to allot funds for the hiring of aides to relieve teachers of such routine chores, implementation of the "relief" clauses has frequently caused difficulties.

Assignments and programming, traditionally a significant discretionary area for the local school administrator, has had a good share of attention in negotiations between teachers' groups and boards of education. In general, particularly in the large city systems, the thrust of teacher organization effort has been to ensure objectivity in the making of assignments by insistence on the use of the seniority concept or on the rotation of choice positions. In a number of systems the contract establishes that both seniority and the principal's judgment as to teacher competency will be given consideration in making assignments. It has proven, however, to be quite difficult to impose a precise and wholly objective system of rotation and/or seniority in view of the complex assignment and programming problems encountered in the large city schools. Recognizing the inevitable imprecision of the process, many boards have insisted on retaining a large degree of discretion and flexibility for those responsible for assignment and programming activities.

Many negotiated agreements contain clauses covering class size. A number of boards in the first round of bargaining argued that class size was a matter of educational policy in the school district, and as such was not a proper subject for negotiation or inclusion in the collective agreement. Teacher organizations countered, however, with the argument that class size was clearly a "working condition" intimately affecting the basis on which teachers provide their services. Most boards finally acknowledged the inevitability of bargaining over class size, and in most cases their fears that negotiating on the subject might result in significant compromises on a crucial basic policy issue proved groundless. A number of the class size clauses merely memorialize existing practices and represent nothing more than affirmation of the status quo. In other instances, boards have been in complete support of reduction, or they have made contractual commitment to reduce the size of classes contingent on the availability of funds. In still other cases, the bargained agreement provides specifically for reductions, but qualifications such as "insofar as possible" and stated reasons for exceptions may appear in the agreement, largely to protect the school board with regard to the significant budgetary implications of the class size issue.

While there is little evidence that the process of negotiations by itself has been responsible for a dramatic reduction in pupil-teacher ratios, including class size provisions in the agreement and making them subject to the grievance procedure has in some instances forced school administrations to make shifts to assure that averages for all teachers become maxima for each teacher.

In at least one major system in the United States the teacher organization has given much attention in several different rounds of negotiations to the working conditions of the substitute teacher. As a result, substitutes in this system now enjoy substantial job security, including seniority on their jobs vis-à-vis other substitutes, the protection of their position in the district afforded by the grievance and arbitration procedure, and the use of a central placement agency established by the administration.

In a number of systems, teachers have alleged that the dispensing of desired summer school positions has not been handled according to any objective principles or guidelines and has constituted a form of "patronage," with favoritism rife. Thus, in a number of instances, collective agreements in the schools provide for specific standards to be followed in the making of summer school assignments, including seniority, rotation, preference to teachers who have not previously had an opportunity to teach summer school, and guarantees that all teachers within the system will be offered summer school opportunities before any persons outside the system are hired.

The contents of a teacher's official file is of great interest and concern to the individual because of the file's implications for personnel decisions within the system and its potential impact should the teacher desire to seek a job elsewhere. Thus, a number of negotiated agreements provide teachers the right to first, examine their files at their request, and second, in some instances, make a formal, written rebuttal to any derogatory material therein. Generally, the negotiation of these clauses has not produced significant conflict, although, in most cases, the administration has insisted on the insertion of a clause exempting "confidential" material (recommendations from schools, other employers, etc.) from teacher scrutiny.

In sum, negotiations on "working conditions" in the schools have to some extent substituted centralized decision-making for decentralized decision-making on the management side. School principals *have* lost significant discretion in this process. In a number of systems they not only resent this loss, but are actually undertaking organization themselves in order to secure a stronger voice in such centralized decision-making, if not also to check and reverse the trend itself. However, although the impact of the negotiated agreement on the local school principal and on other administrators in the hierarchy is often considerable, what school administrations believe to be at least a necessary minimum of discretion and flexibility is being maintained and protected.

☐ "Policy" and "Professional" Issues

School boards and administrators frequently express the fear that formal negotiations in education will divest the community of control over its schools and submerge any opportunity for creative administrative leadership in the inflexible common rule of the collective agreement. As if in confirmation, the teacher organizations proudly assert that increased control over basic district policy and a determinative voice in "professional" considerations are two of the primary goals in the drive for negotiations in education.

First, it should be noted that it is exceedingly difficult to distinguish between "educational policy" and "salaries and working conditions" where teacher bargaining is concerned. For instance, it is generally accepted that the salary schedule and teacher benefits are "bargainable" if anything is. However, if raising teacher salaries in a district as a result of bargaining forces a budget reallocation of sums set aside for textbooks, hiring of additional professional personnel, building maintenance, or even new school construction, a decision on school district "policy" is clearly involved and may, indeed, be discussed as such, although all that is ostensibly under consideration is the salary schedule. As another example, consider the problem of teacher transfers. Transfer rules and procedures have long been considered, in both private and public employment, as falling clearly within any reasonable definition of "working conditions." Yet, in our major cities, where schools in lower socioeconomic areas have a grossly disproportionate share of the system's inexperienced teachers who are minimally qualified in terms of training and advanced degrees, the problem of fairly and equitably balancing teaching staffs, and thus curtailing the right of transfer by seniority, has become a "policy" issue of great significance. Examples of this kind, which point up the difficulty of distinguishing between "policy" and "working conditions," can be cited endlessly. Similarly, no really satisfying distinction can be made between "policy" matters and many so-called "professional" issues. For instance, basic decisions concerning many aspects of curriculum, methodology, or textbook selection are clearly both "policy" questions for the board or the administration and "professional" concerns for the teaching staff. However, despite overlap and untidiness, it is necessary and possible for purposes of analysis and discussion to establish rough, somewhat arbitrary categories of "policy" and "professional" issues.

It is, of course, true that in many school systems in this country, teachers, through one medium or another, have exercised significant influence over numerous policy and professional questions long before the advent of formal collective negotiation relationships. However, the discussion here will focus on the extent to which collective negotiations in the schools has been used as a vehicle for gaining a greater measure of teacher control over or participation in decisions in these areas.

The evidence from the districts investigated in the USOE-UC study, a survey of substantive collective negotiation agreements around the country, and an awareness of the reality behind many seemingly significant contract clauses, have led to the conclusion that there are few cases where negotiations have actually forced a significant shift in basic school district policy on an unwilling board, and few examples of a board being blocked from initiating action or change on a basic policy matter solely as a result of teacher power exercised through the negotiation process.* Also, administrative discretion in areas calling for significant exercise of professional judgment, although it has been curbed or modified in certain instances, has rarely been radically altered.

It should be remembered, though, that collective negotiation in education is a quite recent and immature phenomenon, and there is evidence that the potential clearly exists for the power generated by negotiations to bring about significant changes in the distribution of authority among boards, administrators, and teacher organizations with respect to policy and "professional" matters.

As yet, there are relatively few instances where specific, substantive issues that might be considered in the policy or "professional" realm have become the focus of pointed conflict at the bargaining table.† However, while bargaining over such issues may still be

---

* As we saw earlier, teacher power exercised in negotiations on salary and other cost items has resulted in significant reassessment of budget priorities and forced boards to make reallocations with definite policy consequences, at least in the short run. Our present focus, however, is on the impact of negotiations in policy areas that are not directly budget-related.

† There are exceptions, of course, and dramatic ones at that. The most recent significant instance in which a policy question provided bargaining table conflict occurred in the fall of 1967 between the New York City Board of Education and the United Federation of Teachers. A key teacher demand in New York was for the extension to more inner-city schools of the expensive "saturation services" More Effective Schools program. The board, which had judged that the additional outlay for the MES program had not been justified by the results and that extra sums could better be spent on alternative compensatory educational activities, argued that the issue was clearly an educational policy

rare, negotiation is being used as a vehicle for establishing procedures and structures for interaction that will assure teachers a voice in so-called policy and "professional" matters outside and independent of the process of negotiations over the collective agreement. For instance, a number of contracts have provided for the establishment of committees for a wide variety of research, deliberative, and decision-making purposes embracing such subjects as curriculum, methodology, textbook selection, promotion to the principalship, screening and recommendations of candidates for openings at any level in the system, including the superintendency, methods of achieving pupil and teacher integration in the system, pupil discipline, and many more. In some instances the establishment of committees for such purposes has constituted a dramatic departure from past practice. In other cases, the functioning reality behind the exciting contract clause may be anything but impressive.*

Besides providing a modus operandi in many contracts for teacher participation in policy or professional matters on a non-bargaining, continuing basis during contract term, negotiations *have* resulted in a number of specific, often novel contract clauses involving policy or professional areas. Some examples are:

1. Granting teachers the right to challenge administrative judgment on teaching methods through the grievance procedure
2. Provision for the election of department heads by teachers
3. Provision for peer evaluation of teachers in the event of disagreement over the principal's rating of a teacher

---

matter, not appropriate for resolution through collective bargaining. Ultimately, the issue was resolved through a compromise in which a committee was established that included parent and community representatives. Also, of course, in the fall and early winter of 1968 the teachers in New York City struck three separate times in the struggle over decentralization and community control. The community control dispute in New York is most complex and constitutes an escalation of basic conflict that far transcends the "normal" negotiating process.

* It has been suggested that we may ultimately evolve in the public schools a system of adversary, conflict-oriented bargaining over salaries and a narrowly defined range of working conditions *coupled with* an effective parallel interaction structure along university departmental committee and faculty senate lines to provide for teacher participation and involvement in professional and policy matters. See, Daniel E. Griffiths, "Board—Superintendent—Teacher Relations: Viable Alternatives to the Status Quo," in Frank W. Lutz and Joseph J. Azzarelli (eds.), *Struggle for Power in Education* (New York: The Center for Applied Research in Education, Inc., 1966).

A number of contracts provide for the establishment and operation of school and central office committees. It is generally stipulated that teacher representatives (appointed by the teacher organization) at the levels of school and central office are to meet with the principal and the superintendent, respectively, on a periodic basis during the contract term. The purpose of these meetings is communication and discussion (not negotiations) on matters having to do with, for instance, "educational policy and development," and the application and administration of the bargained agreement.

Generally, in districts investigated as part of the USOE-UC study, the accomplishments of these committees were not particularly impressive. In most instances, although the central office meetings did provide a channel for continuing communication between the superintendent and teacher organization leadership, substantive gains or results were few and far between. The primary reason for this lack of productivity was that the teacher organization almost invariably held back major requests or demands for use during contract negotiations. The organization's need to achieve highly visible, numerous, and substantial "victories" at negotiations curbed the extent to which it could afford to accept one-at-a-time gains throughout the entire year or two of contract term. Also, of course, substantial "concessions" from the board and administration were much less likely to be forthcoming during contract term, no matter how aggressively sought, since the compulsions and pressures to "settle" engendered by formal bargaining at the expiration of the contract were absent.

The school level meetings (often monthly) with the local school principal tended to be preliminary or anticipatory grievance meetings, with a substantial amount of time devoted to airing informal complaints. Substantive discussions most frequently centered around the interpretation, application, and administration of the bargained agreement. Teachers in some districts did feel that these local meetings were valuable in providing a formal communication link between the principal and the local school teacher leaders. They also felt that the meetings aided considerably in the "smooth" implementation of the collective agreement and allowed teachers a participatory voice for the first time in a number of areas of educational management not necessarily covered by the agreement. Other teachers were more negative in their reactions to the local meetings, denigrating them as being mere "gripe" sessions. Evidently the personalities of participants in these meetings and the attitudes of principals and organization leaders toward what can be accomplished in the local meetings are important determinants of success.

☐ Dynamics of School Bargaining

With respect to the dynamics of negotiations in the schools, the projections and hypotheses deriving from our experience in private sector bargaining as to what we would find in collective bargaining in education bore up rather well in the USOE-UC study:

1. Collective bargaining is, in at least some school districts, a power relationship and a process of power accommodation, the essence of which is compromise and concession-making on matters over which there is conflict between the teacher organization and the board. While concessions and compromises may not be demanded by the concept of good faith bargaining, it is a practical fact that in the context of the power relationship that marks true collective bargaining, discussions for the purpose of mutual decision-making often result in compromising subjects under dispute between the board and the teacher organization.

2. When collective bargaining is practiced in education, the teacher organization is a political institution, which, like any union in private industry, must have something to "deliver" or "take back" to its membership.

3. School boards and administrations frequently "play the bargaining game" much as management does in private industry. They attempt at least to make it appear in negotiations that the teachers were successful in "getting more" than they would have in the absence of negotiations and collective pressure. They allow the organization to have a function at the bargaining table so that organization leadership will not be threatened, teacher group expectations will be fulfilled, and strikes or serious impasse problems will be avoided. A few boards have accommodated themselves to the bargaining facts of life and learned to employ appropriate tactics; more are learning rapidly. School administrators, in particular, though, often find it distasteful to "fool" the teacher team by holding back until late in negotiations something that might have been

given freely at the outset. A few boards, however, particularly those who have members with industrial relations experience in the private sector, are proving quite adept at hiding even relatively large sums of money, which are released for salary purposes only at the eleventh hour. The additional amount can then be claimed by the teacher organization as a victory for the exercise of teacher power and the efficacy of the negotiating process.

The necessity for boards to bargain over money matters has, in terms of tactics, been handled in a variety of ways, depending on the fiscal structure of the district, the power of the teacher organization, the board's sophistication, and numerous other factors. In some communities, for instance, the board will use a fact-finding result favorable to the teachers as an instrument for obtaining more funds from the fiscal authorities than might have been forthcoming in the ordinary course of events. In other communities, the board has simply committed itself in bargaining to the expenditure of more funds than it had available, in the expectation that the city council or other governing body would ultimately produce the necessary monies rather than risk the disruptive effects of displeasing the large and powerful teacher organization. In still other communities, bargaining over money matters has been a tripartite affair, with city or state authorities "finding" additional funds not previously allocated to education, funds that are finally pledged to avert an eleventh-hour strike or impasse situation.

4. The first contract that is bargained in a school district is often a most difficult hurdle to get over. The high expectations engendered during organization campaigns, the desire of the teacher organization to "make everything up at once," the board's and the administration's desire to "go easy" and not relinquish their prerogatives too readily or create dangerous precedents for the future, all dictate the presence of some hostility and conflict during initial contract bargaining. Indeed, if the teacher group is pushing hard, and the board is making a reasonable effort to avoid, to paraphrase a cliché of private sector industrial relations, "giving the system away," some hostility, acrimony, and even a modicum of bitterness should be accepted as a healthy norm despite the repugnance it arouses in school administrators and many board members.

5. Competition between teacher organizations or factionalism within the organization increases or heightens overt conflict with

the administration and adds to the stresses and strains of the relationship (more grievances, tougher and more unrealistic bargaining demands, a heightening of irrationality generally, etc.) .

6. In the schools, as elsewhere, when realignment of power relationships and organization structures accompanies the advent of collective bargaining, there is also a preoccupation with procedure and a large measure of confusion and uncertainty on the side of management as to the roles to be played in the new process by top administrative and policy-making personnel.

Although strong feeling is frequently expressed within the profession that the adversary role in the negotiation relationship should not be assumed by the superintendent, surveys indicate that in a majority of bargaining situations, the superintendent bears at least the initial responsibility for conduct of the relationship on the management side. There is some evidence that as relationships mature, boards of education find negotiating too time-consuming and are glad to delegate the chore, while the superintendent finds that if he wishes to maintain a desired degree of control over the administration of his system, he had better assume responsibility for the negotiation relationship even though he may not actually conduct the face-to-face bargaining sessions.

7. In education, as elsewhere, because they are suddenly forced to meet the "crisis" of a new collective bargaining relationship, top administrative personnel may ignore the needs and interests of middle and lower level supervision. We have already mentioned that the initial practical impact of a negotiated agreement in a school system falls most heavily on the local school principal. If representatives of this group have not had a voice in the drafting and bargaining of the contract, resentment and disaffection often follow. Problems also have arisen, when bargaining has been concluded, from the failure to train all of those with supervisory responsibility in the interpretation and principles of proper administration of the negotiated agreement.

8. It seems clear that the teacher organizations, which are presently in control in medium and large school districts, whether they are associations or unions, will retain and entrench their power, just as the majority of unions in private industry have.

Both union locals and association affiliates have become highly sensitized to the basic institutional issues that go to the heart of the organizations' security, survival, and prosperity. In some districts, the victors in the organizing and representational campaign have displayed an almost embarrassing and professionally unbecoming eagerness to suppress the vanquished foe, and lose no opportunity to manifest overt hostility toward any efforts by the minority organization to retain or gain any institutional rights or privileges in the school system. Use of mailboxes, bulletin boards, and other school facilities for purposes of communication and meeting, privilege of dues checkoff, the right to represent teachers in the grievance procedure, the right to receive data on salaries and working conditions, and even the right to be heard at school board and budget hearings, have all been claimed, with varying degrees of success, as privileges that can be enjoyed only by the majority representative. In some districts, requests by the majority representative for such exclusive privileges have been readily granted by a school administration that did not want to risk the complications that might occur if rival minority organizations were allowed to flourish. In any event, one can expect organizations of teachers and other public employees that do not as yet enjoy the significant union security protections (closed or union shop, agency shop) that are commonplace in the private sector, to be occasionally preoccupied with some of the lesser forms of institutional preference.

□ The Ultimate Impact

One must judge that collective negotiations, at least where they have been practiced along largely private sector lines, have been quite compatible with the educational enterprise. The tradition of the single salary schedule long before the advent of bargaining, the lack of any objective, widely acceptable standards by which to judge teacher performance, and, thus, the absence of teacher accountability and "merit" pay differentials, the widespread use, before the negotiations movement, of seniority and other objective standards for the movement and placement of teachers in large scale bureaucratic organizations, are all factors that virtually assured the easy transfer of collective bargaining principles and practices to the allegedly "professional" field of public school teaching.

Collective bargaining in the private sector of the American economy is, of course, hardly a revolutionary phenomenon. It is essentially an affirmation of and an adaptation to the status quo. From the evidence at hand, there are few good reasons to assume that the impact of collective negotiations on education will be radically different.

Indeed, the significant question at the moment is not whether teacher bargaining is itself a process likely to revolutionize education. Instead, the question is what is likely to be the impact of collective negotiations on education with respect to "freezing" the present structure and administrative practices of our educational enterprises?

1. The abolishment of the single, uniform salary schedule in the schools (pursuant to which, for example, math or science teachers in relatively short supply are paid the same as, say, social studies teachers in relatively plentiful supply) has long been urged by those concerned with economic inefficiency in our educational enterprises. What effect will a well-entrenched system of collective negotiations have on a school that attempts, as many surely will in the years that lie ahead, to depart from or modify significantly the uniform, single salary schedule concept?

2. If the new systems analysis approach is applied to the organization and administration of schools and to the measurement of the effectiveness of the schools, it will definitely call for wide differentiation of task, status, and role, and rewards and remuneration within the presently relatively undifferentiated teaching force. As the Supreme Court of the United States long ago observed, collective bargaining is a process "which looks with suspicion on individual advantage," and which, because of its internal political dynamics, tends inevitably toward the uniform, undifferentiated pay scale and the application of the common rule in general. Based on experience in the private sector and on some hints from developments in school districts, one can predict that the systems analysis approach to differentiation of tasks and rewards among the teaching force may meet some stout resistance at the negotiating table.

3. What is likely to be the impact of collective bargaining on the decentralization of some of the larger educational bureaucracies in the big cities? Certain of the plans that have been advanced for decentralization of the city systems would seem to be compatible with central, city-wide negotiations and with the uniform application of policies regarding hiring, promotion assignment, dismissal,

pay scales, and so on. However, any decentralization plan that grants significant autonomy to local school districts or to individual schools on subjects previously covered uniformly in a city-wide contract will undoubtedly meet powerful resistance from teacher organization interests.

4. In recent years, school boards and lay community groups have frequently, although without much success, insisted on the adoption in local school districts of some form of "merit" pay plan to reward "superior" or outstanding teaching effort. It is expected that, with the new emphasis on higher teacher salaries resulting from the new "teacher militancy," community insistence that outstanding service and capability be rewarded will increase. Once again, we might predict that the net effect of power generated by teachers through collective negotiations will be to make experimentation with and installation of input-output measurement of teacher accountability and pay differential plans based on classroom performance much more difficult for school boards and administrations.

5. What impact is collective negotiations in the schools likely to have on the adoption of the new automated teaching methodologies? Teaching machines, teaching by television, and various forms of "computerized" instruction have not received widespread implementation as quickly as some might have guessed a few years ago. Nonetheless, the new teaching methodologies are going to have a major impact on education in the future. Are teachers likely to use collective negotiations to resist the adoption of the new instructional methodology when it has been perfected and become widely available? Automation of the teaching task clearly has potential for the replacement of teaching personnel; with growing surpluses in the teacher labor market, is it possible that adoption of automation in education could, in the years which lie ahead, proceed at such a pace as to result in widespread teacher unemployment? Or will implementation of automation in education allow adequate lead time for the market, operating through enrollment in teacher training institutions, to adjust to a future need for fewer teachers as a proportion of student population?

6. Finally, the power generated by collective bargaining in most major cities, primarily through the insistence on the application of at least a modified form of seniority in the making of teacher transfers, has blocked necessary modification of these systems to meet the

needs of the inner-city schools. The problem of adequately staffing inner-city schools with experienced and integrated staffs is an immensely complex one, and it existed long before the advent of collective bargaining. It is not our intention to single out the preferences of teachers, as manifested through their bargaining agents in these cities, as the primary obstacle to an adequate solution of the staffing problem. However, it provides still another example of the fact that collective bargaining can be used to "freeze" existing practices in the face of strong pressure for change from a school board and administration or from interested parent and community groups.

As we have seen, the gains and accomplishments (realized and potential) of collective teacher power in local school districts are clearly substantial. It remains for school boards, administrators, teachers, and consumers of education alike to ensure that bargaining in the schools continues to play a dynamic and adaptable role in helping meet the public education needs of the future in the United States.

NOTES

[1] Edgar B. Wesley, *NEA: The First Hundred Years, The Building of the Teaching Profession* (New York: Harper & Row, 1957), p. 23.

[2] NEA *Proceedings,* 1913, p. 365. The speaker was Henry Suzzallo.

[3] *Ibid., loc. cit.*

[4] William McAndrew, quoted in Carter Alexander, *Some Aspects of the Work of Teachers' Voluntary Associations in the United States* (New York: Columbia University Teachers College, 1910), pp. 49–50.

[5] D. Felmley, "The Next Step in the Salary Campaign," NEA *Proceedings,* 1906, p. 189.

[6] NEA *Proceedings,* 1918, p. 49.

[7] Albert Byron Crawford, "A Critical Analysis of the Present Status and Significant Trends of State Associations of the United States," *Bulletin of the Bureau of School Service,* University of Kentucky College of Education, 4 (June 1932), 127.

[8] Willard E. Givens, "Teacher Welfare to the Front," NEA *Journal,* 25 (October 1936), 202.

[9] Quoted in Howard K. Beale, *Are American Teachers Free?* (New York: Scribner, 1936), p. 586.

[10] NEA Executive Committee, "The Professional Way to Meet the Education Crisis," NEA *Journal*, 36 (February 1947), 47.

[11] Lester A. Kirkendall, *et al.*, *Goals for American Education* (Chicago: AFT, 1948), p. 60.

[12] AFT, "Policies of the American Federation of Teachers" (Chicago: AFT, n.d.), n.p. (mimeographed).

[13] AFT, *Convention Proceedings*, 1962 (abridged) (Chicago: AFT, 1962), pp. 150–151.

[14] NEA *Proceedings*, 1962, p. 394.

[15] For "box score" on election confrontations, see *American Teacher*, 52 (October 1967), 8.

[16] See *Negotiations Research Digest*, Vol. 1 (June 1968).

[17] D. Richard Wynn, "Policies of Educational Negotiation; Problems and Issues," Tri-State Area School Study Council Research Monograph (University of Pittsburgh, October 1967), p. 4.

[18] *Chicago Division of Illinois Education Association* v. *Board of Education, City of Chicago*, 76 Ill. App. 2d 456, 222 N.E. 2d 243 (1966).

[19] *Oakland County Sheriff's Dept.* v. *Metropolitan Council No. 23, AFS-CME, AFL-CIO*, 1968 Labor Opinion 1, reported in 227 *Government Employee Relations Report F-1* (GERR F-1); thus far, all lower court challenges in Michigan to the validity of "agency shop" clauses in teacher collective agreements have been unsuccessful. See, for example, *Clampitt* v. *Bd. of Ed. of Warren Consolidated Schools*, No. X-67-2865 (Macomb County Circuit Ct., July 19, 1968), reported in 256 GERR E-1.

[20] See Richard Albin, "New York City's Perpetual Fiscal Crisis," *The Wall Street Journal*, October 30, 1967, p. 14.

WHITE-COLLAR ORGANIZATION IN THE FEDERAL SERVICE

by LEO TROY*

Throughout the 1960s a boom in union representation has been underway in the public economy. It began in the late 1950s among employees of local government, but after President John F. Kennedy's Executive Order 10988 of January 1962, unionism[†] among federal employees in the executive agencies moved ahead more rapidly. White-collar workers[‡] participated in the general advance. The extent and significance of their participation are the subjects of this paper.

I propose to analyze how white-collar organizations function under Executive Order 10988, what special problems and opportunities they have under the order, and how professionals, an occupational group of growing importance in the federal service, are reacting to the spread of unionism. Trends in white-collar membership will be traced. Finally, I shall offer some judgments on the character and prospects of growth for white-collar unionism in the executive agencies of the government. I will begin with a sketch of the historical antecedents of President Kennedy's Executive Order 10988.

* Professor of Economics, Rutgers—The State University. I wish to thank Professor Albert Blum and Dr. Herbert Lahne of the U.S. Department of Labor for taking the time to read my paper and for their valuable suggestions for improving it. I also wish to acknowledge the efforts of Sandra Troy, my wife, and two student assistants, Barry Frank and Albert Schechterman, for their aid in putting together the statistical data. I wish to thank Miss Mary Williams for her typing and preparation of the manuscript.

† The terms "union," "labor organization," "association," and "employee organization" will be used interchangeably, so long as the group is subject to and functions under the Executive Order. In 10988, all such groups are referred to as employee organizations.

‡ Most of those grouped as white collar are covered by the U.S. Civil Service Commission's General Schedule of occupations.

☐ Historical Background

President Kennedy's Executive Order 10988 built upon precedents established by the Lloyd-Lafollette Act of 1912, the experience of the private economy under the National Labor Relations Act of 1935, and legislation proposed but never enacted to implement federal employees' right to organize.

The right of government employees to organize was first sanctioned by Congress in the Lloyd-Lafollette Act of 1912. However, such organization was tolerated rather than encouraged by the terms of the act and was technically limited to unions of postal employees. Under the act, union membership did not constitute cause for discharge or for reduction in rank or pay. In order for its members to be eligible for this protection, a union had to give up the right to strike.

Employees in departments and agencies other than the Post Office were permitted to petition Congress individually or in groups. Congress made a distinction between the postal and other government employees because there was little or no organization outside the Post Office in 1912. When unions were established in other agencies, these agencies began to apply the Lloyd-Lafollette Act to the new unions provided they, like the unions of postal employees, renounced their right to strike.

The next important legislation that contributed to labor policy affecting federal employees was the National Labor Relations Act of 1935. Although federal employees were excluded from its jurisdiction, the act had a marked impact on the labor practices of some governmental agencies, notably the Tennessee Valley Authority (TVA). Almost from its inception, the Tennessee Valley Authority entered into collective bargaining relations with its blue- and white-collar employees and its service workers. In 1940 TVA negotiated its first agreement with blue-collar employees represented by the Tennessee Valley Trades and Labor Council-AFL. Four years later TVA negotiated an agreement with a panel of white-collar and service employees' unions representing chemists, engineers, technical, office and clerical, and security and maintenance workers. The authority has periodically renewed these agreements. Because of its extensive history in dealing with white-collar unions, TVA's labor relations with its white-collar employees will be examined later as a possible model for other agencies of the government.

Strikes, which were cause for discharge under the Lloyd-Lafollette Act, were declared unlawful by section 305 of Taft-Hartley in 1948. When it was rewritten in 1955, section 305 continued to declare strikes by federal employees unlawful. In addition, it made strikers subject to fine and imprisonment.

From 1949 to 1961, unions in the federal government tried to amend the Lloyd-Lafollette Act, to include changes patterned on the National Labor Relations Act's positive protection of the right to organize. Just as the unions were about to succeed, President Kennedy met their central objectives with Executive Order 10988.

The order grew out of a report of a Presidential task force set up to study the issue of employee-management relations in the federal service. The task force, appointed June 22, 1961, consisted of the Secretaries of Labor and Defense, the Postmaster-General, the director of the Bureau of the Budget, the chairman of the Civil Service Commission, and the Special Counsel to the President. Arthur J. Goldberg, then Secretary of Labor, was the chairman.

The task force held hearings in seven cities, circulated questionnaires to government agencies and labor organizations, and had special reports prepared by its staff and by some agencies and departments. On November 30, 1961, the task force issued its report. On January 17, 1962, President Kennedy embodied its principal recommendations in Executive Order 10988, which went into effect on July 1, 1962.

In May 1963, the Executive Order was supplemented by the Standards of Conduct for Labor Organizations and the Code of Fair Labor Practices, which governed both management and labor. The Standards are the counterpart of the provisions of the Labor-Management Reporting and Disclosure Act (1958) regulating the internal practices of unions, while the Code is the counterpart of the unfair labor practices of the National Labor Relations Act, as amended.

☐ Key Provisions of E.O. 10988 Applicable to White-Collar Organization

The task force's recommendation and the Executive Order's provision most affecting white-collar organization is protection of the right of employees in the executive branch of the federal government "to form, join and assist any employee organization or to refrain from any such activity."[1] As is evident, this crucial section of the order was based on section 7 of the National Labor Relations Act, as amended. Excluded from the order's coverage are employees of the FBI, the CIA, and similar executive agencies, offices, bureaus, and entities.

Other key provisions of the Executive Order applicable to the organization of white-collar employees are those on bargaining units and types of recognition. These will be discussed below.

All key provisions generally promote the growth of white-collar unions and membership. They also influence the type of employee organizations. For example, professional associations that wish to retain their distinction from traditional unions, while participating in the employee relations program encouraged by E.O. 10988, are able to do so because of special types of recognition provided by the Executive Order. (Parallel provisions are not found in the National Labor Relations Act.)

Although the Executive Order encouraged most white-collar employees to join unions (Table 5), limitations on the participation of some key employees have doubtless stopped them from becoming union members. These limitations are contained in the conflict-of-interest provision, section 1(b), of the Executive Order.

Conflict of Interest

Under this provision, certain white-collar employees are ineligible to lead or represent employee organizations, even though they are eligible for membership in them. According to the Executive Order, the right "to form, join and assist any employee organization" does not "extend to participation in the management of an employee organization, or acting as a representative of any such organization, where such participation or activity would result in a conflict of interest or otherwise be incompatible with law or with the official duties of an employee."[2]

Theoretically, therefore, the same individuals who are ineligible to lead or represent an organization may, as members, advocate policies for the union which, as agency management, they must oppose! While this may be a purely hypothetical situation, it nevertheless illustrates an important anomaly implicit in the Executive Order.

From a practical standpoint, the problem of this proviso is to identify the white-collar employees who do, in fact, have a conflict of interest. Determination of a conflict of interest is made by agency management, usually with the advice of the Civil Service Commission. To date the provision has been applied to management officials, supervisors with "significant" managerial responsibilities, personnel officers other than those doing clerical work, negotiators with employee organizations, and assistants to management.[3] We shall refer to these groups simply as management officials.

In general, the Civil Service Commission has defined the groups we call management officials as "persons who make or recommend management policies or who direct, control, or supervise government operations or personnel, and those associated with or assisting in such direction or control and who therefore generally carry responsibilities incompatible with leadership in an organization of rank and file employees."[4]

Because of the broad scope of this guideline, individual agencies can and do differ in their definition of management. The ambiguities resulting from these differences in definition have exacerbated relations between white-collar organizations and agency management. Generally, management has adopted a broad definition of conflict-of-interest occupations, while the unions have pressed for a narrow definition or near total abolition of the concept.

Disputes between management and unions over application of the conflict-of-interest proviso may go to advisory arbitration, but agency management is free to reject the arbitrator's award. To this writer, the procedure points up another conflict of interest in the Executive Order, namely, the conflict confronting agency management when it assumes the role of either complainant or defendant, as well as that of final arbiter. Unless changed, this conflict of interest may, in the long run, have more serious consequences for government labor relations than the one affecting managerial occupations.

The conflict-of-interest proviso is of great practical importance to white-collar organizations[5] because it deprives them of members, and, more importantly, of potential leaders. The American Nurses Association (ANA) has claimed that the "application of this policy conflict-of-interest has probably been the greatest single difficulty for organizations representing professional and supervisory employees."[6] For example, the ANA in 1963 found it necessary to stop its efforts to gain bargaining rights for nurses at hospitals of the Veteran's Administration because the VA's position barred "every VA nurse in a management position whether or not they had significant authority from serving as an official of the ANA or any of its constituent organizations."[7] Subsequently, the Veteran's Administration changed its approach. Instead of barring from union membership all first-line supervisors, none of whom could hire or fire, it undertook a case-by-case consideration of conflict of interest.

The American Nurses Association also contends that the conflict-of-interest proviso creates an artificial cleavage between experienced professionals (who are usually found in the managerial and supervisory category of employees) and novice professionals, and, therefore, injures the "effective conduct of public business," the stated goal of E.O. 10988.

As a solution to the problem of conflict of interest, the ANA has proposed the "multipurpose organization," which has aspects of both a professional association and a union. As a professional group, the multipurpose organization could take advantage of the rights and benefits accorded professional associations in government; as a union, it could represent its members in bargaining. Removal or reinterpretation of the conflict-of-interest provision of E.O. 10988 might enable the ANA and similar groups to achieve this goal. If so, a new form of labor organization, probably limited to the public sector, may be in the making. This will be one of the more interesting possible developments to be watched in the evolving system of labor relations in the federal government.

An example of the widespread impact of the conflict-of-interest proviso on the leadership of white-collar organizations is indicated by a survey made in February 1963 by the National Federation of Federal Employees (NFFE), an independent national union. Of the NFFE's 600 locals, nearly half had officers and representatives who potentially or actually were affected by the conflict-of-interest provision. The NFFE found 57 locals with presidents whose Civil Service rank could have been grounds for a conflict of interest, 109 locals whose presidents were supervisory officials, 78 locals with professionals as presidents, and 50 locals with personnel officials serving as presidents. In addition, the NFFE reported that prior to its survey thirty-one local presidents and forty-three other officeholders had been officially notified by agency management that they must resign their union offices. Meanwhile, the survey showed that thirty-nine other officeholders had resigned after notification that their union offices posed a possible conflict of interest with their official duties.[8]

Because it was so adversely affected by the conflict of interest provision, the NFFE initially opposed Executive Order 10988, and even took steps to test its constitutionality in the courts. Meanwhile, the organization's opposition to E.O. 10988 caused it to lose members to its rivals, which, in turn provoked a successful challenge to its incumbent leaders. After the change in leadership, the case against the order was dropped and the federation began to compete actively for recognition under the order.

The conflict-of-interest provision in the Executive Order reversed previous policy and practice under the Lloyd-Lafollette Act. As the NFFE's survey revealed, many officials ineligible to lead or represent employee organizations under the Executive Order had held union office under the Lloyd-Lafollette Act. Because of this change in policy, the growth of some white-collar unions has probably been less than it might have been. It is very likely that those individuals affected by a conflict of interest have dropped their membership or have declined to join organizations in which they cannot fully participate.

That many managerial, high-ranking supervisory and personnel employees were members under the Lloyd-Lafollette Act is indicated by the findings of the Presidential task force. According to its report, "a feature distinctive with organizations of federal employees, as contrasted with established trade and craft unions, is the frequent appearance among the general membership of supervisors, often of high rank." Moreover, the report continued, this was "one of the most *uniform features* reported by the agencies, 38 of them noting that supervisors are members of employee organizations with which such agencies deal."[9]

The incongruities of the conflict-of-interest provision are also evidenced by the ambiguous status that it accords to organizations consisting solely of managerial officials. Under a strict interpretation of the provision, it is questionable whether such organizations could even be formed. Even though these organizations avoid a conflict arising from a mix of the supervisors and the supervised in the same organization, there is a possibility that an *organizational* conflict of interest might arise when a union of supervisors sought at the same time to bargain with and execute the directives of top management.

In the private economy this organizational conflict of interest was resolved by the Taft-Hartley amendment, which removed supervisors from the jurisdiction of the National Labor Relations Act. The exclusion effectively terminated foremen's unions and, thereby, virtually mandated that supervisory personnel are to be considered management.

In the federal government, the problem of organizational conflict of interest was side-stepped. Conflict of interest is not interpreted to deny self-organization to managerial employees. However, organizations of such employees are denied full bargaining rights. Instead, they are accorded recognitional rights (informal and formal recognition), which fall short of the right to bargain and to sign contracts.

Informal and formal recognition do not exist under the National Labor Relations Act. These types of recognition will be discussed in detail later; it suffices here to note that informal and formal recognitions facilitate the formation of new organizations of managerial employees and the continuation of those formed prior to Executive Order 10988. Such preexisting managerial organizations are further protected by the Executive Order's grandfather clause, section 16, which permits agencies to "consult or deal with any representative of its employees or other organizations dealt with prior to the time that the status and representation rights of such representative or organization were determined in conformity with this order."

Because the conflict-of-interest provision has caused so many disputes, it is one of the leading issues between white-collar unions and management. Because the disagreement is largely a question of definition, the white-collar organizations have argued that agency managers and the Civil Service Commission who advises them, have manufactured an issue. The issue is significant to unions because it may deprive them of able leaders and members. To be realistic, the unions assert, the conflict-of-interest proviso should be applied only to the highest level of agency management.

However, such a redefinition would also create problems for employee organizations. Under E.O. 10988, rank-and-file members would discover that their grievances were directed against fellow members of the bargaining unit,[10] and the union would have to choose between the two. Obviously, its decisions could divide the organization into factions. Despite this potential "booby-trap," it appears that at the moment, most white-collar organizations prefer a definition of management which would exclude only top agency management.

In the future it is likely that practical experience will lead to the "crafting out" of managerial groups into separate organizations and the granting of full bargaining rights to them. The federal service thus is likely to have a greater degree of organized representation and collective bargaining by managerial and supervisory employees than is the case in the private economy.

Bargaining Units

The second key provision of Executive Order 10988 that affects organization of white-collar employees is the provision concerning the setting up of units appropriate for collective bargaining. The order provided great flexibility in the scope of the bargaining unit. However, it left to agency management the final determination of the appropriate unit. Although a union can challenge an agency's decision and take the dispute to arbitration, the award is only advisory and can be set aside by management. Actually, fewer than 100 of the more than 1,800 exclusive units (reported in Table 2) have involved advisory arbitration.[11]

Agencies can establish a unit on the basis of any plant, installation, craft, function, or any other employment relationship so long as the unit will "ensure a clear and identifiable community of interest among the employees concerned."[12] However, agencies are not permitted to create a unit "solely on the basis of the extent to which employees in the proposed unit have organized."[13] This forestalls the possibility of the organization and recognition of splinter units at the expense of "the community of interest" of a larger group of employees.

For white-collar employees, the order contains two important requirements affecting the determination of bargaining units. The first is a ban on "mixed" units. The second assures professional employees of the right to have their own units.

Like the conflict-of-interest proviso, to which it is closely tied, the ban on mixed units may also adversely affect white-collar organization. On the other hand, "self-determination" for professional employees has probably assisted the growth of organization among this occupational group.

Mixed Units. The ban on mixed units prohibits units that include both rank-and-file white-collar employees and managerial, executive, and personnel officers (exclusive of those doing purely clerical work), and supervisors who "officially evaluate the performance of employees . . . whom they supervise."[14]

The ban on mixed units is a product of the conflict-of-interest proviso just discussed. Therefore, it is characterized by a similar inconsistency: Although an individual must be excluded from a unit because of his official position, he is nevertheless eligible under the order to be a member of the union representing the unit.

When the logic of both the conflict-of-interest provision and the ban on mixed units is applied, it is readily apparent that Executive Order 10988 permits executives, personnel officers, and supervisors to join unions that include rank-and-file employees, but not to lead or represent these unions, nor to be represented by them.

Exceptions to the ban on mixed units are permitted because of past practice, prior agreement, or special circumstances. However, exceptions to the rule prohibiting mixed units are not common.

Professional Units. Under section 6 (a) of Executive Order 10988, professionals may not be included in bargaining units together with nonprofessional employees unless the professionals vote for inclusion. An election is therefore mandatory in units involving professionals, in contrast to the general procedure for determining exclusive recognition.[15]

The problem of defining a professional is left to each agency, but no agency management may change an occupation classified by the Civil Service Commission as professional into a nonprofessional classification. Agencies can therefore expand the definition, but they may not contract it. Consequently, some units classified as consisting of professionals may include employees defined by the Civil Service Commission as nonprofessionals.[16]

Generally, requests for professional self-determination have presented some of the least difficult problems in unit determination.[17] However, the professionals' right to self-determination was called into question when the Navy Department attempted to set up functional units that were to be installation-wide. In all arbitration cases dealing with this issue, the Navy's unit was rejected and separate units were declared appropriate. The main criterion in granting self-determination for professionals was education,[18] since this is the key factor distinguishing them from other groups.

Although most professional units are local in scope, the National Association of Internal Revenue Service Employees (NAIRE) has tried to secure a national unit of professionals in the Internal Revenue Service. In June 1962, NAIRE requested that the Internal Revenue Service (IRS) create separate national units for nonsupervisory employees, supervisors, and professionals. The agency rejected the proposal, contending that only localized and district units were compatible with the historic decentralization of authority in the Internal Revenue Service. NAIRE then sought advisory arbitration of the issue. However, the arbitrator upheld the decision of the agency, pointing out that "meaningful negotiations" were possible at the local level and that NAIRE had not shown any special circumstances that warranted the creation of national units.[19]

About two years after the decision, the IRS and NAIRE began to consider three-tier negotiations—local, regional, and national. However, in July 1967, the Commissioner of the Internal Revenue Service, with the Civil Service Commission in agreement, decided to reject the idea of multiunit negotiations. NAIRE will continue to press for wider units of bargaining and this will doubtless remain the leading issue between the union and the IRS for some time to come.

Types of Recognition

The third key provision of Executive Order 10988 that is important to white-collar organization deals with types of recognition. In contrast to the National Labor Relations Act, which provided only for exclusive recognition, the order permits three types of recognition—informal, formal, and exclusive. The first two types are of great importance to white-collar organizations, particularly those that lack the membership strength or the desire to bargain collectively and sign contracts, and those that are denied exclusive recognition.

To be qualified for any form of recognition under E.O. 10988, an organization must give up the right to strike, must not discriminate in its membership requirements because of race, color, creed, or national origin, and must not advocate the overthrow of the government of the United States. In addition, the Standards of Conduct, issued by the President in May 1963 pursuant to E.O. 10988, require employee organizations to maintain democratic procedures and practices, exclude Communists and adherents of other totalitarian movements from holding office, prohibit financial conflicts of interest by officers and agents of the union, and safeguard the fiscal integrity of the organization. If an organization meets all the qualifications for recognition, the Code of Fair Labor Practices, which contains the rules governing labor-management relations in the federal service, requires agency management to accord the appropriate recognition.

Informal Recognition. Informal recognition is the most limited of the three types of recognition. Organizations that are accorded informal recognition represent members only, not bargaining units, and, therefore, are not required to have any specified membership following. Moreover, informal recognition may be extended to one organization even though "any other employee organization has been accorded formal or exclusive recognition as representative of some or all employees in any unit."[20] Thus, informal representation can overlap the other two types of recognition.

The purpose of informal recognition is to extend "the right to be heard."[21] It does not carry with it the right to negotiate agreements or to process grievances. The informally recognized organization can request management to discuss personnel matters affecting their members, but management need not honor the request.

As already indicated, informal recognition is significant for many white-collar organizations because it enables them to participate in the federal labor relations system even though they cannot or do not wish to qualify for exclusive recognition and collective bargaining. Among the white-collar groups most interested in a limited role in the federal labor relations system are professional associations. For them, informal (and formal) recognition are *goals* rather than *steps* toward exclusive recognition and collective bargaining.

For this reason, many professional organizations have sought and gained informal recognition, and they favor its retention in the federal labor relations program. In hearings before the Presidential committee reviewing the operation of Executive Order 10988, the National Society of Professional Engineers (NSPE) urged that informal recognition be retained in the federal labor relations program because it enables professional organizations to present their views to agency management without the necessity of engaging in collective bargaining. The NSPE encourages its members to get informal or formal recognition but not exclusive recognition. At the beginning of 1968, some twenty groups associated with NSPE, representing 1,200 engineers, held formal or informal recognition.

In addition to professional associations, other white-collar organizations also regard informal (and formal) recognition as a useful way for them to participate in the goals of E.O. 10988. In November 1967, the National Federation of Federal Employees (NFFE), an organization with a large white-collar membership, held a total of 273 informal recognitions, far more than any other single organization. Affiliates of the AFL-CIO had 545 informal recognitions among blue- and white-collar workers. (See Table 1.)

Table 1. Types of Recognition* by Affiliation, November 1967

	Informal	Formal	Exclusive
AFL-CIO Affiliates	545	652	1,232
National Independents	366	479	566
Local Independents	120	41	15
Total	1,031	1,172	1,813

* Includes 7 national exclusive units in the Post Office Department, but excludes 24,500 exclusive units in local post offices.

SOURCE: U.S. Civil Service Commission, "Union Recognition in the Federal Government, August 1966 and November 1967" (mimeo), February 26, 1968.

However, as Table 1 shows, AFL-CIO affiliates account for the bulk of exclusive recognitions, the only type that provides for collective bargaining and agreements. And although AFL-CIO affiliates also have a substantial number of informal and formal recognitions, their ultimate intent is to bargain and obtain agreements. For them informal and formal recognitions are but steps toward exclusive recognition, bargaining, and agreements.

Therefore, in contrast to professional associations and other like-minded groups, the AFL-CIO (and independent unions with experience in collective bargaining) have requested the abolition of informal recognition. In their view, the fact that informal recognition overlaps with formal and exclusive recognition adds to confusion and thwarts the Executive Order's intention of promoting collective bargaining.[22] It is likely, too, that critics of informal recognition oppose it because it facilitates the survival of splinter groups[23] and permits professional associations to avoid making a decision to enter the union movement. Reports indicate that the AFL-CIO demand for the abolition of informal recognition will be met, and the President's committee reviewing the operation of E.O. 10988 will recommend such an action.[24]

Formal Recognition. Formal recognition, the second type of recognition available under E.O. 10988, has also been actively sought by many white-collar organizations. Some are simply forced to settle for formal recognition. Others seek it because they lack sufficient membership to gain exclusive recognition, or because they do not desire to bargain and write contracts.

Under present policy, groups consisting solely of managers, high-level supervisors, and high-ranking personnel officers cannot be accorded exclusive recognition and, therefore, must accept the second strongest form of recognition, formal recognition. For example, the National Association of Naval Technical Supervisors (NANTS), the National Association of Planners, Estimators and Progressmen (NAPEP), and the National Association of Supervisors (NAS) hold formal recognition (and on a national level) in the Navy Department. Similarly in the Post Office Department, the National League of Postmasters and the National Association of Postal Supervisors have received formal recognition. Other organizations with formal recognition are the Organization of Professional Employees in the Department of Agriculture (OPEDA), the Association of Engineers, Architects and Scientists, and the Professional Engineers in Government (PEG).

Formal recognition requires management to consult with the organization on all personnel policy of concern to the membership. Subjects for consultation can include the development and operation of grievance and appeal systems, physical conditions at the place of work, tours of duty, joint committees on cooperation, scheduling of vacations, opportunities for training, and disciplinary practices.

To gain formal recognition an organization must have a stable membership of at least 10 percent of a unit. If the unit is national in scope, the agency may accept a lower percentage. The number of members (or locals) need only be sufficient in the judgment of the agency. In addition to the membership requirement, the union must file the names of its officers, its constitution, and a statement of its objectives.

Unlike informal recognition, formal recognition cannot be accorded in a unit where there is an exclusive bargaining representative. On the other hand, in the absence of an exclusive unit, an agency may extend formal recognition to more than one organization in a unit.

Although groups that hold formal recognition do not participate in collective bargaining and agreement writing, this form of recognition, unlike informal recognition, very likely will be retained if Executive Order 10988 is amended. However, the requirements for obtaining formal recognition probably will be stiffened. One likely change is that the required percentage of a unit that must belong to the organization will be increased from 10 to 30 percent.[25]

Exclusive Recognition and Collective Bargaining. Organizations enjoying exclusive recognition, the third type of recognition, have as their central purpose the writing of agreements through collective bargaining. Subjects for bargaining include all those just enumerated in the discussion of formal recognition.

Topics that are not subject to collective bargaining include the mission of the agency, its budget, its organization, assignment of personnel, and the technology involved in the performance of its work. In addition, all agreements are subject to existing and future laws, regulations, and policies set forth in the *Federal Personnel Manual* as well as agency regulations.

Some relaxation of the restrictions on the subject matter of negotiation are likely in the near future. The President's review committee is expected to recommend that unions be allowed to negotiate job assignments, the impact of technological changes, retraining, and transfers.[26]

The agreement must be approved by the head of the agency or his authorized deputy. If the parties fail to reach an agreement there is no mechanism to resolve the impasse: strikes are forbidden and there is no provision for compulsory arbitration. The parties can seek mediation to help settle the dispute, but the final decision rests with the top management of the agency.

Similarly, final resolution of grievances also rests with top management. Advisory arbitration is available, but as it is only advisory, agency management can reject the award.

In the near future, it is likely that impasses in negotiation will be settled by binding arbitration.[27] It is expected that the arbitration panel will consist of the chairman of the Civil Service Commission, the chairman of the National Labor Relations Board, and the Secretary of Labor. When a contract dispute involves one of these three agencies, the member concerned would step aside in favor of a substitute.

The Presidential committee reviewing E.O. 10988 is also expected to recommend that grievances terminate in an award binding in principle, if not in law. In units represented by organizations, the committee is expected to suggest limiting grievance representation to a single representative in any agency. Presumably the larger one would be selected as the only representative. Eventually, this would probably eliminate the smaller organizations and end representation by more than one union in formally recognized units.

The terms of an agreement must apply equally to all employees in the unit irrespective of membership, and the representative must represent all employees without discrimination, even if some hold membership in an organization holding informal recognition in the same unit.

When an employee organization is accorded exclusive recognition, it may not deny membership to any employee in the unit unless the individual fails to meet reasonable occupational standards uniformly required for admission, or fails to pay initiation fees and dues uniformly required of members. Under the Code of Fair Labor Practices, employee organizations (whatever their type of recognition) are prohibited from interfering with or restraining an individual's rights of membership or non-membership and from attempting to induce an agency to do so.

To attain designation as an exclusive representative, an organization must meet the standards of formal recognition and, in addition, demonstrate that it represents a majority of employees in a unit. This requirement can be fulfilled through a check of membership cards, written authorization by a majority of employees, or by a representation election.

When elections are held, an organization can win exclusive recognition if it obtains a majority of votes, provided at least 60 percent of those eligible vote. Consequently, thirty-one votes per hundred eligible for the winning organization is the minimum needed to gain exclusive recognition. In a run-off election, the 60 percent requirement need not be met.[28]

Once exclusive recognition for a given unit has been won, the bargaining representative normally retains recognition rights for at least one year. A contract may extend the duration of exclusive recognition for a second year and it may then be renewed on an annual basis unless the union loses exclusive recognition.

Challenges and decertifications of exclusive recognition must be filed between the ninetieth and sixtieth day prior to the terminal date of the agreement. In addition, 30 percent of the employees in the unit must petition for a change in representation.

An agency can withdraw recognition at any time if the employee organization violates any of the conditions required for eligibility or engages in practices prohibited by the Code of Fair Labor Practice. For example, an agency can withdraw recognition if the union practices racial discrimination.

There are important limitations on exclusive recognition. For example, it does not preclude an individual from processing his own grievances, nor does it prevent an agency from meeting with a veterans' organization to discuss veterans' affairs. Exclusive recognition does not hinder an agency from consulting or dealing with any religious, social, or fraternal group concerning subjects of mutual concern.[29]

Exclusive recognition is the predominant type of recognition currently accorded labor organizations of white- and blue-collar employees in the federal service (Table 2). Of over 4,000 recognitions,

Table 2. Recognitions and Agreements in Executive Agencies,
U.S. Government, 1962–1967

	Total	Annual Increase	Informal	Formal	Exclusive	Agreements
1962	529*	—	289	155	85*	37*
1963	1,309	780	531	377	401	111
1964	1,848	539	662	569	617	272
1965	2,504	656	785	782	937	467
1966	3,263	759	903	981	1,379	689
1967	4,016	753	1,031	1,172	1,813	882

* Includes 29 exclusive recognitions and agreements existing prior to 1962.

SOURCE: U.S. Civil Service Commission, "Union Recognition in the Federal Government," November 1967 (mimeo), p. 37.

45 percent are exclusive. Surprisingly, the 1,813 exclusive recognitions have led to 882 agreements.

However, the number of exclusive recognitions and agreements is far less prevalent among white-collar workers than among blue-collar workers in the federal government. Perhaps the absence of a means for resolving these impasses may account for the discrepancy between the number of exclusive recognitions and the number of grievances. A BLS study of collective bargaining agreements in the federal service in late 1964, about two and a half years after E.O. 10988 was issued, disclosed only thirty-three agreements covering 21,000 white-collar employees.[30] This figure did not include installation-wide agreements, which included an undetermined number of white-collar employees. Of the agencies with large groups of white-collar employees, only the Department of Health, Education, and Welfare (HEW), and the Department of Labor had any significant number of employees under agreement. HEW reported just over 11,000; the Labor Department, about 4,100.

Based on this report, the BLS observed that, "comparing these figures with corresponding employment, it is clear that except for the Post Office, unions still face major organizing tasks."[31] Since 1964, the unions have made some advances among white-collar workers but this general assessment remains accurate.

☐ **White-Collar Organization Before and After E.O. 10988**

General Trends

In response to Executive Order 10988, existing unions and new ones swiftly gained representation among white- and blue-collar employees in the executive departments and agencies of the federal government. Within six years of the announcement of E.O. 10988, the number of white- and blue-collar employees under exclusive recognition* jumped from 521,000 to 1,239,000, a gain of almost 720,000 (Table 3). However, a substantial part of this growth re-

Table 3. Employees Under Exclusive Recognition in the Federal Government, 1962–1967

	All Agencies	Annual Increase	All Agencies except Post Office	Annual Increase
Dec. 1962	520,800		42,300	
Dec. 1963	648,000	127,200	180,200	137,900
May 1964	718,000	70,000	246,600	66,400
July 1965	835,000	117,000	319,700	73,100
Aug. 1966	1,054,400	219,400	434,900	115,200
Nov. 1967	1,238,700	184,300	629,900	195,000

SOURCE: December 1962 and December 1963 figures from the files of U.S. Civil Service Commission, except that the figure for all agencies in December 1962 includes a figure for Post Office representation that was obtained by averaging the figures for October 1961 and December 1963. All other figures from public reports of the Commission, except that that for May 1964 was obtained by adding the figure for the TVA (16,063) to the published total (701,948) and rounding.

sulted from the order's recognition of union representation that existed prior to E.O. 10988. On the eve of the order, in October 1961, union representation and membership in the federal government was estimated at 762,400.[32] Therefore, about 50 to 60 percent of the 1,238,700 persons represented in late 1967 had probably been members or were represented by unions prior to 1962. The Presidential task force also found that as of October 1961, union membership and representation was "larger among craftsmen and other blue collar workers; smaller among white collar workers."[33]

Table 4 shows that the number of employees under exclusive

* The number of employees under formal and informal recognition is not known.

Table 4. Extent of Employment Represented Under
E.O. 10988, 1962–1967 (percent)

	All Agencies	All Agencies except Post Office
Dec. 1962	19.8	2.2
Dec. 1963	14.8	9.6
May 1964	28.7	12.9
July 1965	32.6	16.3
Aug. 1966	39.9	22.3
Nov. 1967	45.3	31.1

SOURCE: Employment figures for December 1962 through July 1965, from U.S. Civil Service Commission *Monthly Report of Federal Employment;* those for August 1966 and November 1967, from U.S. Civil Service Commission, "Union Recognition in the Federal Government, August 1966 and November 1967," February 26, 1968, p. 2. The employment figures for December 1962 through July 1965 are not strictly comparable to those for August 1966 and November 1967, because the exclusions made by the Commission for these two months could be made for the others. These exclusions refer to employees of security agencies of the federal government. Employees in exclusive units are from Table 3.

recognition grew much faster than total employment between 1962 and 1967. Because the Post Office was already largely unionized, organization grew much faster in other agencies. By July 1965, the percentage of government employment represented by unions (including the Post Office Department) equalled the proportion on the eve of the Executive Order. In October 1961, one-third of all federal employees was represented by unions.[34]

The number of dues-paying members is unknown, but it is certainly less than the number in exclusive recognition units. For example, as of August 1966, the American Federation of Government Employees (AFGE), the largest union in the federal government, represented 207,700 employees.[35] However, its average dues-paying membership for the fiscal year ending June 30, 1966 was 168,500.* The number of employees represented by the AFGE was thus more than 20 percent larger than its dues-paying membership.

In the federal service the number of employees represented by

* Calculated from per capita receipts, charter fees, and initiation fees. Hence, the figure is slightly above annual average dues-paying membership.

organizations with exclusive recognition should exceed the number of members in these organizations* substantially because the union shop and other forms of compulsory membership are prohibited under E.O. 10988. If the ratio of the AFGE's dues-paying membership to the number of employees it represents is typical in government service, total membership in November 1967 would be approximately 1 million and the percentage unionized about 38 percent, a figure well above that in the private economy. For 1966, the Bureau of Labor Statistics estimated that 28 percent of all nonfarm employees were members of unions.[36]

Union membership in the federal service may be slightly larger than the estimated 1 million, however, since figures on employees in informal and formal units are not available. Normally, unions with formal recognition have at least 10 percent of the employees in a unit as members, while no special number is required in informal units. Among the largest unions with formal recognition are the Postal Supervisors (31,700 members) and the National League of Postmasters (18,000).[37]

White-Collar Trends

White-collar employees shared in the general gains that labor organizations made in the federal government between 1962 and 1967. In fact, as Table 5 shows, white-collar organizations added well over 250,000 to the number of employees under exclusive recognition in the period.

Compared to blue-collar labor organizations, which added over 320,000 to the number they represented, the white-collar organizations have remained a fairly stable percentage (ranging from 40 to 46 percent) of the total after 1962.

Members of white-collar unions make up a much greater proportion of the entire union population in the federal service than in

* In the case of one union, the National Federation of Federal Employees, dues-paying membership exceeds the number exclusively recognized. However, this exception is probably attributable to the union's initial opposition to E.O. 10988 and its limited participation under its procedures. At the same time this union holds the largest number of informal and the second largest number of formal recognitions, which explains why its membership exceeds the number it represents in exclusive units.

Table 5. Exclusive Recognition Among Blue- and White-Collar
Employees in the Federal Government, 1962–1967*

	Blue	White	White-Collar Percent of Total*
Dec. 1962	18,300	24,000	57
Dec. 1963	96,900	83,300	46
May 1964	140,000	106,600	43
July 1965	191,400	128,300	40
Aug. 1966	243,500	191,400	44
Nov. 1967	338,700	291,300	46

* Excludes the Post Office Department.

SOURCE: Tables 3 and 9.

the economy as a whole, or in the private economy. In part, this phenomenon probably results from the fact that there is a greater proportion of white-collar employment in the federal government than in the private economy. Another contributing factor is probably the greater ease of organization in the federal government.

Whatever the cause, however, the figures given in Table 5 and others from the U.S. Bureau of Labor Statistics indicate that white-collar unionism comprises about three times as much of the total unionism (excluding the Post Office) in federal employment as in private employment. Whereas white-collar representation* in the federal government comprised 44 percent of all employees represented in 1966 (Table 5), in the economy as a whole white-collar membership made up only 14 percent of the total.[38] For the private economy alone, the white-collar percentage of total union membership would be even lower.

Another measure of the success white-collar unions have had in the federal government is a comparison of representation (or membership) with total employment. As Table 4 has shown, the over-all extent of organization (excluding the Post Office Department) rose rapidly between 1962 and 1967, from 2 to 31 percent. However, if blue- and white-collar workers are taken separately, the percentage organized by each of the two groups differs significantly (Table 6). In 1964, over one-fourth of all blue-collar workers in the federal service were represented, and by 1967 over one-half of the

* Representation is treated as a proxy for membership; since the comparisons are relative comparisons, this seems a valid procedure.

Table 6. Extent of Organization, Blue- and
White-Collar Employment,* 1964–1967
(percent)

	Blue-Collar	White-Collar
1964†	27	10
1965†	38	11
Aug. 1966‡	40	15
Nov. 1967	54	21

* Excludes the Post Office Department.

† Because of the lack of occupational employment figures for the same month as union representation figures, we compared the union representation of May 1964 with the employment figures (partially adjusted) for December 1964; similarly, we compared union representation figures as of July 1965 with employment figures (partially adjusted) for December 1965. White-collar employment for December 1964 and December 1965 are from U.S. Bureau of Labor Statistics, *Occupational Employment Statistics, 1960–66,* BLS Bulletin 1579 (January 1968), Table 22, p. 30. Representation figures for blue- and white-collar employees are from Table 5. Extent of organization for August 1966 and November 1967, U.S. Civil Service Commission, "Union Representation in the Federal Government, August 1966 and November 1967," p. 2.

‡ A check for 1966 shows the "mixed" estimate for the percentage of blue-collar workers represented at 40.1 (compared to 40 percent published by the Civil Service Commission and reported in the above table) and 16.1 for white-collar employees compared to the 15 percent in Table 6.

federal blue-collar workers were organized. Comparable figures for white-collar employees were one-tenth in 1964 and just over one-fifth in 1967. On the other hand, the 21 percent rate of unionization among federal white-collar employees is more than double the national average of 9.5 percent for all white-collar employment.[39]

When the *composition* of the federal white-collar employees who are represented by unions is analyzed, it appears that most are in the lower occupational ranks. Furthermore, among the occupations and departments counted in the official statistics as "white-collar" are service groups such as hospital attendants, fire fighters, security inspectors, and employees in food and commissary service.

In contrast, professionals comprise a small proportion of exclusively represented white-collar employees. As shown in Table 7, professionals did not exceed 18 percent of all exclusives in the federal government from 1962 to 1967. If Table 7 indicates any trend in professional organization it appears to be that their percentage is declining.

Table 7. Professional and Other White-Collar Employees Under
Exclusive Recognition, 1962–1967

	Professional	Other White-Collar	Percent Professional of Total White-Collar
Dec. 1962	3,000	21,000	14
Dec. 1963	12,900	70,400	18
May 1964	16,500	90,100	18
July 1965	19,400	108,900	18
Aug. 1966	25,000	166,400	15
Nov. 1967	37,300	254,000	15

SOURCE: See Table 9.

The low degree of organization among professionals is indicated
by the figures in Table 8. Professionals are less organized than
nonprofessionals in the federal service and, as Table 8 shows, the
gap between them is growing.

Table 8. Extent of Organization, All White-Collar and Professional
Employees, 1964–1967 (percent)

	All White-Collar Employees	Professional Employees	Percentage Points Difference
1964*	10.0	7.7	2.3
1965*	11.2	8.6	2.6
1966†	16.1	11.1	5.0
Nov. 1967	21.1	13.0‡	8.1

* See Notes to Table 6.
† Representation from Table 9; employment from U.S. Bureau of
Labor Statistics, *Occupational Employment Statistics, 1960–66*, BLS
Bulletin No. 1579 (January 1968), Table 22, p. 30.
‡ H. Lahne, "Unit Determination in the Federal Service," Twenty-
first Annual New York University Conference on Labor, May 16, 1968
(typescript), p. 4.

Over 80 percent of all nonprofessional white-collar employees are
in the three military services, the Veteran's Administration, the
Treasury, and the Department of Health, Education and Welfare
(Table 9). Together these six agencies accounted for 209,000 of the
254,000 nonprofessional white-collar employees under exclusive recognition in November 1967. Over one-third of the 37,300 professionals in exclusive units in November 1967 were in the Treasury,
and all of these were in the Internal Revenue Service. The next
largest groups were the 4,900 professionals in the Army, 3,700 in the

Table 9. Exclusive Recognition Among White-Collar Employees, Selected Agencies, 1962–1967

Agency	Dec. 1962		Dec. 1963		May 1964		July 1965		Aug. 1966		Nov. 1967	
	P*	Other	P	Other	P	Other	P	Other	P	Other	P	Other
Labor	1,000	3,600	1,100	3,800	1,100	3,800	1,300	3,300	1,400	6,900	1,500	7,400
TVA	1,600	4,700	1,500	4,300	1,600	4,600	1,300	3,900	1,400	4,000	1,500	4,400
Treasury			8,100	9,100	9,000	10,500	9,100	13,100	10,900	16,300	15,700	22,400
Justice					100	600	100	600	200	2,200	300	6,000
HEW		3,300		12,500	500	14,400	600	15,800	800	19,900	700	25,500
Navy	200	3,000	900	11,500	900	16,000	900	18,300	400	25,700	1,600	36,500
Air Force			100	4,200	100	6,200	500	10,500	600	23,000	1,300	32,600
VA	100	1,300	600	9,500	700	14,900	1,500	17,700	2,500	30,400	3,700	44,400
Army	100	1,300	200	6,800	500	8,300	700	11,200	1,900	19,000	4,900	44,800
Agriculture		3,400		3,600	800	3,800	2,400	3,900	2,400	4,700	2,800	5,400
Total of above	3,000	20,600	12,500	65,300	15,300	82,100	18,400	98,300	22,500	152,100	34,000	229,400
Total all agencies	3,000	21,000	12,900	70,400	16,500	90,100	10,400	108,900	25,000	166,400	37,300	254,000

* P = Professional.

SOURCE: November 1967, and total for 1966, U.S. Civil Service Commission, *Union Recognition in the Federal Government*, Statistical Report, November 1967. Detail for 1966 and all figures for other years were estimated by the writer.

Veteran's Administration, and 2,800 in the Department of Agriculture. One of the most important white-collar gains came in the Labor Department. In August 1962, the American Federation of Government Employees won exclusive recognition within the Department of Labor in the District of Columbia, and in December 1965 it gained exclusive recognition for the entire Department.

Table 10. Percent of White-Collar Employment Represented, Selected Agencies, November 1967

Agency	Nov. 1967
Labor	90
TVA	79
Treasury	46
Justice	37
HEW	26
Navy	22
Air Force	21
VA	21
Army	19
Agriculture	8
All agencies	21

SOURCE: U.S. Civil Service Commission, *Union Recognition in the Federal Government,* Statistical Report, November 1967.

As of November 1967, white-collar unionization in the Labor Department was the most extensive of the major agencies (Table 10). The TVA ranked second to the Labor Department. Lowest ranked was the Department of Agriculture.

White-Collar Unions

The leading unions in the campaign to organize white-collar workers in the federal service (outside the Post Office) are the American Federation of Government Employees (AFGE), AFL-CIO, the National Association of Internal Revenue Service Employees (NAIRE), independent, the National Federation of Federal Employees (NFFE), independent, and the National Association of Government Employees (NAGE), independent. Small groups of white-collar employees have been organized by the Metal Trades Department, AFL-CIO (almost all of these in the Navy) and the Machinists, AFL-CIO.

The National Federation of Federal Employees is the oldest white-collar union in the federal service. It was founded in 1917 and was affiliated with the AFL from that date until 1932 when it withdrew over a policy dispute.[40] Its jurisdiction has always been industrial in type, that is, it has always sought representation irrespective of occupation. While it includes both blue- and white-collar workers, the majority of its members has usually consisted of white-collar employees.

The largest union of white-collar employees in the federal government is the American Federation of Government Employees (Table 11). It accounted for nearly two-thirds of all white-collar employees recognized by the end of 1967. The AFGE, which began

Table 11. Exclusive Recognition White-Collar Employees, Selected Unions, November 1967

	Professional	Other	Total
AFL-CIO Affiliates			
AFGE	7,400	179,300	186,700
Metal Trades Dept.		2,000	2,000
Machinists	*	1,400	1,400
Subtotal	7,400	182,700	190,100
Independent Unions			
Nat. Assn. of I.R.S. Empls. (NAIRE)	12,800	19,600	32,400
Nat. Fed. of Federal Empls. (NFFE)	3,200	16,300	19,500
Nat. Fed. of Gov't. Empls. (NAGE)	1,300	17,700	19,000
Subtotal	17,300	53,600	70,900
Total, above unions	24,700	236,300	261,000
Total, all unions	37,300	254,000	291,300
Percent above unions of total white-collar unions (8/9)	66.2	93.0	89.5

* Less than 50.

SOURCE: U.S. Civil Service Commission, *Union Recognition in the Federal Government,* August 1966 and November 1967, p. 3.

as a faction that seceded from the National Federation of Federal Employees, was chartered by the AFL in August 1932. Initially, its jurisdiction was limited to clerical and office employees, but it now seeks to organize all civilian federal employees of the United States and District of Columbia. From an early membership of 4,000 in 1933, the AFGE rose to become the largest single union in the federal service, including the Post Office. In 1966, its average dues-paying membership reached 168,500, while the number of employees it represented stood at 207,700. In 1967 the AFGE pushed its total representation to 326,400, the largest number represented by a single union. Of this number, 57 percent (186,700) were white-collar employees.

The National Association of Internal Revenue Service Employees (NAIRE) is second to the AFGE in white-collar representation (32,400). In fact, its entire representation and dues-paying membership (estimated at 26,200) is white collar, and is thus far limited to the Internal Revenue Service. Recently, NAIRE amended its constitution and jurisdictional claims to enable it to go outside that single jurisdiction. Its rapid growth in numbers and importance since 1962 has impelled NAIRE to reorganize its structure from a confederation of autonomous locals into a more centralized organization. It also has a full-time paid president for the first time in its history.

Both the National Federation of Federal Employees (NFFE) and the National Association of Government Employees (NAGE) have their largest following in the military services. In addition, NFFE holds recognition for nearly 1,000 employees in the Interior Department, and about 1,100 each in the Commerce Department and Veteran's Administration. NAGE represents about 5,000 white-collar employees in the Transportation Department, with the majority in the Federal Aviation Administration.

Most professionals are represented by independent unions and associations. Among these (in addition to NAIRE, NFFE, and NAGE) are the National Association of Federal Veterinarians, (Agriculture Department), the National Education Association (in the Army and Air Force), the Patent Office Professional Association (in Commerce), two independents at the National Labor Relations Board, and two at TVA.

The preference shown by professionals and many white-collar

workers for independent unions is underlined by the BLS' recent finding that the proportion of white-collar members in local and regional independent unions is double that in national and international unions.[41] Evidently, even when professionals and white-collar unionists join a labor organization, they retain some desire for distinction from the main symbols of unionism.

Membership Turnover and Mergers

A concomitant of the rapid growth in representation in the federal service since 1962 has been a high turnover of membership. John F. Griner, president of the American Federation of Government Employees, reported to the national convention of the union in September 1964 that in the prior twenty-three months, the organization added over 113,000 members and dropped nearly 84,000, for a turnover rate of 74 percent. While various reasons account for the turnover of membership, unwillingness to pay dues was singled out as the leading cause.[42]

Nine months prior to Griner's report, on January 1, 1964, the Civil Service Commission revised its regulations on dues check-off to permit voluntary allotments. As a result of this measure and as a result of improved union services and communications with members, President Griner was able to report to the next AFGE convention in 1966 that the rate of membership turnover had dropped from 74 to 55 percent.[43] Griner attributed the continuing high drop-out rate to employment turnover and deauthorizations of the dues check-off.

Merger and affiliation movements among white-collar unions in the federal service have thus far been few. A small independent of 600 members, the Custom Inspectors Association in New York, joined the AFGE early in 1967.[44] On the other hand, a few months earlier the National Association of Internal Revenue Service Employees rejected a merger bid from the AFGE.[45]

The National Federation of Federal Employees at its convention in December 1966 called upon other independent unions of federal employees to form a Council of Independents. The organizations invited to join in the council were the National Postal Union (66,000 members), NAIRE (28,000), the National Alliance of Postal and Federal Employees (126,000), and the National Association of

Government Employees (44,500).[46] However, nothing has come of this bid. Within the AFL-CIO, the Government Employees Council, consisting of thirty-four unions, pools the resources and energies of AFL-CIO affiliates in the federal service.

Far from embracing mergers and affiliation, rivalry between white-collar independents and AFL-CIO affiliates is intense. The AFGE, AFL-CIO sees the independents as "company unions" or "dues collection agencies" that are eventually doomed to extinction. The independents depict the AFGE as "constantly embarrassed by deep-rooted jurisdictional and other conflicts in the AFL-CIO."[47] With time, some mergers are likely, but as in the private economy, there is room for both independent and affiliated white-collar unions.

□ Continuing Issues

Professionals and Unionism

The leading labor relations issue facing white-collar employees in the federal government (as in the private economy) is whether or not to join unions. This has been the central issue since E.O. 10988 was issued and it remains so today. A corollary is the dilemma facing professional associations: Can they survive and function effectively in a labor relations system that shows signs of becoming a system of organized union representation? The answers to these questions will have a significant impact for employee relations in the federal service, particularly for professionals.

While total federal civilian employment has grown slowly in the past decade (from 2.4 million in 1957 to 2.9 million in 1967[48]), employment in professional, administrative, and technical occupations has grown very rapidly. As a result, there has been a change in the composition of federal white-collar employment in favor of the professional, high-level administrative and technical groups. As recently as June 1962, employment in clerical grades exceeded employment in the professional grades by 112,000; but by the beginning of fiscal 1965 the two groups were almost equal in size, "each representing approximately one-third of total full-time white-collar employment."[49] The largest increases were in the (professional) categories of physical and medical sciences, and engineering.[50]

The trend toward occupations requiring greater skill and education in the federal service will continue. Of the projected increase of 100,000 in white-collar employment for 1966 to 1970, over two-thirds are expected to be in professional, administrative, and technical occupations. The remaining one-third is expected to be in the lower-graded clerical, aide, and assistant occupations.[51]

In the professional occupations, the largest future gains (to 1970) are expected in engineering, education, mathematics and physical science.[52] In this group only the teachers have shown any marked propensity to enroll in unions. Among administrative and technical occupations, the most sizable growth is anticipated in the physical sciences, computer services and management services, and engineering support. Thus far there is very little employee organization among these employee groups. On the other hand, among lower-graded white-collar occupations, in which the propensity to join unions is greatest, employment is expected to grow the least.

Given that high-level occupations are expected to increase in number and importance in the federal government and given their low susceptibility to unionism, the growth that unions experienced in the last six years will doubtless begin to slacken. At the heart of the challenge to the organization of white-collar employees are the professional associations. Will they remain aloof, enter the union fold, modify their organizations so as to become unions, or seek, as many already have, a role under E.O. 10988 that is limited to informal or formal recognition? Since informal recognition is expected to be abolished soon, the professionals will have to seek formal recognition. However, formal recognition will become more difficult to secure if the minimum membership requirement goes to 30 percent as expected. If that happens formal recognition is on the brink of exclusive recognition. The impetus to go over the brink is the ban on any formal recognition coextensive with exclusive recognition.

Nevertheless, the pressures on professionals to seek exclusive recognition and bargaining are not yet overpowering. Collective bargaining in the federal service does not yet encompass many subjects that are crucial to agreements in the private sector and in many local governments. Wages, hiring, promotion, transfer, suspension, demotion, discharge, or other disciplinary action—all these are either entirely outside the scope of collective bargaining or so dependent on laws and regulations that the exclusive relationship cannot materially affect them. Hence, in the final analysis, to obtain a raise in pay, professionals will have to go to Congress, and lobbying can be done at least as effectively by a professional body as by a union.

It thus seems probable that most professional associations will not seek exclusive recognition and bargaining. Added support for this view is provided by the experience of professional unionism in the TVA. It appears that the special circumstances that have made collective bargaining for professionals possible in the TVA cannot be reproduced elsewhere in the federal government without drastic changes in Executive Order 10988 and the Code of Fair Labor Practices.

The TVA Model

Professional unionism, bargaining, and agreements have flourished in TVA, largely because of the unusual degree of support and encouragement TVA management has displayed toward unions. Almost from its inception, TVA management has "subscribed to the principle of 'democratic management,' and as a corollary to its belief in democratic management, both blue collar and white collar employees have been *encouraged* . . . to join and support employee organizations."[53]

Despite this managerial encouragement, Arthur Thompson and Irwin Weinstock found that barely 25 percent of TVA's white-collar employees believed that union membership was consistent with professional status, and most TVA professionals viewed union membership as unprofessional. An equally surprising finding was that TVA white-collar workers held a generally unfavorable opinion in regard to how well their organizations represented them.[54]

Thompson and Weinstock's most significant finding (in view of the importance of professional and technical employees in the federal service) was that support of unions varied inversely with the level of education.[55] The most unfavorable views were held by those who had done some graduate work or who held an advanced degree. In addition, the younger employees and those with the shortest length of service also registered unfavorable reactions to the compatibility of union membership and professionalism. In fact, only those fifty years of age and over and those with over twenty years' service expressed any measure of favorable opinion.

What, then, was the "equalizer" that countered these negative views and made white-collar unions viable at TVA?

The answer to this question lies in the attitude of the TVA management. At TVA, according to Thompson and Weinstock, "the degree of employee interest in unions varies significantly among employees according to age, length of service and education, although *the key variable seems to be management's posture toward collective bargaining.*"[56] At TVA, "there can be little doubt that the attitudes of white-collar TVA employees toward unions and the obvious success of collective bargaining have mainly been the product of TVA management's affirmative willingness to share its decision-making powers with unions in matters affecting the employees."[57]

The key factor in management's support of unionism and bargaining at TVA is its encouragement of union membership. The articles of agreement between TVA and its white-collar unions negotiated December 5, 1950 and reaffirmed May 7, 1964, state that "[union] membership and . . . participation are among the positive factors of merit and efficiency to be considered in selecting employees for promotion, transfer and retention."[58]

Because these agreements were negotiated prior to the Executive Order, they are legal under section 16, the order's grandfather clause. However, such management support is prohibited by the order and the Code of Fair Labor Practices in all agreements negotiated since the Executive Order.

Section 1(a) of the order directs each agency head to take positive action so "that no interference, restraint, coercion or discrimination is practiced within such agency to encourage or discourage membership in any employee organization." Section 1(a) also declares that an employee's right not to join, as well as his right to join, an employee organization must be protected. Similarly, the Code of Fair Labor Practices prohibits "encouraging or discouraging membership in any employee organization by discrimination in regard to hiring, tenure, promotion or other conditions of employment."

When TVA first agreed to the preferential shop in 1952 "the

membership rolls showed a considerable influx of new members."[59] Despite the premium put on membership, the Thompson-Weinstock survey estimated that from 10 to 20 percent of the eligible employees are still not union members.[60]

Thompson and Weinstock concluded that if their findings can be applied to other white-collar government employees, "they spell trouble for organizers . . . given the rising educational level among white collar employees and the declining average age of labor force participants resulting from the influx of young workers and earlier retirement."[61]

An even more important drawback is that other agencies cannot, under the Executive Order, adopt TVA's principles of "democratic management," and its attendant support for union membership. Without this "equalizer," it is unlikely that unionism will develop readily among professionals elsewhere in the federal government. Unlike TVA, other agencies may consider membership as a factor in personnel actions only when dealing with professional associations that are outside the scope of E.O. 10988. Only in the case of professional associations not participating in E.O. 10988 can management encourage and support membership as "positive factors of merit and efficiency to be considered in selecting employees for promotion, transfer and retention." As soon as a professional group seeks or receives even informal recognition, agency management must terminate its encouragement of membership and can no longer use membership as a criterion for promotion or transfer.

In fact, one of the major grievances expressed by professional associations (in addition to the problems of conflict of interest and mixed units) is that under E.O. 10988 they must give up managerial encouragement of membership. For the same reason they must also surrender such a tangible benefit as time off with pay while attending professional meetings.[62] It is partly because they lose such managerial support and encouragement that professional groups like the American Nurses Association have advanced the notion of a "multipurpose" organization, that is, one that would accept preferential treatment based on professionalism but would also retain the rights of an employee organization under E.O. 10988. In effect, the Nurses Association seeks the same preferential treatment white-collar unions receive from the Tennessee Valley Authority.

Federation of Professional Associations

Outside the TVA, the dilemma that professional associations have encountered in regard to defining their status, functions, and goals since the inception of E.O. 10988 has led a small number to seek exclusive recognition. For example, exclusive recognition has been won by the Association of Scientists and Engineers at the federal arsenal in Watertown (Mass.), the National Association of Federal Veterinarians in the Department of Agriculture, the Trademark Society in the Patent Office, and NLRB Professional Association at the National Labor Relations Board.

Most professional associations, however, are still in the process of resolving their status. Many have sought informal or formal recognition, but others, perhaps a majority, remain outside the scope of Executive Order 10988. Even those who have elected to participate continue their professional associations. Thus, in late 1965, six professional groups set up a short-lived Council of Federal Professional Associations limited to organizations that participated under E.O. 10988.[63]

A new group, the National Federation of Professional Organizations (NFPO), was formed in July 1966 and formally organized in November 1966. Initially it considered limiting membership only to those groups that did *not* operate under E.O. 10988, but finally decided to accept both participants and nonparticipants. Although member groups were to be free to participate in E.O. 10988, it was decided that NFPO itself would not.[64]

At its inception in November 1966, NFPO had six affiliates with a claimed membership of 24,000. These were the Air Traffic Controllers Association (5,000), the Association of Senior Engineers, Naval Ship Systems (600), the National Association of Federal Veterinarians (1,300), the National Society of Professional Engineers (8,000 engineers in the federal government), the Patent Office Professional Association (1,100), and the Organization of Professional Employees of the Department of Agriculture (7,600). Three others, the National Association of Naval Technical Supervisors (1,000), the Society of Real Estate Appraisers (485), and the Federal Quarantine Inspectors (300) joined on a provisional basis. The American Nurses Association, claiming to represent 40,000 employees in the federal service, considered joining on a special basis, rather than as a regular member, but has not yet affiliated. Fourteen other professional groups were invited to join.[65]

The Federal Professional Association (FPA), although one of the original authors of the plan to create the NFPO, decided against affiliation and offered itself as a rival federation. The FPA criticized the NFPO because it was inadequately financed, gave equal voting strength to each affiliate regardless of size, and accepted occupational groups that were not truly professional. The Federal Professional Association, founded in 1962, had itself been established in response to E.O. 10988. One of its founders and principal spokesmen has been Robert Ramspeck, former chairman of the Civil Service Commission.

Despite the challenge of FPA, the National Federation of Professional Employees seems to be the principal federation of professional associations in the federal service. By November 1967, a total of twelve associations, with a combined membership in excess of 30,000, had affiliated with the NFPO.

The AFL-CIO made a bid to the professional associations by establishing a council of Scientific, Professional, and Cultural Employees (SPACE) in mid-March 1967. SPACE's purpose is to "maintain a friendly attitude toward professional associations with the aim in mind to eventually bring them into the mainstream of the labor movement, either within the framework of existing unions or as separately charted AFL-CIO international bodies."[66] SPACE noted that "the vast majority of scientific, professional and cultural employees belong to professional associations."[67] At the time this chapter was written, it was still too early to judge SPACE's success in attracting professional associations; however, it has thus far obtained no known professional affiliations.

Similarly, an invitation to professionals at the end of 1967 by the National Federation of Federal Employees received little response. At that time, the NFFE offered to charter locals consisting solely of professionals, whereas it had previously enrolled only those professionals who belonged to locals in combination with other workers.[68]

What, it may be asked, inhibits the professional association from becoming a union, affiliating with one, or seeking exclusive recognition under E.O. 10988. Why are so many professional associations opposed to unionism?

The associations have several objections, and these are not limited to fears of loss of status. In terms of pay, the professionals feel that membership in a union representing both professionals and nonprofessionals, even in separate units, must eventually mean that the demands of the most numerous lower-paid members will be favored and therefore that the differential between the two groups will be reduced. (This is much the same problem that an industrial union that comprises both skilled and unskilled blue-collar workers faces when it bargains.)

The objection to separate unions and exclusive recognition appears to be that the short-run gains in wages that might be secured by collective bargaining are outweighed by other considerations. Most important, professionals protest that collective bargaining places restrictions on managerial prerogatives. Whereas unionists strive to limit management prerogatives, professionals, according to the National Society of Professional Engineers, believe that "most of the things professionals want can only be obtained by the exact reverse of this process."[69] In essence, many of the goals of the professional are not to be found in grievance procedures, seniority and overtime provisions, disciplinary procedures, the check-off, and work assignment clauses; that is, elements that are the substance of collective bargaining and agreements.

Economic, Bargaining, and Political Issues

Although professionals generally may not favor the process of collective bargaining, they are concerned about wages and other economic issues. The National Federation of Professional Organizations, the Federal Professional Association, and the National Association of Government Engineers have strongly urged the President, Congress, and the Civil Service Commission to bring the salaries of government professionals up to the level of those paid in private industry. Comparability, promised in the Salary Reform Act of 1962, has yet to be achieved, according to these groups. For example, the NAGE claims that (as recently as 1967) federal pay for their group lagged from 16 to 37 percent behind that of private industry.[70]

Another economic issue, one that affects blue-collar as well as white-collar employees and that may assume far greater importance in the future, is contracting out for goods and services. On the one hand, Budget Bureau Circular A-76 appears to place general reliance on private enterprise to supply the government, thus lending support to the practice of contracting out. On the other hand, the circular does not absolutely obligate the government to contract with the private sector. Currently, the Budget Bureau feels that its policy on contracting out has been "reasonably satisfactory."[71] However, if the line between in-house production and contracting out shifts toward more contracting out, it could reduce employment, and could exacerbate relations between unions and agency management.

An important issue in employee-management relations in the federal service are the claims by some unions that agency management, especially in the military services, is anti-union.[72] When the Civil Service Commission called on agency management to ensure that employees would not be denied access to personnel officers and supervisors and that the agencies maintain an "open door" policy, the National Federation of Federal Employees denounced the directive as a "pathetic commentary on management attitudes toward organized employee relations at this stage of labor history."[73]

Increases in the number of black employees in the government and upgrading in their job status may test the ban on racial discrimination by unions and agencies. Thus far, few cases involving unions have arisen. As a general principle, however, local unions in government are not doing a satisfactory job in equal employment opportunity, according to an officer of the Equal Employment Opportunity Committee.[74]

In the political realm, some white-collar unions, notably the American Federation of Government Employees, AFL-CIO, appear to be preparing the groundwork for a drive to obtain a change in the Hatch Act that would facilitate greater participation by unions and their members in politics. Illustrative of the problems are the following queries put to the Civil Service Commission by a local of the American Federation of Government Employees:

1. Is the union an entity apart from its members and therefore not subject to the Hatch Act?
2. Would a union officer who is also a federal employee violate the Act by serving on the AFL-CIO Committee on Political Education?

3. Can a local request donations for COPE on government property?[75]

Other unions, particularly the Government Employees Council of the AFL-CIO, have joined in the demand for revision of the Hatch Act. The Civil Service Commission has also recommended some changes to liberalize the Act, but its proposals are more limited than those of the AFL-CIO unions. The National Federation of Federal Employees, independent, opposes any changes. This also is the attitude of many of the professional associations and the National Civil Service League.[76]

☐ Summary and Conclusions

In this report we have tried to explain how white-collar unions function under Executive Order 10988, what problems and opportunities they have, and how professionals are reacting to the order. In addition, we have attempted to describe trends in white-collar organizations in general and in detail. At this point, we offer some judgments on the character of the organization of federal employees and the prospects for continued union expansion.

Based on the statistical profile, it is evident that Executive Order 10988 spurred labor organization in the federal government among all groups of employees, both blue and white collar. A substantial portion (50 to 60 percent) of the increased union membership, however, resulted from formalization under E.O. 10988 of representation that existed prior to the new program. Nevertheless, organization moved ahead in the federal sector, while the level of union membership in the private economy barely kept pace with the increase in employment.

The unions' advance in the federal government was not uniform. Blue-collar workers joined in larger numbers than white-collar workers. Furthermore, among white-collar employees, those in lower-graded occupations have joined in far greater numbers than have higher-graded professional, administrative and technical employees. Moreover, over two-fifths of all professional representation is in one agency, indicating the narrow confines and limited growth of union membership among professionals.

The basic policy of Executive Order 10988 is to protect the right of federal employees in the executive branch of the government to belong to labor organizations. Despite the invitation to organize, serious obstacles beset the enrollment of white-collar employees in unions. Primary among these are the conflict-of-interest issue, mixed bargaining units, and the attitude of professional employees and their associations. Although white-collar employees' attitudes range from overt opposition to enthusiastic joining, most either oppose or desire only limited participation in the new program; that is, they seek informal or formal recognition, both of which fall short of collective bargaining.

One of the responses to this variety of viewpoints has been the idea advanced by the Nurses Association, the multipurpose organization. A multipurpose organization seeks to gain the best of both worlds, professionalism and unionism. It would be professionally oriented, include all but the highest levels of management, receive the support and encouragement historically given professional membership, but it would also seek exclusive recognition and agreements. To permit management support, there would have to be important revisions in the Executive Order and the Code of Fair Labor Practices. The multipurpose organization, if it does evolve, would partially duplicate the relationship of the TVA to its white-collar unions.

The role of professional and technical employees is regarded as the keystone to the future of white-collar unionism in the federal government. Professional, high administrative, and technical occupations are growing faster than low-level white-collar occupations. On the basis of the limited unionization that took place among professionals in the years from 1962 to 1967, the future trend in the structure of employment portends small union gains.

An interesting exception to the general weakness of unionism among professional and technical workers in the federal government is the Tennessee Valley Authority. White-collar unions have been active in the TVA since the early 1940s. However, this model is not regarded as portable, primarily because the special ingredient, TVA management support and encouragement of unionism and union membership, cannot be duplicated elsewhere in the federal government without revising the Executive Order and the Code of Fair Labor Practices.

The most likely resolution of the dilemma facing professional associations is a limited participation under E.O. 10988. This will be facilitated if informal recognition is retained in the order. If it is not, professional associations will seek formal recognition. Exclusive recognition will be sought less actively. Mergers with established unions is unlikely.

Meanwhile, federations of professionals will continue to accentuate professional interests and to move toward a more active role in representing professionals before Congress. In sum, the role of professional associations is likely to depart from the previous attitude of professional disinterest, but is not likely to evolve into full-scale unionism and collective bargaining.

The character of union growth in the federal government since 1962 sets the movement apart from other episodes of upsurge in the history of American labor. By any standard, labor organization in the federal service has been accomplished with little opposition and strife. This is no doubt due to the type of occupations involved, the nature of the employer, and the lessons of the past. In addition, the leader of the major unions now organizing government workers are experienced in the ways of institutionalized, mature unionism. Members and potential members decide on the exercise of their rights while enjoying a living standard that workers of the thirties would have associated with employers. Ideology is absent.

The public charter underpinning the organization of federal employees also contrasts sharply with that governing employees in the private economy. Executive Order 10988 evokes the atmosphere of the personnel office, while the National Labor Relations Act conjures up the strike and the picket line. Where E.O. 10988 converts the theories of personnel management and human relations to justify an executive policy of improving the effective conduct of public business, the National Labor Relations Act encouraged unions as a countervailing force to the business cycle and managerial power.

Despite the differences between the federal and private systems of industrial relations, the likelihood is that the two systems will steadily move closer together. While each may be expected to borrow from the other, the direction of change is almost certainly toward the system that has evolved in the private economy.

NOTES

1 *Executive Order 10988,* January 17, 1962, section 1(a).

2 *Executive Order 10988,* section 1 (b).

3 U.S. Civil Service Commission, "Letter 700–1," *Federal Personnel Manual,* p. 4.

4 *Op. cit.,* p. 3.

5 For a contrary view, see H. Lahne, "Unit Determination in the Federal Service," Twenty-first Annual New York University Conference on Labor, May 16, 1968 (typescript), p. 11.

6 Presidential Review Committee on Employee-Management Relations in the Federal Service, *Hearings,* October 24, 1967 (mimeo), pp. 189–190.

7 "Testimony of the National Federation of Professional Organizations before the President's Committee on Federal Employee-Management Relations," October 22, 1967 (mimeo), p. 6.

8 Willem B. Vosloo, *Collective Bargaining in the United States Civil Service* (Chicago: Public Personnel Association, 1966), p. 101.

9 Quoted in "Testimony of the National Federation of Professional Organizations . . .", *op. cit.,* October 26, 1967, p. 4. Emphasis added.

10 See Lahne, *op. cit.,* p. 12.

11 *Ibid.,* p. 5.

12 *Executive Order 10988,* section 6 (a).

13 *Ibid., loc. cit.*

14 *Ibid., loc. cit.*

15 U.S. Civil Service Commission, "Employee-Management Cooperation," *Federal Personnel Manual,* June 30, 1964, pp. 711–716.

16 A leading case on the definition of professional and the grouping of professionals to constitute an appropriate unit is "In the Matter of the Arbitration between Manhattan District, Internal Revenue Service, U.S. Treasury Department, Agency and American Federation of Government Employees, Lodge 15, AFL-CIO, Petitioner, and National Association of Internal Revenue Service Employees, Intervenor," Case No. 111-IRS-6, award dated August 23, 1966.

17 Lahne, *op. cit.,* p. 9.

18 U.S. Department of Labor, Office of Labor Management Policy Development, *Federal Employee Unit Arbitration,* June 1964, pp. 18–19.

19 "In the Matter of the Petition of the National Association of Internal Revenue Service Employees for Determination of Appropriate Unit for Exclusive Recognition in the Internal Revenue Service," Advisory Decision 91-IRS-5, April 7, 1965.

[20] *Executive Order 10988,* section 4 (a) , p. 3.

[21] *A Policy for Employee-Management Cooperation in the Federal Service, Report of the President's Task Force on Employee-Management Relations in the Federal Service,* November 30, 1961, p. 13. Hereafter cited as *Report of the Task Force.*

[22] Statement of George Meany to the Presidential Review Committee on Employee-Management Relations in the Federal Service, Bureau of National Affairs, *Government Employees Relations Report,* No. 215, October 23, 1967, p. D-3. Hereafter cited as *GERR.*

[23] See *GERR,* No. 212, October 2, 1967, pp. A-6, A-7, in which professional groups express the view that elimination of informal recognition will hasten the elimination of professional associations in government.

[24] *The New York Times,* April 11, 1968, p. 28. The Presidential committee reviewing E.O. 10988 was set up by President Lyndon Johnson on September 8, 1967. (See *GERR,* No. 209, September 11, 1967, p. A-5.)

[25] *New York Times, loc. cit.*

[26] *Ibid., loc. cit.*

[27] *Ibid., loc. cit.*

[28] U.S. Civil Service Commission, *Federal Personnel Manual,* Letter 711–4, May 23, 1966.

[29] *GERR,* No. 136, April 18, 1966, pp. A-1, A-2.

[30] U.S. Department of Labor, *Collective Bargaining Agreements in the Federal Service, Late Summer 1964,* BLS Bulletin, August 1965.

[31] *Ibid.,* p. 6.

[32] Vosloo, *op. cit.,* appendix B, pp. 178–179, citing *Report of the Task Force,* pp. 10–11.

[33] *Report of the Task Force,* p. 3.

[34] *Ibid.,* p. 1.

[35] U.S. Civil Service Commission, "Union Recognition in the Federal Government, August 1966 and November 1967," February 26, 1968, p. 4.

[36] U.S. Bureau of Labor Statistics, "News Release," September 4, 1967, p. 2.

[37] Figures are from the Bureau of Labor Statistics, *"Directory of National and International Unions, 1967,"* BLS Bulletin No. 1596.

[38] U.S. Bureau of Labor Statistics, "News Release," March 18, 1968.

[39] *Ibid.*

[40] L. G. Reynolds and C. C. Killingsworth, *Trade Union Publications* (Baltimore: Johns Hopkins Press, 1944) , Vol. I, p. 319.

[41] BLS "News Release," March 18, 1968.

42 *Report of the National President to the 19th Convention of the American Federation of Government Employees*, September 7, 1964 (mimeo) , p. 1.

43 *Report of the National President to the 20th Convention of the American Federation of Government Employees*, August 29–September 2, 1966 (mimeo) , p. 2.

44 *GERR*, No. 177, January 30, 1967, p. A-8.

45 *GERR*, No. 157, September 12, 1966, p. A-4.

46 *GERR*, No. 169, December 5, 1966, p. A-6. The figure for NAGE is the number represented exclusively as of November 1967.

47 *GERR*, No. 162, September 17, 1966, p. A-6.

48 *GERR*, No. 208, September 4, 1967, p. C-3.

49 U.S. Civil Service Commission, *Federal Work Force Outlook, Fiscal Years 1966–1969*, November 1965, p. 5.

50 *Ibid., loc. cit.*

51 U.S. Civil Service Commission, *Federal Work Force Outlook, Fiscal Years 1967–1970*, May 1967, p. 5.

52 *Ibid.*, p. 6.

53 Arthur Thompson and Irwin Weinstock, "White Collar Employees and the Unions at TVA," *Personnel Journal*, 46 (January 1967) , pp. 14, 15. Emphasis in the original.

54 *Ibid.*, p. 16, Table 1, p. 17.

55 *Ibid.*, p. 20.

56 *Ibid.*, p. 14, emphasis added.

57 *Ibid.*, p. 21.

58 *The Articles of Agreements and Supplementary Agreements*, p. 35, and quoted by Thompson and Weinstock, *op. cit.*, p. 15.

59 Arthur Thompson, "Collective Bargaining in the Public Service—The TVA Experience and its Implications for Other Government Agencies," *Labor Law Journal*, 17 (February 1966) , p. 93.

60 Thompson and Weinstock, *op. cit.*, n. 7, p. 15.

61 *Ibid.*, p. 21.

62 U.S. Civil Service Commission, *Federal Personnel Manual System*, Letter 711-5, August 1, 1966; *Bulletin* 711-11, April 25, 1967; and from interviews with CSC officials.

63 *GERR*, No. 167, November 21, 1966, p. A-4.

64 *Ibid.*, pp. A-2, A-3.

65 *GERR*, No. 167, November 21, 1966; No. 168, November 28, 1966.

[66] *GERR,* No. 184, March 20, 1967, p. B-5.

[67] *GERR, loc. cit.*

[68] *GERR,* No. 220, November 27, 1967, pp. A-1, A-2.

[69] *GERR,* No. 169, December 5, 1966, p. D-5.

[70] *GERR,* No. 186, April 3, 1967, pp. A-5, A-6.

[71] *GERR,* No. 189, April 24, 1967, p. A-4.

[72] *GERR,* No. 158, September 19, 1966, p. A-13.

[73] *GERR,* No. 202, July 24, 1967, p. A-2.

[74] *GERR,* No. 177, January 30, 1967, p. A-8.

[75] *GERR,* No. 177, September 11, 1967, p. A-3.

[76] *GERR,* No. 193, May 22, 1967, pp. A-5 to A-7.

Selected Bibliography

The Office Employee

Barry, Carol A. "White-Collar Employment: II—Characteristics," *Monthly Labor Review,* February 1961, 139–147.

Blackburn, R. M. *Union Character and Social Class—A Study of White Collar Unionism.* London: B. T. Balsford, 1967.

Blum, Albert A. *Management and the White Collar Unions.* New York: American Management Association, 1964.

———. "The Prospects for Office Employee Unionization," *Annual Proceeding* (Madison, Wisconsin: Industrial Relations Research Association) , 1963, 182–193.

———. "Why Unions Grow," *Labor History,* Winter 1968, 39–72.

Burr, John, *et al. White Collar Restiveness: A Growing Challenge.* New York: Industrial Relations Counselors, Inc., 1963.

Caskey, Clark C. "White Collar Employees—A Union Dilemma and a Management Challenge," *Management of Personnel Quarterly,* Spring 1962, 10–13.

Coughlin, Howard. "Unionism in Offices Is on the Rise," *The American Federationist,* May 1955, 13–15.

———. "White Collar Unionism in the United States," *Free Labor World,* September 1961, 391–394.

Developments in White Collar Unionism. A panel discussion by Harold T. Gibbons, Everett M. Kassalow and Joel Seidman. Chicago: A. G. Bush Library, Industrial Relations Center, University of Chicago, Occasional Papers No. 24, 1962.

Douty, H. M. *Employment Trends and White Collar Employee Organizations in the United States.* Winston-Salem, N.C.: Wake Forest College, 1968 Labor Symposium, September 18–19, 1968.

———. "Prospects for White-Collar Unionism," *Monthly Labor Review,* January 1969, 31–34.

Dufty, N. F. "The White Collar Unionist," *The Journal of Industrial Relations,* October 1961, 151–156.

Helfgott, R. B. "The Computer and the Prospects for Office Unionism," *Quarterly Review Economic Business,* Spring 1969, 19–28.

Kassalow, Everett M. "Organization of White-Collar Workers," *Monthly Labor Review,* March 1961, 234–238.

——. "The Prospects for White-Collar Union Growth," *Industrial Relations,* October 1965, 37–47.

——. "White-Collar Unionism in the United States." Madison, Wisconsin: Industrial Relations Research Institute, University of Wisconsin, Reprint series no. 77, 1966, 305–364.

Kepes, Sherwin. "A Study of White-Collar Satisfaction and Attributes toward Unions" (unpublished master's thesis, Wayne State University, 1962).

Kleingartner, Archie. *Professionalism and Salaried Worker Organization.* Madison, Wisconsin: Industrial Relations Research Institute, University of Wisconsin, 1967.

——. "The Organization of White-Collar Workers," *British Journal of Industrial Relations,* March 1968, 79–93.

Lachter, Lewis E. "Growing White-Collar Unionization," *Administrative Management,* April 1965, 20–26.

Lange, William H. "Target for Tomorrow: The White Collar Employees," *Office Executive,* February 1958, 14–18.

Lombardi, Vincent, and Andrew T. Grimes. "A Primer for a Theory of White-Collar Unionization," *Monthly Labor Review,* May 1967, 46–49.

Mills, C. Wright. *White Collar.* New York: Oxford University Press, 1951.

Solomon, Benjamin, and Robert K. Burns. *Unionization of White Collar Employees: Extent, Potential and Implications.* Chicago: Industrial Relations Center, University of Chicago, Reprint series no. 110, 1963.

Snyder, Carl Dean. "The U.A.W. and White Collar Unionization," *Management of Personnel Quarterly,* Winter 1966, 11–19.

Strauss, George. "White Collar Unions are Different," *Harvard Business Review,* September–October 1954, 73–82.

Sturmthal, Adolf F., ed. *White-Collar Trade Unions: Contemporary Developments in Industrialized Societies.* Urbana, Illinois: University of Illinois, 1966.

White Collar Workers in Industry. Summary Report of Staff Seminar, Industrial Union Department, AFL-CIO, December 3, 1960.

The Retail Clerks

Estey, Marten. "The Grocery Clerks: Center of Retail Unionism," *Industrial Relations,* Vol. 7, No. 3, May 1968, 249–261.

——. "Patterns of Union Membership in the Retail Trades," *Industrial and Labor Relations Review,* Vol. 8, No. 4, July 1955, 557–564.

——. "The Strategic Alliance as a Factor in Union Growth," *Industrial and Labor Relations Review,* Vol. 9, No. 1, October 1955, 41–53.

Harrington, Michael. *The Retail Clerks*. New York: Wiley, 1962, vii and 99.

Kirstein, George G. *Stores and Unions*. New York: Fairchild Publications, 1950, x and 246.

Knight, Robert E. L. "Unionism Among Retail Clerks in Postwar Britain," *Industrial and Labor Relations Review*, Vol. 14, No. 4, July 1961, 515–527.

Northrup, Herbert R., and Gordon Storholm. *Restrictive Labor Practices in the Supermarket Industry*. Philadelphia: Industrial Research Unit Study No. 44, University of Pennsylvania Press, 1967, 202.

Engineers and Their Unions

Dvorak, Eldon. "Will Engineers Unionize?" *Industrial Relations*, 2, May 1963, 45–65.

Goldner, Fred, and R. R. Ritti. "Professionalization As Career Immobility," *American Journal of Sociology*, 72, March 1967, 489–502.

Goldstein, Bernard. "Unionism Among Salaried Professionals in Industry," *American Sociological Review*, 20, April 1955, 199–205.

———— and Bernard P. Indik. "Unionism As A Social Choice: The Engineers' Case," *Monthly Labor Review*, 86, April 1963, 365–369.

Graham, D. M. "Organizing Scientists and Engineers," *Industrial Relations*, 9, March 1967, 92–96.

Kleingartner, Archie. "Unionization of Engineers and Technicians," *Monthly Labor Review*, 90, October 1967, 29–35.

————. "The Organization of White Collar Workers," *British Journal of Industrial Relations*, 6, March 1968, 79–93.

————. "Professionalism and Engineering Unionism," *Industrial Relations*, 8, May 1969, 24–35.

Kuhn, James W. "Success and Failure In Organizing Professional Engineers," *Proceedings*, Sixteenth Annual Meeting, Industrial Research Association, December 1963, 1–15.

Mooney, Joseph D. "An Analysis of Unemployment Among Professional Engineers and Scientists," *Industrial and Labor Relations Review*, 19, July 1969, 517–528.

Strauss, George. "Professional or Employee-Oriented: Dilemma for Engineering Unions," *Industrial and Labor Relations Review*, 17, July 1964, 519–533.

Walton, Richard. *The Impact of the Professional Engineering Union*. Boston: Graduate School of Business Administration, Harvard University, 1961.

Teachers and Collective Negotiations

American Federation of Teachers, *American Teacher*. Washington, D.C.

Blum, Albert A., ed. *Teacher Unions and Associations: A Comparative Study*. Urbana, Illinois: University of Illinois Press, 1969.

Bureau of National Affairs, Inc., *Government Employee Relations Report*. Washington, D.C.

Carlton, Patrick W., and Harold I. Goodwin, eds. *The Collective Dilemma: Negotiations in Education*. Worthington, Ohio: Charles A. Jones Publishing Co., 1969.

Corwin, Donald G. "Militant Professionalism, Initiative, and Compliance in Public Education," *Sociology of Education*, 38, Summer 1965, 310–330.

Doherty, Robert E., and Walter E. Oberer. *Teachers, School Boards, and Collective Bargaining: A Changing of the Guard*. Ithaca, New York: Cornell University, Cuyuga Press, ILR Paperback No. 2, May 1967.

Educational Service Bureau, Inc., *Educators Negotiating Service*. Washington, D.C.

Elam, Stanley M., Myron Lieberman, and Michael H. Moskow, eds. *Readings on Collective Negotiations in Public Education*. Chicago: Rand McNally, 1967.

Hanslowe, Kurt L. *The Emerging Law of Labor Relations in Public Employment*. Ithaca, New York: Cornell University, Cuyuga Press, ILR Paperback No. 4, October 1967.

ISR Journal, Institute for Staff Relations and Governance at New York University, New York.

Lieberman, Myron, and Michael H. Moskow. *Collective Negotiations for Teachers—An Approach to School Administration*. Chicago: Rand McNally, 1966.

National Education Association, *Negotiation Research Digest*. Washington, D.C.

Shils, Edward B., and C. Taylor Whittier. *Teachers, Administrators, and Collective Bargaining*. New York: Crowell, 1968.

Steffenson, James P. *Teachers Negotiate with School Boards*. U.S. Office of Education, Bulletin OE-23036, Washington, D.C., 1964.

Stinnett, T. M., Jack H. Kleinmann, and Martha Ware. *Professional Negotiation in Education*. New York: Macmillan, 1966.

"Symposium: Labor Relations in the Public Sector," *Michigan Law Review*, 67, 5, March 1969.

Taylor, George W. "The Public Interest in Collective Negotiations in Education," *Phi Delta Kappan*, 48, September 1966, 16–32.

Weber, Arnold R., chairman. "Impasse Resolution, The Community, and Bargaining in the Public Sector." Madison, Wisconsin: Industrial Relations Research Association, *Proceedings* of Twenty-First Annual Winter Meeting, 1969.

Wildman, Wesley A., Robert K. Burns, and Charles R. Perry. *Collective Action by Public School Teachers, Final Report.* [This is a 4-volume study completed at the Industrial Relations Center of the University of Chicago under a grant from the U.S. Office of Education.] Washington, D.C.: ERIC Clearinghouse on Teacher Education.

Wildman, Wesley A., and Charles R. Perry. "Group Conflict and the School Organization," *Phi Delta Kappan,* 47, January 1966.

————. *The Impact of Negotiation in Public Education: The Evidence from the Schools.* Worthington, Ohio: Charles A. Jones Publishing Co., in print.

White-Collar Organization in the Federal Service

U.S. Department of Labor, *Collective Bargaining Agreements in the Federal Service,* Bulletin No. 145, Late Summer 1964.

————. *Federal Employee Unit Arbitration, A Summary and Analysis Up to December 31, 1963.*

U.S. Government Documents, *Federal Personnel Manual,* U.S. Civil Service Commission.

————. "Union Recognition in the Federal Service," August 1966, November 1967, and (mimeo) February 26, 1968.

————. *Union Recognition in the Federal Government,* Statistical Report, November 1967.

U.S. President, "Review Committee on Employee-Management Relations in the Federal Service," *Hearings,* 1967 (mimeo).

————. "Task-Force on Employee-Management Relations in the Federal Service," *Hearings* on Staff Reports.

————. "A Policy for Employee-Management Cooperation in the Federal Service," November 30, 1961.

Thompson, Arthur A. "Collective Bargaining in the Public Service—The T.V.A. Experience and Its Implications for Other Government Agencies," *Labor Law Review,* February 1964, 89–98.

———— and Irwin Weinstock. "White Collar Employees and Unions at T.V.A.," *Personnel Journal,* January 1967.

Vosloo, Willem B. *Collective Bargaining in the United States Civil Service.* Chicago: Public Personnel Association, 1960.

Index

A

B

C

Note: The index was prepared by Miss Gerard Fiala and Mr. Allen Ponak.